The Social and Political Thought of Michael Bakunin

Recent titles in Contributions in Political Science
Series Editor: Bernard K. Johnpoll

Governor Rockefeller in New York: The Apex of Pragmatic Liberalism in the United States
James E. Underwood and William J. Daniels

Neo-Marxism: The Meanings of Modern Radicalism
Robert A. Gorman

The Politics of Pressure: American Arms and Israeli Policy Since the Six Day War
David Pollock

Congress, the Executive Branch, and Special Interests: The American Response to the Arab Boycott of Israel
Kennan Lee Teslik

Third World Policies of Industrialized Nations
Phillip Taylor and Gregory A. Raymond, editors

"For Immediate Release": Candidate Press Releases in American Political Campaigns
Jan Pons Vermeer

The Vice President as Policy Maker: Rockefeller in the Ford White House
Michael Turner

A Contemporary Crisis: Political Hostage-Taking and the Experience of Western Europe
Clive C. Aston

Socialism of a Different Kind: Reshaping the Left in France
Bernard E. Brown

Aging and Public Policy: The Politics of Growing Old in America
Edited by William P. Browne and Laura Katz Olson

Influence, Change, and the Legislative Process
Janet Miller Grenzke

Coherent Variety: The Idea of Diversity in British and American Conservative Thought
Michael D. Clark

The Social and Political Thought of Michael Bakunin

RICHARD B. SALTMAN

CONTRIBUTIONS IN POLITICAL SCIENCE,
NUMBER 88

GREENWOOD PRESS
WESTPORT, CONNECTICUT • LONDON, ENGLAND

Library of Congress Cataloging in Publication Data

Saltman, Richard B.
The social and political thought of Michael Bakunin.

(Contributions in political science, ISSN 0147-1066; no. 88)
Bibliography: p.
Includes index.
1. Bakunin, Mikhail Aleksandrovich, 1814-1876.
2. Anarchism and anarchists—History. 3. Marx, Karl, 1818-1883. 4. Communism—History. I. Title. II. Series.
HX915.B3S24 1983 335'.83'0924 [B] 82-9348
ISBN 0-313-23378-0 (lib. bdg.)

Library of Congress Catalog Card Number: 82-9348
ISBN: 0-313-23378-0
ISSN: 0147-1066

First published in 1983

Greenwood Press
A division of Congressional Information Service, Inc.
88 Post Road West
Westport, Connecticut 06881

Printed in the United States of America

10 9 8 7 6 5 4 3 2 1

Copyright Acknowledgments

Permission is gratefully acknowledged for the use of excerpts from the following:

Shlomo Avineri, *The Social and Political Thought of Karl Marx*, by permission of Cambridge University Press.

Michael Bakounine, *Etatisme et Anarchisme*, Vol. III of *Archives Bakounine*, ed. Arthur Lehning, 1967, by permission of E. J. Brill Publishing Co.

Kenneth J. Kenafick, *Michael Bakunin and Karl Marx*, by permission of Freedom Press.

Arthur Lehning, ed., *Michael Bakunin: Selected Writings*. Reprinted by permission of Grove Press, Inc. Translations by Steven Cox and Olive Stevens, © 1973 by Jonathan Cape Ltd., London. This edition © 1974 by Grove Press, Inc. ALL RIGHTS RESERVED. By permission of Grove Press outside of the British Commonwealth and Empire territories. By permission of Jonathan Cape Ltd. for rights in the British Commonwealth and Empire including Canada.

Reprinted from *The Political Philosophy of Bakunin: Scientific Anarchism*, G. P. Maximoff, Ed. Copyright 1954 by The Free Press, a Division of Macmillan Publishing Co., Inc.

To Denise

Contents

Preface

In most contemporary circles, Michael Bakunin is rather poorly regarded as a political thinker. There is a generally held presumption among both academics and activists alike that Bakunin lacked a coherent political theory, and that as a result his writings contain little of present-day value or significance.

It seems to me that this perception of Bakunin as exclusively historical and atheoretical has deprived us of a useful conceptual tool. Bakunin took the position that Marx's theory of social authority was too narrowly defined to fulfill socialism's liberatory potential. He acknowledged the validity of Marx's economic critique of capitalism yet rejected the political and social conclusions that Marx drew from that critique, seeking instead a form of post-industrial socialism that could not devolve into a new authoritarian or bureaucratic state. And while Bakunin's position bears a certain resemblance to the "left socialist" arguments advanced by later Marxists like Luxembourg, Lukacs, and on occasion even Trotsky, Bakunin's theory has a fundamentally different structure that sets it apart from even the most democratic of orthodox Marxist arguments.

Bakunin's theory of collectivist anarchism appears to be capable of infusing a new and important perspective into the current effort to develop a truly participatory form of government. Precisely because he insisted upon the centrality of self-activity and self-administration to *all* aspects of organization, his work can serve as a powerful corrective to the tendency of twentieth-century regimes to sink into bureaucratic and repressive forms of authority. Further, Bakunin's concept of social authority is much closer to the reality of popular desires within contemporary society: certainly the French Communist party gleaned little comfort from the events of May 1968, and the Yugoslavian experiment with worker's control and market socialism sends ever-increasing shivers down the centralized spine of the Soviet state bureaucracy. In short, the current theoretical dialogue would be simultaneously richer and more realistic if it included Bakunin's collectivist-anarchist argument.

It was with this potential contribution in mind that I wrote this study of Bakunin's political philosophy. Its organizational structure emerged in response to two central questions which must be a part of any contemporary reconsideration of Bakunin's thought. First, it was necessary to present a full statement of Bakunin's political argument, both to counter traditional misunderstandings and to provide a common ground upon which to discuss the importance and usefulness of his theory. And secondly, in keeping with the intellectual rule of thumb that all political theory since 1850 has been a dialogue with Marx, it seemed logical to compare Bakunin's argument with that of his most respected teacher and rival. These two concerns together served to determine the organizational framework which follows. Chapter 1 explores the intellectual inadequacies of the traditional interpretation of Bakunin's thought. The substance of Bakunin's political argument is then presented in chapters 2 and 3, and his strategy for implementing his theory is discussed in chapter 4. In the final section of the work, the differences between Bakunin's argument and that of Marx are explored in chapter 5, and the value of Bakunin's theory is evaluated in chapter 6.

My analysis of Bakunin's political argument is based primarily upon the available published editions of his own unedited manuscripts. Although Bakunin began a goodly number of works during his mature collectivist-anarchist period, he never managed to finish and publish more than a handful of letters and short pamphlets. His work is now in the process of being published in a definitive fifteen-volume edition by the Bakunin Archiv at the International Institute for Social History in Amsterdam, under the direction of Arthur Lehning. Those volumes, along with a six-volume collection of his work edited by Bakunin's colleague James Guillaume and published in Paris between 1895 and 1913 by Stock, are the most comprehensive and reliable editions of his works. Both of these collections are in French, however, which was the language in which Bakunin generally wrote. Thus, while I relied upon them extensively in my research, I actually cite these two compendia as a source only when I was unable to find a reasonably accurate translation in one of the several English language collections of his writings. Of these, the best is a one-volume paperback collection edited and introduced by Lehning entitled *Michael Bakunin: Selected Writings*, published by Grove Press in 1974. Lehning's introduction to the volume deserves mention as perhaps the most accessible and accurate summary of Bakunin's political thought currently available in English. Additionally, I found Georgi

Maximoff's *The Political Philosophy of Michael Bakunin* (Free Press, 1953) to be a useful and generally reliable source. However, inasmuch as Maximoff attempted to overcome the diffuse character of Bakunin's unedited drafts by compiling citations on the same topic under subject headings, his book alone gives a rather disjointed and disorienting picture of Bakunin's intellectual style. Unfortunately, the most readily obtainable English language edition of Bakunin's writing, Sam Dolgoff's *Bakunin on Anarchy*, was apparently conceived as an effort to make Bakunin's manuscripts more accessible to present-day political activists: it takes substantial liberties in its translations, and as a result must be used with a degree of caution.

Acknowledgments

This work would have been far more difficult to complete had I not had the direction, the support, and in some cases the forbearance of numerous teachers and friends. I would like to express my gratitude to Charles Drekmeier of Stanford University, for his continual intellectual support and encouragement, and to Nannerl Keohane, now of Wellesley College. Additionally, I am very much indebted to two former teachers, Joseph Paff of Stanford and Henry Ehrmann of Dartmouth College, each of whom gave me intellectual guidance and taught me to value serious critical thought. I would also like to thank Stephen Slaner for many hours of spirited discussion, the Lamperti family for their many kindnesses, and my parents, Ruth and Phil Saltman, for their encouragement. Finally, I would like to thank my wife, Denise, without whose intellectual and emotional support this project could not have been finished.

The Social and Political Thought of Michael Bakunin

1 *Bakunin under Western Eyes*

Within the standard literature of intellectual history, Bakunin has been uniformly regarded as a paradoxical figure. Whether a political commentator explored Bakunin's historical activities, his political arguments, or the linkages between the two, he always seemed to arrive at the same conclusion: Bakunin had pursued a hopelessly contradictory and inconsistent course. The fundamental tenets of this analysis are now broadly accepted by classical liberals and Marxists alike, and its central conclusion has emerged almost by default as the sole respectable interpretation of Bakunin as either socialist revolutionary or theoretician.

The major difficulty with this conventional intellectual wisdom, though, is that it cannot adequately account for Bakunin's actual impact upon the nineteenth-century socialist world. By its exclusive concentration upon Bakunin's supposedly inchoate nature, this analysis is unable to explain satisfactorily the substantial theoretical power which Bakunin exercised, and which his arguments still carry today within the European socialist movement. While the various works which adopt this standard interpretation of Bakunin's work might be internally cogent, therefore, and though they might disagree among themselves over certain issues, they all suffer from the same basic limitation: they cannot adequately explain what in fact occurred.

For convenience of reference, various proponents of this standard interpretation of Bakunin have been grouped under the collective rubric of the Paradox school. The name was chosen with an eye primarily toward this argument's traditional conclusion, although it also hints at the interpretation's explanatory failings. This chapter will explore the intellectual and ideological sources of this Paradox argument, in order both to demonstrate its inadequacies and to dispel its aura of reasoned neutrality.

At first glance, it might appear that the Paradox argument could have grown out of structural problems within Bakunin's manuscripts. Certainly, since its fundamental perception was of the contradictory and inconsistent character of Bakunin's theoretical position, the Paradox conclusion could have readily emerged from some major obstacle to comprehension within Bakunin's expository style. This possibility makes it necessary to examine the basic structure of Bakunin's written work, and to evaluate the likelihood that internal flaws had generated the Paradox interpretation.

There are two aspects of Bakunin's manuscripts that could make his argument more difficult to understand. The first problem is inherent to the unfinished form in which he left nearly all his work. With the exception of *State and Anarchy*—which was itself the introduction to a broader study—Bakunin published only a few short topical pamphlets during his mature collectivist-anarchist period. The bulk of his writings remained uncompleted and unedited first drafts, which often broke off in mid-sentence. As might be expected, these manuscripts contain the confusions of topic and syntax usually found in such drafts.

Their unedited character compounds the impact of a more important yet less easily resolved difficulty in Bakunin's written work. This second problem is the apparent imprecision with which Bakunin sometimes employed certain crucial terms. This difficulty does not seriously disturb the cogency of Bakunin's overall argument, but it is an additional source of confusion, and it requires some critical explication. Most Paradox commentators, however, have been content to respond only with an uncomplicated, literal, and consequently "contradictory" interpretation.

Had they pursued this issue farther, these commentators would have found a quite different explanation for these politically sensitive lapses. Rather than reflecting an inconsistent theoretical position, Bakunin's problem was an inevitable by-product of the broad political and educational function which these manuscripts were intended to fulfill. He had posed as the central tenet of his argument the necessity to both "educate and organize" the European working classes. This revolutionary program had to overcome the essentially circular, and potentially self-defeating, character of its approach: each of these two endeavors could be effective only if it had been preceded by the other. More specifically, while in general agreement with Marx's materialist analysis of capitalism, Bakunin believed that Marx's abstracted literary style had left his work inaccessible to the as-yet-uneducated working classes, and had thereby left Marx's own revolutionary efforts vulnerable to this circular tendency. Therefore, to minimize this danger, Bakunin assumed a style of discourse which would be immediately accessible to those he wanted to reach. In effect, he infused into all his work the unadorned language of the common man.

His desire to popularize, however, was in no way an intention to dilute, and he thus directly confronted the political limitations of the popularly acknowledged language. Bakunin had set himself the task of describing the fundamental socialist structure of both the pre-revolutionary historical process and a post-revolutionary society by means of a language which had long since taken on specifically bourgeois connotations. It was his difficulty in conveying the fundamental differences of a new socialist frame of reference, but in the popularly recognized language of the old regime which it was to replace, which generated Bakunin's terminological inconsistencies. Lacking a universally defined popular language, which could describe social arrangements in their most general form, and yet quite obviously unwilling to adopt Marx's didactic academic solution, Bakunin had little choice but to employ the specific, reductive, and therefore inappropriate language of bourgeois relationships.

This interpretation of Bakunin's seemingly contradictory language can be illustrated by his usage of the term "politics." Paradox commentators have always been quick to conclude that Bakunin's central political argument was overtly contradictory since, on the one hand, he regularly called for the "total abolition of politics"[1] which he condemned as the "art and science of dominating and exploiting the masses,"[2] yet on the other, in his descriptions of a post-revolutionary federation, he wrote favorably about the need to institute a "true politics of the people."[3] How, they wonder, could any logical individual preach the "total abolition" of what he considered to be a quintessential source of social evil, and then subsequently describe that same concept as the "true" basis of a completely different, fully liberated society?

The answer was that Bakunin had been condemning the specific bourgeois variant of parliamentary politics, which he believed only facilitated conflict resolution within the ruling elite, while at the same time opposing to that discarded concept a different, socialist definition of politics that was rooted in a tightly defined, historically generated process of mutual influence and collective self-discipline. In fact, in the very paragraphs from which some Paradox commentators took their "contradictory" quotations, Bakunin quite explicitly differentiated between these two opposite definitions of the term. Writing of the International Workingmen's Association, which was to be the general vehicle of working-class "education and organization," Bakunin stated:

> But at the time it was founded there was no other politics in the whole world but the politics of the Church, monarchy, aristocracy, or bourgeoisie. . . . they all were equally based upon the exploitation of the working masses and had no

> other aim than to contest the monopolizing of this exploitation. The International then had to begin by clearing the ground, and, since every form of politics, from the point of view of the emancipation of labor, was tainted by the touch of reactionary elements, the International had to throw out of its midst all the known political systems in order to found, upon the ruins of the bourgeois world, the true politics of the workers, the politics of the IWA.[4]

With this passage, Bakunin clearly indicated that although he had utilized the same term, he was in fact describing two very different conceptual entities, and that he himself was quite well aware in his own mind of what differentiated one from the other. Severely constricted by the specific political content of the popularly acknowledged language, Bakunin conveyed his meaning by in effect using that language against itself. That he was successful in this effort is apparent in the passage cited: whatever initial confusion this dual definition creates can be dispelled by a careful second reading of the text.

A similar structural problem produced by this attempt to popularize socialist conceptions through reductive bourgeois language was Bakunin's apparently unintentional tendency to invest several key terms with both a negative-bourgeois, as well as a positive-socialist connotation. To cite a second example favored by many Paradox commentators, Bakunin generally understood the term "anarchy" to imply a new, affirmative self-ordering of popular life. Yet he would sporadically revert to that word's negative, specifically bourgeois connotation of social chaos, as when he referred to Hobbes' "supposition" that, in a state of nature, men would "offer the spectacle of the most terrifying anarchy, where the stronger would exploit and slaughter the weaker."[5] This form of terminological confusion clearly indicated little more than a conceptual lapse by Bakunin into what remained the common understanding of the word, and would probably have been rectified if he had edited his manuscripts. Most commentators, however, preferred to ascribe this problem not to any structural impediments created by the political content of bourgeois language, but rather to the essentially contradictory character of Bakunin's political argument.

As the two above examples illustrate, the structural problems within Bakunin's manuscripts aren't serious enough to explain satisfactorily the Paradox School's central conclusion about the coherence of Bakunin's political argument. Neither their first-draft form nor their occasional terminological imprecision made his work inaccessible to serious study. One must conclude, consequently, that the reasons for which Paradox commentators were disoriented by these structural problems must lie elsewhere.

Certain theoretical limitations of this Paradox approach to Bakunin's political thought are apparent within the works of those commentators who adopted it. With the exception of K. J. Kenafick's commentary,

Michael Bakunin and Karl Marx, and Arthur Lehning's excellent but very short introduction to a one-volume collection of Bakunin's works, the Paradox School encompasses most well-known English-language studies of Bakunin. The Paradox list includes E. H. Carr's *Bakunin*, Eugene Pyziur's *The Doctrine of Anarchism of Michael Bakunin*, James Joll's *The Anarchists*, Max Nomad's *Apostles of Revolution*, and more recently, Anthony Masters' *Father of Anarchism* and Arthur Mendel's *Michael Bakunin*. These same analytic limitations also can be found in those works which harbor a "libertarian" bias, such as George Woodcock's *Anarchism* and Paul Avrich's *The Russian Anarchists*, as well as within various other efforts: Camus' *The Rebel*, Martin Malia's *Alexander Herzen and the Birth of Russian Socialism*, Edmund Wilson's *To the Finland Station*, and Isaiah Berlin's *Karl Marx* and *Russian Thinkers*. Additionally, as will be considered separately, Marxist commentators like George Lichtheim and Julius Braunthal adopted most key Paradox propositions as the basis for their own "socialist" commentaries on Bakunin's work. Despite their otherwise diverse nature, all of these authors share the central conclusion of the Paradox approach: in the final analysis, Bakunin's political thought was theoretically inconsistent and contradictory, without serious intellectual or political merit.

In arriving at this common conclusion, these commentators incorporated within their respective analyses of Bakunin's works two fundamental assumptions. First, they presumed that if Bakunin had ever held a consistent theoretical position, and if his collectivist anarchism was grounded in a comprehensible system, then he of necessity had to have held that position and maintained that system throughout his entire life. By means of this analytic contrivance, these commentators variously insisted that Bakunin's 1837 interest in Fichte, his 1842 publication of a left-Hegelian article, his 1848 address to a Slavic Congress, and his 1851 "Confession to Tsar Nicholas" must all have correlated fully with the works of his collectivist-anarchist period (approximately 1866 to 1874). Through their pursuit of a unitary framework with which to explain a life of a substantial intellectual change, and which only crystallized into a consistently articulated system in the last ten years of Bakunin's life, these authors created a distorted evaluatory structure. In effect, through their artificial insistence upon lifelong theoretical consistency, most Paradox commentators could only demonstrate an equally artificial inconsistency within Bakunin's mature political thought.

The second theoretical assumption common to most Paradox commentary concerns the selection of Bakunin's intellectual mentors. Most commentators, on the one hand, insisted upon placing Bakunin within intellectual traditions to which he was at best only tangentially related. They concentrated particularly upon the late eighteenth-century exponents of egalitarian communism via coup d'état, Babeuf and Buonarotti, these exponents' nineteenth-century counterpart, Blanqui, and the last major spokesman of utopian French socialism, Proudhon. Additionally, certain commentators like Carr attributed what they considered Bakunin's "extreme individualism" to the influence of Max Stirner.[6] In this emphasis, these commentators located Bakunin within the realm of pre-industrial utopian theory, among the traditionalist backlash against the disruptive effects of industrialization.

On the other hand, these same commentators neglected the dominant influence which both idealist philosophy and evolutionary theory had upon Bakunin's thought. Beyond an occasional unappended citation, most Paradox authors never acknowledged or explored Bakunin's substantial intellectual debt to Hegel and Feuerbach. Further, these commentators themselves appear to be unfamiliar with Hegel's argument that individual freedom must be sought within and through the collective structure of human society. In their analyses of Bakunin's work, consequently, Paradox commentators invariably split apart and create separate analytic categories for concepts which, within Bakunin's frame of reference, were comprehensible only as the partial elements of a larger integrated whole. Similar difficulties also arise from these commentators' ignorance of Bakunin's debt to Lamarck for his perspective on the physical world.

Moreover, most Paradox proponents undervalued Bakunin's intellectual obligation to Marx. Bakunin himself considered his collectivist anarchism to be a refocussed and decentralized variant of Marxian socialism, and intentionally incorporated major segments of Marx's political economy. Most adherents of the Paradox interpretation, however, never attempted any theoretical comparison between Bakunin and Marx. Worse, those few who noted some proximate similarity were so limited in their own perception of Marx that their comparisons read like journalistic caricatures. Pyziur, for example, ascribed an absolutely determined historical materialism to Marx, which he then contrasted to the absolutely ahistorical volitionism which he discerned within Bakunin's thought. And Nomad concluded that Marx and Bakunin alike were attempting to implement a New Deal style reform of capitalist democracy.

The ideological consequences of these various structural and theoretical presumptions are not difficult to discern. By their insistence upon a strict literal reading of Bakunin's manuscripts and the resultant misunderstanding of his terminological imprecision, most Paradox commentators believed they had demonstrated inconsistency and contradiction. In a parallel development, by assuming a lifelong theoretical consistency and then adamantly relegating his political thought to the pre-industrial utopian dustbin, on the one hand, while ignoring the two intellectual traditions which point toward the coherency of his argument on the other, these commentators are again able to prove inconsistency and contradiction.

For the purposes of this discussion, the probable causal linkage of these misapprehensions is unimportant. What is crucial, on the contrary, is the combined impact of these presumptions upon the ability of most Paradox commentators to reach a rather convenient ideological conclusion. Having systematically invalidated any possibility of coherence within Bakunin's political argument, these commentators had thereby freed themselves to discover a safe, non-political explanation for Bakunin's political position. In short, their false dilemma produced a false solution.

The true source of consistency within Bakunin's argument, most Paradox commentators argued, wasn't in his theoretical works at all, but in his eccentric personality. E. H. Carr contended that the key to Bakunin's thought could be found in "the pure instinct to rebel, independently of the object or the reason of the rebellion," which "has never been more strikingly expressed than in the personality of Michael Bakunin."[7] This peculiar trait, Carr submitted, was indicative of a truncated personal development, and was unilaterally explanatory of Bakunin's disdain for bourgeois capitalism and his clear incapacity to formulate a consistent analysis of it.

> Indiscriminate insubordination to authority is a necessary phase in the development of every normal individual. Bakunin spent his whole life in a phase which most human beings outgrow at some time between the ages of ten and thirty. In this respect, he enjoyed the secret not so much of perpetual youth as of perpetual childhood.[8]

Carr's effort to integrate Bakunin's thought through a deviant character structure was paralleled by a more broadly psycho-historical thesis suggested by Max Nomad. Bakunin's alleged need to rebel, now descried as Bakunin's "romantic desire to act the terrible man,"[9] was combined by Nomad with an equally powerful lust for political authority and power. These emotional compulsions forced Bakunin to assume a calculated political stance which would be "fundamentally different from all other revolutionists,"[10] and thereby enable him to "outdo them in the race for the 'favor of the masses.' "[11] Nomad summarized his motivational analysis by simultaneously trivializing and mystifying not only Bakunin, but Muhammed and Lenin as well.

> This titanic adolescent who, born in another period, might have become a legendary hero of popular folksongs, the founder of a militant religion, like Mohammed, or the God-Emperor of an authoritarian state, like Lenin...[12]

The most fully nuanced psycho-historical argument, however, appears in James Joll's 1964 work, *The Anarchists*. Generalizing beyond Bakunin alone, Joll discerned within all anarchists the character structure of the religious fanatic. He then argued that central tenets common to all anarchist theory were comprehensible only in terms of their therapeutic value for this pathological personality structure. Setting out the broad contours of his argument, Joll wrote:

> What emerges from any study of heretical religious movements is that certain kinds of people feel a recurrent need to react violently against the existing order, to question the right of the existing authorities to rule, and to assert instead that all authority is unnecessary and evil. And this revolt against society and its leaders is accompanied, according to the temperaments concerned, either by a belief in the healing properties of violent destruction, the importance of revolution as an end in itself, or else by a boundlessly optimistic belief in the possibilities of an immediate and radical change for the better.[13]

Armed with this absolutist and millenarian assessment of anarchist theory, which facilely consolidated its extreme Lockean-individualist and its collectivist-Hegelian materialist factions, Joll concluded that "it is the heretical religious temperament that drives men to become anarchists," because "the myth of the revolution satisfied the temperamental need for action of those who, in earlier ages, might have embarked on a crusade or a religious revolt."[14]

This general analytic structure was then applied specifically to Bakunin's political activity. Joll described Bakunin as "a violently rebellious young man" whose "violent nature really wanted action."[15] This deviant drive could be satisfied, in the nineteeth century, solely by the cathartic release of anarchist political behavior: as Joll phrased it, "his later revolutionary activity seems to be the direct expression of a complex and turbulent temperament."[16] While Joll had indicted all anarchist theory in his general psychological model, he himself chose to scrutinize only Bakunin's political actions. However, this assumption of a therapeutic relationship between Bakunin's personality and his political stance wasn't confined to his political acts alone. George Woodcock, for example, extended this psycho-historical approach to the substantive theoretical arguments of Bakunin and Marx, insisting that for both men "the differences in personality projected themselves in differences of principle."[17]

This psycho-historical model had a second advantage, since it could also be used to explain the size of Bakunin's political following. Many Paradox commentators found that his political attractiveness grew out of another fortuitous element in Bakunin's character, his charisma. And although some commentators viewed this aspect of Bakunin's personality in a positive light—for instance Joll's reference to Bakunin's "charm and conviction"[18]—most Paradox adherents described this trait in a more derogatory fashion. Typical of this second group was Edmund Wilson's comment that "Bakunin had a peculiar combination of childhood candor with Russian slyness, which, together with his enthusiasm and his grandiose presence, enabled him to perform miracles of persuasion."[19] Wilson, in fact, extended this psycho-historical model to its logical limit, making explicit what other Paradox commentators had only implied. "Surely," Wilson observed, "Bakunin was a little cracked."[20] Wilson was joined in this conclusion by Paul Avrich, who alluded without explanation to "the hints of derangement that sometimes appeared in Bakunin's words and actions."[21]

In short, most Paradox commentators would have one believe that the strength and intensity of Bakunin's political support was also a consequence of certain unstable elements within Bakunin's personality. In a sense, having once resorted to a psycho-historical explanation of Bakunin's political argument, these commentators were trapped within the ahistorical character of their own logic. They had little choice but to extend that psychological model of motivation to those groups that Bakunin had mobilized, and through those groups to Marx as well. Indeed, one might speculate that, beyond its convenient ideological safety, it was this model's transmissibility that many commentators found so seductive: they could utilize it to explain literally everything. They evidently failed to notice that, as a result, it could explain little of value about anything.

Most Paradox misrepresentations of Bakunin's position appear attributable to some combination of the three analytic flaws just described—the false imposition of lifelong theoretical consistency, the incorrect attribution of Bakunin's intellectual lineage, and the subsequent psychological solution—with the additional problem of these commentators' evident unfamiliarity with Bakunin's actual manuscripts. The supportive interplay among these four factors, as well as the inadequate interpretations which they inevitably produced, can be observed within most Paradox commentators' treatment of two central components of Bakunin's political thought: his attitude toward revolutionary violence, and his concept of freedom.

Despite minor variations in emphasis, most Paradox adherents concluded that Bakunin's theory of revolutionary violence could be explained by what Joll described as Bakunin's "belief in the virtues of violence for its own sake, and a confidence in the technique of terrorism."[22] Since this "belief" directly contradicted the known facts about Bakunin's daily life, one might expect that this conclusion would give pause to serious partisans of the psycho-historical approach. Yet only one commentator recognized a possible inconsistency here, and he then dismissed it without elaboration: "While all we know of his life suggests that in action he was the kindest of men, his imagination . . . was always ready to be stirred by melodramatic dreams of blood and fire."[23]

Most of these commentators, on the contrary, choose to invest great significance in two specific sentences which Bakunin wrote—one from the 1842 article "Reaction in Germany," the other from his 1848 "Appeal to the Slavs" —and in certain aspects of Bakunin's fifteen-month relationship with Sergei Nechaev in 1869 and 1870. Inasmuch as the problems raised by the Paradox interpretation of these two sentences differ somewhat from those associated with the Nechaev question, they will be explored separately.

Most Paradox commentators' interpretation of the 1842 and 1848 sentences incorporated at least two of the four analytic improprieties noted above. First, both of these sentences were written well before Bakunin's mature collectivist-anarchist period—in fact, the 1842 article was Bakunin's first published piece. Consequently, whatever their content, these sentences are of import not to the structure but rather only the etymology of Bakunin's mature political thought. Second, these commentators were unable to understand the 1842 sentence because they evidently have little knowledge of Hegelian philosophy, and/or had failed to locate Bakunin's work within the intellectual tradition of Hegel and Feuerbach. Published in Berlin, "The Reaction in Germany" was a formulation of the left-Hegelian position that Bakunin had just recently reached. At the culmination of what was widely applauded by his contemporaries as a prescient restatement of Hegel's political argument, Bakunin summarized the Young Hegelian real-must-be-made-rational reading of the master with these two sentences: "Let us therefore trust the eternal spirit which destroys and annihilates only because it is the unfathomable and eternally creative source of all life. The passion for destruction is a creative passion, too."[24] That this clearly Hegelian conception of "destruction" didn't require either physical bloodshed or the demolition of buildings to fulfill itself escaped the notice of every Paradox commentator. Woodcock, for example, wrote that "there is a true Bakuninist feeling in the apocalyptic tone and the emphasis upon destruction."[25] Even Camus, himself a philosopher, concluded from this sentence that for Bakunin "the struggle against creation will therefore be without mercy and without ethics, and the only salvation lies in extermination."[26]

The standard Paradox interpretation of the 1848 sentence is equally deficient, although for different reasons. The sentence in question was aimed at democratically oriented Eastern Europeans just after the failure of the 1848 wave of bourgeois rebellions, and it capsuled Bakunin's desire to see all nations within the Russian Empire freed of the tsar's hand: "the star of revolution will rise high and independent above Moscow from a sea of blood and fire, and will turn into a lodestar to lead a liberated humanity."[27] A cursory glance at the "Appeal" itself, an acquaintance with Bakunin's personal experiences during the 1848 uprisings, or an awareness of the human slaughter with which the "forces of order" had suppressed not only past peasant rebellions within Russia, but the 1848 Paris Commune as well, would bring one to relate this "sea of blood and fire" to the great cost which both bourgeois and autocratic states alike would inevitably exact from a successful revolutionary movement. Yet for most Paradox commentators this phrase only confirmed their certainty that Bakunin, in the words of Robert Wesson, "took unusual glee in violence."[28]

The third and final pillar of the Paradox analysis of Bakunin's theory of violence concerned Bakunin's involvement with Nechaev, and most particularly with the 1869 *Catechism of a Revolutionary*. Although a full exploration of this question must be left to chapter 4, that discussion's conclusion is quite relevant here: it was Nechaev, not Bakunin, who wrote the disputed document. And while some of the means by which this point can be established are of fairly recent discovery (Bakunin's final letter to Nechaev, for example), the crucial element in this determination is the immediately evident degree to which the *Catechism* contradicted every direct statement which Bakunin made in his mature collectivist-anarchist period about revolutionary violence. Had these commentators read Bakunin's manuscripts with any dispassion this disparity would have been obvious. They evidently preferred to believe that Bakunin had associated himself with Nechaev, qua Camus, "because he recognized in that implacable figure the type of human being that he recommended and what he himself, in a certain manner, would have been if he had been able to silence his heart."[29] Alternatively, some commentators invoked the contradictory-child explanation from their psycho-biographical arsenal:

> That he was not totally converted to Nechaev's tactics is shown by the disgust he displayed when Nechaev began to put them into action. Bakunin may have been as devoid of middle-class morality as Alfred Doolittle, but he retained an aristocratic concern for good manners; he would rebuke the young men of the Jura villages for using bad language in front of women, and there seems no doubt that, while in theory he may have found Nechaev's proposals delightfully horrific, in practice he saw them as merely caddish.[30]

Despite substantial evidence to the contrary, then, most Paradox commentators resolutely concurred with Joll's judgment that Bakunin and Nechaev were equally enamoured with the techniques of terrorism expounded in the *Catechism*.

Overall, this three-legged Paradox analysis of Bakunin's theory of violence can be seen to contain all four analytic improprieties detailed above. The Paradox approach distorted Bakunin's chronological development, ignored his early Hegelian tendencies even while evaluating an article he wrote about Hegel, disregarded his written statements on the subject in question, and, lastly, through its concentration upon Bakunin's "violent" temperament, proffered a psychological explanation with which conveniently to resolve its own self-produced dilemma. One direct consequence of this Paradox interpretation, however, has been that Bakunin is now known as "The Apostle of Pan-Destruction"—an "epithet," Pyziur wrote, that Bakunin "richly deserved."[31] And one can gain a sense of the full impact which this misinterpretation can carry in the following citation from Martin Malia:

> With Bakunin, the chief, indeed almost the sole emphasis was on disorganization, destruction, and negation; the dominant theme of his thought was the anticipated exultation of a new, universal [peasant uprising]. . . .it is difficult to see what, if anything, Bakunin was trying to accomplish in the real world, other than to blow the whole place up for the sheer fun the bang of the explosion would produce.[32]

Most Paradox commentators were even less adept in their interpretation of Bakunin's conceptions of freedom and authority. Having consigned Bakunin to the pre-industrial netherworld of utopian socialism, and being themselves proponents in various degrees of a possessive, negative Lockean freedom from society, these commentators transformed Bakunin's collectivist Hegelian-inspired notion of individual freedom into an absolutist version of their own Lockean assumptions. As E. H. Carr described Bakunin's supposed Stirnerian conception of human liberty, "individualism remains the essence of Bakunin's social and political system."[33] In turn, this contrived emphasis upon an extreme Lockean doctrine of "absolute liberty" was then contrasted with an equally distorted interpretation of Bakunin's theory of revolutionary authority, in which Bakunin's conception of collective self-discipline was portrayed as "the most severe social discipline" whose "culmination would be total despotism."[34] Once they had successfully dichotomized Bakunin's concept of individual freedom through collective solidarity into two entirely separate entities, one derived from Max Stirner and Locke, the other from some combination of Babeuf, Buonarotti, and Wilhelm Weitling, these commentators could firmly conclude that Bakunin's notion of individual freedom contradicted his conception of revolutionary authority. Carr argued, for example,

> In theory a protagonist of absolute liberty, and ready. . .to denounce in the bitterest terms the rigid discipline of communism, Bakunin resorted, in the organization of his revolutionary activities, to methods which were not only the precise contradiction of his own principles, but went far beyond the most extreme ambitions of the dogmatic and dictatorial Marx.[35]

And Avrich, writing in (of all places) a preface to an English translation of Bakunin's manuscripts, employed this standard Paradox misinterpretation to explain Bakunin's insufficiently complete adoption of Avrich's own right-wing "libertarian" individualism:

> While he recognized the intimate connection between means and ends, while he saw that the methods used to make the revolution must affect the nature of society after the revolution, he nonetheless resorted to methods which were the precise contradiction of his own libertarian principles.[36]

Although they agreed upon the existence of this contradiction within Bakunin's works, the Paradox commentators disagreed among themselves as to its meaning. Those like Woodcock and Avrich who were intent upon discovering precursors to their own libertarianism, attributed Bakunin's "authoritarianism" to a lapse in his fundamentally "libertarian" doctrine, stemming from flaws in his personal psychology. Alternatively, commentators like Carr, Nomad, and Pyziur chose to interpret this contradiction as fatal evidence not just that Bakunin was psychologically deficient, but that all anarchist doctrine, suffering from the same theoretical liability, would necessarily and inevitably result in "the infernal reality of dictatorship."[37] In what perhaps gave an indication of their own personal motivations, this second group of commentators generally discerned the Bolshevik Revolution and Leninist Doctrine lurking just behind the facade of Bakunin's theory of authority. Pyziur wrote that "a Bolshevik revolution was needed to expose the true meaning of Bakunin's teaching."[38] And Camus contended that not only had Bakunin "contributed as much as his enemy Marx to Leninist doctrine," but that Bakunin's 1848 outline of a "Slav Empire" was "exactly the same, down to the last details of its frontiers, as that realized by Stalin."[39]

Camus' work, in fact, provides an excellent summary of the intellectual inadequacies of the Paradox interpretation of Bakunin's political thought. In the passage below, he quite clearly coupled the standard Paradox position on Bakunin's theory of violence, his notion of individual freedom, and his theory of revolutionary authority in order to arrive at what Camus concluded was the "inevitable" authoritarian consequence:

> Certainly, [Bakunin] wanted total freedom; but he hoped to realize it through total destruction. To destroy everything is to pledge oneself to building without foundations, and then to holding up the walls with one's hands. He who rejects the entire past, without keeping any part of it which could serve to breathe life into the revolution, condemns himself to finding justification only in the future and, in the meantime, to entrusting the police with the task of justifying the provisional state of affairs. Bakunin proclaimed dictatorship, not despite his desire for destruction, but in accordance with it. Nothing, in fact, could turn him from this path since his ethical values had also been dissolved in the crucible of total negation.[40]

As noted above, the Paradox interpretation of Bakunin's thought was advanced by Marxist as well as Lockean liberal commentators. The most prominent Marxist commentator to assume the Paradox mantle was George Lichtheim. In his various historical works, including *The Origins of Socialism, A Short History of Socialism,*, and *Marxism*, Lichtheim adopted the central tenets of the Paradox approach, departing from its liberal line only to contextualize Paradox conclusions within Lichtheim's own Neo-Bernsteinian Marxism. Lichtheim adhered to the Paradox argument about lifelong theoretical consistency, and he too relegated Bakunin's political argument to the pre-industrial utopian netherworld. Ignoring his own Marxist understanding of Hegel, Lichtheim concluded that Bakunin's defense of individual liberty contradicted his theory of revolutionary authority, noting "Bakunin's peculiar mixture of anti-authoritarian philosophy *in abstracto*, and dictatorial, indeed despotic, practice *in concreto*."[41] Further, Lichtheim accepted Paradox doctrine's psycho-historical solution, and he joined both Wilson in impugning Bakunin's sanity and Joll in condemning the religious underpinnings of anarchism generally.[42] Lastly, having concurred in the Paradox dismissal of Bakunin's political thought as incoherent, Lichtheim found himself in the curious position of ascribing Bakuninist notions and movements to Marx: the European syndicalist movement became "semi-Marxist," and Marx's revolutionary theory called for only "the minimum of effective leadership."[43] In short, despite Bakunin's formal theoretical kinship to Marxist theory, Lichtheim chose to evaluate Bakunin's work through the Lockean liberal eyes of the Paradox school.

Several conclusions can be fairly drawn from this discussion. First, the various structural problems within Bakunin's manuscripts cannot adequately explain how all these Paradox commentators arrived at their common conclusion. That conclusion, on the contrary, is rooted in three fundamental misapprehensions about Bakunin's work: the insistence upon lifelong theoretical consistency, the attribution of an incorrect intellectual lineage, and the imposition of a psycho-historical solution. These misapprehensions were compounded by these commentators' evident unfamiliarity with Bakunin's actual written work. And last, it would appear that the ideological thrust of the Paradox misinterpretation is too conveniently proximate to the ideological conclusions that liberal, libertarian, and Marxist partisans alike might wish to discover within the work of an important collectivist-anarchist thinker. Although the evidence is only circumstantial, the consistency with which these commentators adopted the Paradox conclusion leads to the conclusion that these authors were more interested in dismissing Bakunin's arguments for political reasons than they were in assessing his thought for any contributions to socialist theory or history.

This last point warrants a short digression into socialist history, for although the bourgeois liberal and libertarian motives for reworking Bakunin's political argument have been noted, something has yet to be said of the Marxist interest in this enterprise. Much of the animus which Marxists bear toward Bakunin developed in reaction to the particular political role which Bakunin had within the socialist movement. Bakunin was a contemporary of Marx. They had known each other as students in Berlin, and Bakunin's theoretical debut had appeared in the leading left-Hegelian journal of the period, Arnold Ruge's *Deutsche Jahrbucher*, alongside articles by Marx and Feuerbach. Far from being an apostate, Bakunin was well within the socialist mainstream throughout the 1840's, and was more or less acknowledged as such by Marx himself. Bakunin's differences with Marx developed only in the middle 1860's, with Bakunin's reappearance after twelve years of prison and exile, and their disagreement stemmed from Bakunin's emerging collectivist-anarchist argument and the prominence to which that argument thrust him within the resurgent socialist movement. Their famous split, which Marx felt constrained to engineer at the 1872 Hague Congress, was evidently precipitated by the political character of the events surrounding the 1871 Paris Commune. The Commune's activities were widely acknowledged as confirming Bakunin's revolutionary theory, and even as committed a Marxist partisan as Franz Mehring (Marx's biographer) felt obliged to attribute Bakunin's increased political influence after the Commune to the theoretical reverberations of that revolt.[44] In any case, the dispute between Bakunin and Marx had become political as well as philosophical, and Marx found it necessary to drum Bakunin out of the International on demonstrably trumped-up charges and to transfer the General Council to New York—in effect dissolving the entire International—in order to preserve both the Council and the International from Bakunin's supporters. As might be expected, the intellectual and personal animosities kindled by their clash were long lasting; indeed in some quarters the antagonism still survives. Moreover, from the Marxist perspective the question of Bakunin's claims to any socialist legitimacy had been settled by Marx himself. It was from within a rather long historical frame of reference, then, that commentators like Lichtheim and Braunthal chose to dismiss Bakunin as being of little theoretical interest or consequence.

Although they may have reached it through a different historical logic, Marxists like Lichtheim and Braunthal appear to carry the same partisan political animus toward Bakunin as do defenders of the liberal state like Carr and Pyziur. Further, their joint conclusion about the quality or usefulness of Bakunin's theoretical work seems to be confirmed in the recent strenuous efforts of right-wing libertarians like Woodcock and Avrich to claim Bakunin for their own pre-industrial Lockean individualism. Thus, the overall consequence of these disparate political motivations has been a common desire to discredit and/or ignore the uniquely socialist character of Bakunin's anti-authoritarian argument. Certainly, given the logic of their own political situations, these commentators could be expected to have little interest in explicating the collectivist-anarchist argument which Bakunin actually made, or in raising that argument for contemporary reconsideration.

In a sense, this work is a response to the presumptions and misconceptions that undergird the Paradox interpretation of Bakunin's thought. By going back to Bakunin's published manuscripts, I have attempted to reconstruct a clear statement of Bakunin's political argument as he himself presented it. The following chapters will show that during his mature anarchist period, dating approximately from 1866 to 1874, Bakunin set forth an internally consistent and fully fleshed social theory that bears little resemblance to the standard Marxist, liberal, or libertarian historical wisdom. His argument was based upon a specific understanding of the natural universe, in which the "mutual interaction" of all organic and inorganic matter produced a "natural authority" that dominated all aspects of human life. He analyzed the existent structures of human social organization in terms of this mutual interaction, in order to determine where mankind had interfered with its regular action by imposing arbitrary and static structures of authority upon particular human activities. These arbitrary institutions, Bakunin argued, were abstracted from the true source of free human development, which was grounded in mutual interaction, and they had been established solely in order to enable some men to dominate and oppress other men. On this basis he attacked the structure of abstract authority in four central aspects of nineteenth-century social organization: in the state, including that invested in a state bureaucracy; in a formalized understanding of science; in a capitalist mode of production; and in bourgeois parliamentary democracy. Furthermore, on a particular concrete translation of mutual interaction which I have labeled collective self-discipline, Bakunin constructed both a general theory of revolution and a specific revolutionary program for 1870 Europe.

There are two elements of Bakunin's theoretical work that deserve particular analytic attention. They both derive from his overarching commitment to the tangible social, economic, and political freedom of each individual within and through the collective structure of a socialist society. First, employed critically, this fundamental commitment guided Bakunin's sustained attack on all aspects of human social organization that, from whatever source, would establish an abstracted or reified social authority. This attack explicitly included not only the bourgeois capitalist but also the Marxist conception of state and science, and insisted that all such forms of abstracted authority forced mankind into a "Procrustean bed" of political domination and economic exploitation. Secondly, employed positively, Bakunin's central philosophical commitment led him to insist that all social and economic decision making must be fully participatory. His notion of collective self-discipline was a highly interactive system of individually and collectively exercised authority, which was to permeate all sectors of both pre-revolutionary and revolutionary organization. These two broad aspects of Bakunin's thought lead directly to the conclusion that, far from the anti-political construct described by many of the above-noted commentators, his fundamental argument was political in the best classical sense of the term.

There may be something of value to contemporary political thought in an awareness of how Bakunin arrived at his political argument. Bakunin utilized Feuerbach's anthropological naturalism as the basis for his own social theory, and a substantial number of Bakunin's major points have recognizably Feuerbachian overtones. Bakunin himself acknowledged this debt indirectly,[45] and in itself this theoretical lineage did not distinguish Bakunin from the rest of his socialist peers, including Marx. However, Bakunin's approach diverged sharply from that of Marx in terms of the "energizing principle" with which each man sought to transform Feuerbach's essentially contemplative perspective into an active and directive political force. Marx reached back into the Hegelian tradition by appropriating both the dialectic and, with it, Hegel's notion of man's self-development as coming through man's own labor—primarily an intellectual labor for Hegel, largely a physical labor for Marx via Feuerbach. Bakunin took quite a different theoretical tack, adopting the Lamarckian conception of an evolutionary theory predicated upon the adaptation of species to their surrounding physical environments. By so doing, Bakunin not only maintained but strengthened Feuerbach's subject-predicate inversion of Hegel, and thereby retained Feuerbach's living, sentient man at the center of collectivist-anarchism's political thought. Bakunin's analysis gained its historical dimension by coupling the purposiveness inherent within Lamarckian evolutionary adaptation to Feuerbach's conception of consciousness, and thus arrived at a theory of temporal development and social transformation which didn't in any way sacrifice the anthropological core of Feuerbach's argument.

Chapter five suggests that this approach to Feuerbach through evolutionary theory rather than through the dialectic may have important implications for the overall structure of post-industrial socialist thought. Bakunin, of course, relied upon this theoretical foundation when he criticized Marx's centralized socialist state as an abstracted and thereby oppressive form of social authority. But although he did suggest that Marx's Hegelian heritage was partially responsible for Marx's conception of the state, Bakunin evidently never pursued this line of analysis. I believe that by extending Bakunin's line of reasoning we can raise a series of major questions about the consequences that Marx's appropriation of the dialectic may have had for the overall character of Marx's political and social thought. Specifically, Bakunin's theoretical approach to Feuerbach contains within it the suggestion that Marx saddled himself through the dialectic with an inadequate, narrowly Hegelian theory of social domination. And this suggestion itself indicates that present-day socialists might be well advised to ask of Marx the same questions about the authoritarian character of the dialectic that Feuerbach addressed to Hegel.

2 *Bakunin's Theory of Freedom*

Toward a Bakuninist Ontology

Within the frame of intellectual reference of the Paradox school, most commentators argued that Bakunin's political thought had its primary intellectual roots in French theories of egalitarian communism and Stirner's notion of an absolute individual freedom. Additionally, commentators like Carr and Pyziur drew upon Bakunin's early attraction to Fichte (which preceded his interest in Hegel and Feuerbach) to confirm their own contention that the only consistency within Bakunin's work lay within his own unfettered will. As noted in chapter 1, though, the Paradox school as a whole downplayed the significance of Marx's work upon Bakunin's argument, and they completely missed the importance of Bakunin's Hegelian period in the early 1840's in their assessment of his 1842 article.

The further suggestion is sometimes made that Bakunin's political argument resembles that of Rousseau. While there are certain points of convergence between their respective political theories, these parallels generally appear only at the most basic level of intentions and goals. When one probes further, their theories become substantially less similar. Rousseau understood the relationships among state, society, and the individual to be of a fundamentally different character than that presented in Bakunin's work. While Bakunin located the central source of man's oppression within the structure of the political state as such, Rousseau placed it within the overall structure of civilized society as a whole. And where Bakunin believed that the solution lay in removing the political yoke of the state from the normal functioning of human society,

Rousseau argued that only through the imposition of a properly structured state could man rise above the obstacles created by human society. This distinction had a major impact upon the expectations which each held for the new community he proposed to establish: Bakunin envisioned a powerful and resilient entity rooted in the essential principles of the natural world; Rousseau saw an inherently unstable artifice which threatened to resolve back into its component interests. Consequently, it seems inappropriate to look to Rousseau as the primary intellectual source of Bakunin's collectivist-anarchist theory.

There is, lastly, an often unspoken assumption that Bakunin worked primarily within the utopian socialist tradition of early nineteenth-century France. Again, though, the similarities would seem to be more apparent than real. Bakunin's insistence that science had to be mediated by consciousness and volition, and that it could be of value to mankind only if it was strictly subordinated to a fully participatory process of decision making, bears little resemblance to the all-encompassing scientism of a Saint-Simon. And perhaps more to the point, the counterrevolutionary intentions which led Saint-Simon to propose his new scientific priesthood directly contradicted the entire thrust and purpose of Bakunin's theory.

Of Bakunin's theoretical indebtedness to Proudhon, two things can be said. First, Proudhon's basic argument, quite unlike Bakunin's, was predicated upon a hatred of the luxury and corruption bred by an urban industrialized civilization, and his program was designed to protect the small individual freeholding farmer or self-employed artisan from the encroachments of urban capital. And second, Bakunin himself, despite friendly personal relations with Proudhon, wrote that he had no choice but to agree with Marx's ascerbic dismissal of Proudhon in *The Poverty of Philosophy*, inasmuch as Proudhon's position was fundamentally idealist, metaphysical, and wholly lacking in any knowledge of "natural science."[1] Thus, while there are several intellectual threads that run from Proudhon to Bakunin—most particularly Proudhon's somewhat vaguely developed notion of a mutualist system of authority—each writer placed these concepts within a strikingly different philosophical and social context.

A careful reading of Bakunin's writings on his mature theory of collectivist anarchism points toward a rather different set of intellectual sources from those discussed thus far. The central framework of Bakunin's social theory would appear to have its most important intellectual roots in the work of Feuerbach and Lamarck. This conclusion isn't based on Bakunin's own statements of intellectual acknowledgement, for he made only a few short references to Feuerbach—the most interesting being his comment in *God and the State* identifying Feuerbach as "the disciple and demolisher of Hegel"[2]—and he apparently never mentioned Lamarck at all. Rather, this conclusion can be derived from Bakunin's conceptual approach to man's nature, and in the language and conceptual apparatus through which Bakunin conveyed that approach.[3] From Feuerbach,

Bakunin absorbed a fundamentally anthropological conception of the universe, in which the sentient human individual was simultaneously the center and the purpose of all philosophical endeavor. And from Lamarck, Bakunin acquired a theory of evolutionary development that could explain the progressive character of human history without endangering the centrality of Feuerbach's sentient being. By fusing Lamarck's late eighteenth-century French notion of purposive evolution to Feuerbach's humanist revision of German idealist philosophy, Bakunin arrived at a materialist theory of society that was substantially different from Marx's dialectical conception of materialism, and from which Bakunin could then castigate the "metaphysical" Hegelian undercarriage of Marx's social theory.

The parallels between the philosophical positions of Bakunin and Feuerbach run to the heart of Bakunin's entire intellectual enterprise. With only slight transmutations, Feuerbach's materialist assault upon the Hegelian Absolute reappeared in Bakunin's attack upon all forms of arbitrary authority. Most particularly, Feuerbach's repudiation of the Absolute mirrored almost exactly Bakunin's repudiation of the state as such—a correspondence which (as already implied) has important implications both for Bakunin's critique of capitalist society and for his philosophical dispute with Marx.

Feuerbach based his thought upon the necessity of restoring existing sentient mankind to the center of philosophical concern. His insistence that philosophy must begin with non-philosophy, with an "anti-scholastic" sensuousness ontologically given, directly parallels Bakunin's insistence that state and science must be judged in terms of their impact upon the ongoing daily lives of the popular mass, or "real life." For Feuerbach as for Bakunin, man must recognize that "the life of this world is the true life," and man must come to understand himself as the true center of his universe: "the human is the divine and the finite the infinite."[4] According to Feuerbach, however, man can never so experience himself as long as he remains subservient to the twin alienating and abstracting falsehoods of divine religion and Hegelian philosophy. Both the notion of God in religion, and of the Absolute in Hegel, "posit the essence of nature outside nature, the essence of man outside man," thereby stripping man of his own real and concrete being and alienating "man from himself."[5] Moreover, once having set themselves up as abstractions, neither the divine nor the Absolute could ever speak to the real concerns of the concrete, of sentient living man. "A philosophy that derives the finite from the infinite and the determinate from the indeterminate can never find its way to a true positing of the finite and the determinate."[6] Bakunin transmuted Feuerbach's critique of Hegel's Absolute into a broad-scale attack upon all forms of abstracted and alienating authority, criticizing both bourgeois and Marxist notions of state and science, as well as all religion, for precisely the same inability to either comprehend or sustain the concrete conditions required by living individuals within the real world. For Bakunin, as will be explored in chapter 3, abstracted state and science represented arbitrary interference with the complex processes of "real life," and consequently they had to be dismantled if man was ever to obtain true freedom.

Feuerbach and Bakunin both understood mankind to be at the center of a *natural* universe, by which they both meant the external physical environment. For Feuerbach as for Bakunin, man was inherently and inextricably connected to the natural world outside him, separated from other animals only by his capacity to develop rational thought. For Feuerbach, man was linked to the natural world by the fixed ontological character of sensuousness, which required man to be the passively receptive object, as well as the active subject of sensuous reality. Further, Feuerbach considered man's active subjectivity, his mind, to be limited by the naturally determined physical requirements, by the concrete needs of his body, and therefore argued that man could realize himself only through the medium of an independently existing physical nature. For Bakunin, under the influence of Lamarckian evolutionary theory as well as Feuerbach's "passive principle," man was linked to physical nature by ties that totally determined the character of his existence, and from which he could be relieved only by death.

Man, then, was posited by Feuerbach, and after him, Bakunin, to be a sentient being inextricably linked to physical nature, but alienated from himself in the bourgeois world by divine religion and speculative philosophy (the latter as embodied in state and science for Bakunin). To resolve man's plight—to force philosophy, in Feuerbach's words, to "open its eyes to human misery"[7]—both Feuerbach and Bakunin argued that concrete sentient man must regain his own alienated essence from the abstract ideal superimposed over him. For Feuerbach, this meant breaking the hold of religion and Hegelian philosophy; for Bakunin the effort must be to release man from all idealist reifications which prevented him from freely determining—within the fixed structure of the natural world—the course of his own existence. It is particularly instructive to note their similarity on this key point, for much of Feuerbach's criticism of the Hegelian dialectic later appeared in Bakunin's attack on a specifically Marxist state. Feuerbach argued that Hegel's system lacked "the tolerance of space," that it had no room for "the simultaneous totality of nature" which involved "co-ordination and co-existence." Rather, Hegel's system concerned itself solely with the progress of the Absolute toward its self-realization, and tolerated "only succession and sub-ordination" of "a particular and individual totality" in "exclusive time."[8] Consequently, Feuerbach insisted, the dialectic necessarily reduced the fully developed character of real world objects to only those aspects useful for the Absolute's progress toward itself. Bakunin argued, some thirty years after Feuerbach, that a centralized Marxist state would, in effect, suffer from all the inadequacies which Feuerbach attributed to Hegel's dialectic: that it would be an abstraction that would distort the wholeness of real individuals for its own development and satisfaction, that it would impose itself on that wholeness as an external, artificial, and dominant force, and that therefore it would not liberate but only further enslave those whose fates were consigned to it. One should note here that this direct parallel between Bakunin and Feuerbach lends support to an argument that Bakunin himself would only make implicitly, but which should be of fundamental concern to present-day socialists: the likelihood that Marx's state, in consequence of his appropriation of Hegel's dialectic, was indeed the universal and absolute state of Hegel.

Feuerbach's critique of Hegelian philosophy led him to argue that only by freeing the entire natural world from the arbitrary and abstracted straitjacket of the Absolute could concrete sentient man gain his freedom. "Feuerbach's insistence," Hanfi wrote,

> on the anthropological substratum of theology and speculative philosophy contains a categorical imperative for man to take back into himself all the richness of content—infinity and universality— he has put into God or into his speculative metamorphoses. The practical-emancipatory value of this supersession of man's self-alienation would be his elevation from a morally and socio-politically degraded, impoverished, unfree being into a free and dignified being.[9]

For Bakunin, of course, while the ultimate goal remained Feuerbach's "free and dignified being," the categorical imperative took a practical, concrete form: abolish the authoritarian state, popularize scientific knowledge, and remove the means of economic production from private and/or state-bureaucratic control. Both Bakunin and Feuerbach, however, understood that man could accomplish this restoration of his own human capacities only with and through his fundamental unity with his fellow man. Feuerbach argued that each man's subjective capacity for thought and action was equally grounded with that of all other men in a common shared objective, in the requirements of physical nature. Feuerbach also argued, however, that each man's individual totality as both subject and object of the natural world required that the independent and individual character of each man be preserved within that common objective.

> the single man in isolation possesses in himself the essence of man neither as a moral, nor as a thinking being. The essence of man is contained only in the community, in the unity of man with man—a unity, however, which rests on the reality of the distinction between You and I.[10]

Thus for Feuerbach as for Bakunin, man's individuality was derived from the human collective and could only be attained within and through that unity, yet his individuality carried a distinct and separate character from the shared common structure, and could participate in its commonness only from the perspective of that personal independence.

Implicit within this discussion of a real freedom for a concrete sentient man there lies, lastly, the similarity between Feuerbach and Bakunin on the question of human consciousness. For Feuerbach, it was man's capacity for rational thought—his capacity to become conscious both of himself and of the entire natural world—that distinguished man from all other animals. However, like Bakunin, Feuerbach doesn't posit man's consciousness as a metaphysical ideal that existed in and of itself. Rather, it was a necessary product of man's physical nature, anchored in the very structure of his being. Hanfi suggests that "in the language of Heidegger, the consciousness of Feuerbach is not a metaphysical category, but an existential characteristic belonging to the ontological constitution of man."[11] Bakunin fully shared this notion of human consciousness as a fixed natural aspect of man's physical being. For him, man was distinctive because, unlike all other animals, he was "capable of abstracting himself from the external world" and thereby "rising to the universality of things and beings."[12] Thus Feuerbach's understanding of man as a "species-being," as a creature capable of both consciousness of himself and of all others around him in the natural world, was also a central constitutive element in Bakunin's conception of man.

This shared perspective about the source and character of human consciousness was also valuable to Bakunin in that Feuerbach's notion neatly dovetailed with the strictly materialist argument of Lamarck. Indeed, Lamarck's premise that "every animal faculty whatsoever it be is an organic phenomenon and. . . results from a system or apparatus of organs that gives rise to it,"[13] provided a biological explanation for Feuerbach's philosophical argument. The crucial importance of conjoining Lamarckian evolutionary theory to Feuerbach's notion of concrete sentient man, however, lay in Bakunin's ability to utilize the progressive and developmental character of evolutionary change as the "living spontaneous fact"[14] with which to transform Feuerbach's essentially contemplative analysis into an active, historically contextualized process.

Bakunin's theoretical relationship to Lamarck was similar in both character and importance to his relationship with Feuerbach. Bakunin's central philosophical notion about the character of the natural world, that of the "mutual interaction" of all organic and inorganic entities—from which he derived his conceptions of natural authority, natural law, and collective self-discipline—was very closely based on Lamarckian evolutionary theory. This relationship can be readily observed by comparing their respective intellectual concepts and the language they used to express them.

Lamarck's understanding of the natural world was predicated on his belief that all aspects of both animal and plant life had a biological genesis. Nature was simply a long-term process by which matter became progressively more complex in its organization, resulting in a hierarchy of beings in which man was the "most perfect." "Nature, in producing successively all the species of animals, [began] with the most imperfect and the most simple in order to end her work with the most perfect."[15] This most fundamental statement of Lamarck's evolutionary theory appeared in a somewhat more expanded form in the opening pages of Bakunin's *God and the State*, in which he described

> the natural order from the lower to the higher, from the inferior to the superior, and from the relatively simple to the more complex; . . . the progressive and real movement from the world called inorganic to the world organic, vegetables, animal, and then distinctly human—from chemical matter or chemical being to living matter or living being, and from living being to thinking being.[16]

Lamarck argued that this developmental process reflected the interaction of two distinct and often opposed forces: an initial "power of life" or "stimulating cause" that by chemical or electrical means "excites" basic matter and encourages it to become more complex, and the modifying influence of enviromental factors around that matter which then either assist or inhibit its development.[17] The tension between these two forces accounted for the diversity of species within the natural world, and simultaneously allowed Lamarck to explain that diversity as the product of a dichotomy between a pure, natural, as against the real, actual course of biological development.[18] This two-factor theory of evolution appeared in Bakunin's thought directly in his statement that human society, as one aspect of the natural world, not only "develops" man's capacities but often "halts or falsifies their development." Even more centrally, however, Bakunin subsumed Lamarck's notion of a "power of life" into his own concept of a "universal motive power" which initiated and then maintained that process of perpetual development which he called "mutual interaction."[19] Bakunin argued, in a direct attack on Hegel, that the "motive power which creates the animal and human world" had no "self-consciousness," and was not the "indivisible substantial and single being as represented by the metaphysicians."[20] Rather, this force was "not an idea but a universal fact," which existed as "perpetual movement, manifesting and forming itself as an infinity of relative action and reaction— mechanical, physical, chemical, geologic, and those of the plant, animal and human worlds."[21] Bakunin concluded that, "as a resultant of that combination of relative and countless movements, this universal motive power is all-powerful,"[22] and thereby grounded his own concrete description of that force, mutual interaction, in a thoroughly Lamarckian conception of the natural world.

Beyond this fundamental contribution to Bakunin's thought, Lamarck's two-factor explanation of historical development also appeared indirectly, within Bakunin's perception of a basic tension between the free and dignified creature that man ought to be both in terms of his constitution and the character of "real life," and the reality of what man had become under the distortional impact of artificial, man-made social institutions. In this form, in fact, one could argue that Lamarck's theory itself paralleled a key presumption of Feuerbach's attack on the Hegelian Absolute.

As might be expected for Bakunin's agreement with Lamarck's most basic propositions, his work also paralleled at least four further elements of Lamarck's system. He accepted Lamarck's characterization of nature as a non-intelligent force "which acts only by necessity, and which can execute only what it does execute":[23] for Bakunin, nature acted "unconsciously" through the "inevitability of action."[24] Moreover, as Lamarck believed that the natural world was a well-ordered universe which operated on humanly comprehensible laws, Bakunin wrote of mutual interaction that "thanks to the inevitability of action, universal order can and indeed does exist,"[25] and this natural harmony became the basis for Bakunin's theory of a new collectivist-anarchist order within human society. Bakunin also absorbed Lamarck's rather eighteenth-century notion that animal life was distinguished from plants by "the properties of sensibility and irritability."[26] And lastly, Bakunin accepted Lamarck's proposition that "all animals" that had the physical "faculty to feel" would respond to "felt needs" with an unthinking, automatic, and mechanical reaction which Lamarck labeled the "sentiment intérieur."[27] Bakunin incorporated this concept of a non-rational response into his own notion of "animal will," which he presented as a natural impulse toward self-preservation.

Through his absorption of Lamarckian theory Bakunin was able to acquire a substantive, material, and most importantly, a developmental and historical conception of what Feuerbach had described only as the objective physical needs of mankind within an independent sensuous nature. Bakunin understood as implicit within the notion of mutual interaction the necessity of continual struggle as an inevitable element of the natural world. "The harmony of the forces of nature," which he accepted as a guiding general characteristic from Lamarck, was for Bakunin only "the actual result of that continual struggle which is the very condition of life and movement. In nature and also in society order without struggle is death."[28] Additionally, implicit within both this conception of a continual struggle with nature for survival and the conception of "animal will" which Bakunin had derived from Lamarck's "sentiment intérieur" toward self-preservation, was the notion of the necessity of labor. Bakunin himself used the Lamarckian notion of animal irritability and sensibility to justify first the necessity of nourishment, and through that need a requirement to labor.

> Being a living organism, endowed with the two-fold property of sensibility and irritability, and as such capable of experiencing pain as well as pleasure, every animal, man included, is forced by its own nature to eat, drink and move about. . . . In order to maintain its existence, the organism must protect itself against anything menacing its health, its nourishment, and all the conditions of its life. . . . It must want all these conditions for itself. And directed by a sort of prevision based upon experience, of which no animal is totally devoid, it is forced to work. . . in order to provide for the more or less distant future.[29]

In effect, Bakunin's acceptance of Lamarckian evolutionary theory enabled him to develop a conception of the necessity of perpetual struggle for survival, and of the necessity of human labor as the key constituent element of that struggle, without requiring him to turn to Hegel's dialectic. Where Marx employed the dialectic as an "energizing principle" with which to give Feuerbach's thought a historical dimension, and in order to obtain the key socialist conceptions of class struggle and the necessity of human labor as the motive force toward human liberation, Bakunin was able to adopt Lamarck's conception of a purposive natural drive toward organic perfection as the "living spontaneous fact" which Feuerbach's philosophical approach required.

Furthermore, through his reliance upon a primarily Lamarckian rather than a Hegelian understanding of the natural world, Bakunin could develop a conception of history which was fully transformational and which resulted in continual substantive and qualitative change without being dialectical. For Bakunin, the central characteristic of historical progress was that it was gradual, that it was a long-term development from one state into its opposite: "the development of everything. . . implies the gradual negation of the point of departure."[30] This emphasis on the gradual nature of historical change was clearly derived from an evolutionary rather than a dialectical model of development. For despite Bakunin's reliance upon a negative element within historical transformation—that everything necessarily becomes its opposite—his context and specific examples all point to his having grafted a residual Hegelian term onto a fundamentally evolutionary frame of reference. Thus, where dialectical change presumes a series of continual negations, which generate a series of abrupt historical breaks, Bakunin argued that historical transformations were unilinear. He wrote, for instance, that "as every development necessarily implies a negation, that of its base or point of departure, humanity is. . . essentially the deliberate and gradual negation of the animal element in man."[31] The evolutionary rather than dialectical character of Bakunin's argument is further evidenced by the strictly Lamarckian context within which Bakunin always framed his discussions of historical change. In one of his clearest passages on the subject, he argued that from the moment that this animal origin of man is accepted, all is explained. History then appears to us as the revolutionary negation, now slow, apathetic, sluggish, now passionate and powerful, of the past. It consists precisely in the progressive negation of the primitive animality of man by the development of his humanity. Man, a wild beast, cousin of the gorilla, has emerged from the profound darkness of animal instinct into the light of the mind.[32]

With his adoption of evolutionary theory, Bakunin acquired a concept of historical change that was equally as progressive, and equally as inexorable in its movement toward a final perfect historical condition, as was the dialectic, but which was also fully grounded in the concrete material character of the existent natural world, in the sensuousness of Feuerbach's Nature—which the dialectic clearly was not. From his fusion of Lamarck and Feuerbach, then, Bakunin could envision a fully conscious human being who was the absolutely determined product of an external physical nature, yet who could forge his own real freedom by working within its natural laws, through the processes of natural influence and mutual interaction, toward the satisfaction of his own rationally defined and thereby human needs. Bakunin himself effectively conjoined Lamarck's biology to Feuerbach's philosophy in one long paragraph, in which the core concept of evolutionary theory—the naturally defined and determined hierarchy of animals—introduced the core concept of Feuerbach's vision of the natural world: his "passive principle." After having introduced the notion of a naturally mandated desire for self-preservation among all animals, Bakunin continued:

Inevitable and irresistable in all animals, the most civilized man not excepted, this imperious and fundamental tendency of life constitutes the very basis of all animal and human passions. It is instinctive, one might say mechanical, in the lowest organizations, it is more conscious in the higher species, and it reaches the stage of full self-consciousness only in man, the latter being endowed with the precious faculty of combining, grouping, and fully expressing his thoughts. Man is the only one capable of abstracting himself, in his thought, from the external world and even from his own inner world, and of rising to the universality of things and beings. Being able, from the heights of this abstraction, to view himself as an object of his own thought, he can compare, criticize, order, and subordinate his own needs, without overstepping the vital conditions of his own existence. All that permits him, within very narrow limits of course, and without being able to change anything in the universal and inevitable flow of causes and effects, to determine by *abstract reflection* his own acts, which gives him, in relation to Nature, the false appearance of spontaneity and absolute independence.[33]

It was upon this theoretical foundation that Bakunin constructed his central notions of natural law, mutual interaction, and collective self-discipline, as well as his subsequent social and political argument about capitalist, Marxist, and, finally, collectivist-anarchist conceptions of human society.

Bakunin's Concept of Freedom

The fundamental concern which animated Bakunin's entire social theory was the pursuit and attainment of a viable human freedom. As he summarized his position, in an often quoted aphorism, "I am a fanatical lover of freedom."[34] However, despite the tenacious insistence of Paradox commentators like E. H. Carr, Bakunin never described liberty in the separate, independent, or absolutist terms of Lockean individualism. Far from transcending and thereby divesting itself of social content, Bakunin's notion of human freedom could survive only within a strictly structured social context. Liberty was always the product of a self-sustaining equilibrium among Nature, society, and the individual, and as such it was fully predicated upon its relationship to human society as a whole. Thus Bakunin's concept of liberty can only be properly understood within the particular social framework that could produce it.

Bakunin believed that a society's capacity to sustain human freedom was closely linked to the manner in which it maintained internal order. All human societies, he argued, exercised two distinct forms of social authority over the individuals within them. These two types of authority had very different origins, with substantially different capacities to sustain human freedom, and as a result Bakunin insisted that it was essential to comprehend the "precise distinction" that separated them.[35]

One form of authority was intentionally and consciously imposed upon mankind by the decision of certain individuals within human society. This type of social control, whether exercised by a single individual or a select group, and whether promulgated through physical force or electoral consent, remained an arbitrary man-made system. Bakunin argued that by its very nature this artificial form of social authority developed and maintained only those "political, religious, and civil laws" that served the interests of the society's elite. He generally ascribed this type of authority to the "official, and therefore tyrannical authority of the state-organized society,"[36] although on occasion he extended its purview to the coercive imposition of "any theological, metaphysical, political or even economic idea."[37]

The second form of social authority was that exercised by the fundamental, pre-existing structure of mankind's "physical and social worlds."[38] Bakunin argued that the central components of both man's own nature and of the external environment severely circumscribed mankind's potential activity. Producing fixed and immutable relationships, these elements acquired the impact of natural forces, exerting inexorable and "inevitable power"[39] over human beings and thereby extracting from them "an involuntary and inevitable obedience."[40]

Thus, Bakunin argued that the notion of social authority had to be dichotomized into separate and distinct components: one consciously invoked and controlled by mankind, the other imposed and determined by the pre-existent configuration of the natural world. "One should not," he admonished his followers,

> confuse sociological laws, . . . which are just as immutable and necessary for every man as the laws of physical Nature . . . with political, criminal and civil laws, which to a greater or lesser extent express the morals, customs, interests, and views dominant in a given epoch, society, or section of that society.[41]

Having sundered the notion of social authority, Bakunin could assume a dual posture toward its exercise. On the one hand, provoked by what he perceived as its objective consequence for the working classes, Bakunin excoriated the form of man-made artificial authority embodied within nineteenth-century bourgeois institutions. He argued further that similar results would inevitably flow from any such set of formal political institutions, regardless of the social intentions of the men who erected them. In his manuscripts, the word "authority" was employed almost exclusively as a pejorative reference to this man-made type of social control. Comments like "authority is the negative of freedom,"[42] and "we reject all legislation . . . and all authority"[43] summarized Bakunin's attitude toward this variant of social authority.

Bakunin approached what he called "natural authority," however, from exactly the opposite perspective. Its objective impact upon every human being regardless of social position, Bakunin argued, left every individual with no alternative but to acknowledge and accept the overwhelming power of these naturally mandated "sociological laws." In direct contrast to his attack upon all forms of man-made social authority, Bakunin adopted and even embraced this natural type of social control. "We recognize all natural authority," Bakunin wrote in one passage, "and all influence of fact upon us."[44]

By separating man-made from naturally induced social authority, Bakunin could reject the formal institutionalized authority of the bourgeois state as illegitimate, while simultaneously acknowledging a dominant and universal authority which was exercised upon man by the natural world. This analytic framework provided the central premise for Bakunin's conception of a new, collectivist-anarchist social order. Both his definition of a viable human freedom, as well as the system of collective self-discipline through which he proposed to attain that freedom, were fully predicated upon the mechanisms of natural as against man-made social authority. Bakunin believed that human freedom could be achieved only within a system of social authority that was based upon and patterned after the fundamental framework of natural authority that regulated all aspects of the natural world, including human society. For Bakunin, liberty could be attained not just within a social context per se, but rather within an arrangement of social authority that directly reflected the pre-existing processes of natural authority.

One further introductory point needs to be made, with regard to the contribution that Bakunin believed individual volition could make toward the attainment of human freedom. His conception of the individual's will, in the general sense of volition, was very different from the eighteenth-century idealist notion of a free will. Bakunin argued that Rousseauian postulations of a "free *arbitrary* will, that is to say, the presumed faculty of the human individual to determine himself freely and independently of any external influence,"[45] were no more than an "untenable fiction."[46] Such a "doctrine of 'free will'" was "nonsense" which collectivist anarchism "rejects absolutely."[47] With the exception, then, of several infrequent passages in which he described "rational will" as akin to "free will" in a positive, fully contextualized sense, Bakunin consistently presented the concept of free will as an explicitly metaphysical and negative notion.

Bakunin's denial of "free arbitrary will," however, and with it the denial of any possibility that mankind could be freed *from* the constraints of natural authority, did not in any sense include a rejection of the contrary proposition that mankind could attain freedom *with* and *through* natural authority. "The negation of free will," he argued, "does not connote the negation of freedom. On the contrary, freedom represents the corollary, the direct result of natural and social necessity."[48] A conception of freedom could be meaningful in the actual world, Bakunin contended, only if it was compatible with the immutable conditions which established and defined that world. Freedom must be consistent with natural authority, and with that authority's practical expression in what Bakunin termed "natural law." Thus an individual's personal will could contribute toward his freedom only to the extent that it acknowledged and reflected this determinate natural force. Bakunin argued further that the individual's will could attain this level of development only through the fusion of a knowledge of natural law achieved through reason with man's innate biological need to survive, which Bakunin termed man's "animal will." This coupling of rational intellect to animal will, Bakunin believed, produced within man a "rational will" with which man could pursue his liberation within the actual world by and through the established mechanisms of natural authority.

The general structure of Bakunin's argument should now be apparent. His conception of human freedom, and of the procedures by which man was to attain it, was based on his perception of a pre-existent and ultimately determinant natural world. Consequently, Bakunin's conceptions must be evaluated through the prism of his understanding of natural authority.

Bakunin believed that the preeminent power upon earth, which dominated all living creatures including human beings, was that of Nature. He conceptualized this power as a continual process of change, with the word itself representing simply the static summation of this constant flux. "Nature," Bakunin argued, "is the sum of the actual transformations of things that are and will ceaselessly be produced within its womb."[49] Within this flux, each entity's continual development had a correspondingly continual impact upon its surrounding environment, and thus upon the development if not the actual existence of every other entity within that environment. Each entity was engaged in a constant process of cause and effect with every other entity, and the overall sum of these interactions was the dominant force within the natural world.

> All this boundless multitude of particular actions and reactions, combined in one general movement, produces and constitutes what we call Life, Solidarity, Universal Causality, Nature. . . . the universal, natural, necessary, and real, but in no way pre-determined, pre-conceived, or foreknown combination of the infinity of particular actions and reactions which all things having real existence incessantly exercise upon one another.[50]

It was to this inexorable unfolding of the concrete world that Bakunin referred when he applied the adjective "natural" to an object or a process.

Bakunin believed that this process of mutual interaction and consequent interdependence followed certain established patterns, which were defined by each living entity's innate instinctual drive toward "the conditions necessary for the life of its species."[51] These patterns emerged from daily life as "natural laws" which "manifest themselves in the concatenation and succession of phenomena in the physical and social worlds."[52] Bakunin concluded that all living entities both influenced and were influenced by all other living entities, and that the patterns of mutual interaction which they created formed a set of humanly discernable natural laws.

Human society, or what Bakunin sometimes termed the "social world," was simply one subset of the natural world. Society was "the natural mode of existence of the human collective,"[53] and as such was, like all natural conditions, neither good nor evil. Rather, Bakunin argued, it was "an immense and overwhelming fact, a positive and primitive fact, having existence prior to all consciousness, to all ideas, to all intellectual and moral discernment."[54] Society both precedes and survives the human individual, for "like Nature it is eternal,"[55] and it is governed by its own set of intrinsic laws, "natural laws, inherent in the social body, just as physical laws are inherent in material bodies."[56] As Bakunin viewed it, the existence of such natural laws within human society was to be expected, "since human society is, after all, nothing but the last great manifestation or creation of Nature on earth."[57]

This fundamental conception of a determinant and omnipotent natural world, within which human society was subsumed, greatly narrowed the context within which it was possible to consider the question of human freedom. Bakunin outlined the consequences of natural authority for the liberty of the individual human being in passages such as the following.

> Nature, through its ethnographic, physiological, and pathological action, creates faculties and dispositions which are called natural, and the organization of society develops them or on the other hand halts or falsifies their development. All individuals, with no exceptions, are at every moment of their lives what Nature and society have made them.[58]

He based this conclusion upon the impact that both Nature and society had upon the human individual.

Bakunin considered mankind, like all living species on earth, to be "Nature's product," and he believed that, as such, mankind "exists only by virtue of its laws."[59] Individual human beings were so utterly "pervaded and dominated" by this force that they were completely dependent upon it to create and sustain their very lives.[60] "Let us recognize once and for all," Bakunin wrote,

> that against this universal Nature, our mother who shapes us, brings us up, feeds us, surrounds and permeates us to the marrow of our bones, to the deepest recesses of our intellectual and moral being, and which end[s] by smothering us in her maternal embraces—that against this universal nature there can be neither independence nor revolt.[61]

Even the individual's "most intelligent and abstract thoughts and emotions" were in their essence only "Nature's new creations and manifestations."[62] In the face of such overwhelming force, Bakunin argued, any attempt to separate oneself from this natural authority became either a logical absurdity—"he would revolt against himself"—or suicide.[63]

Man was equally dependent upon the subdivision of Nature which pertained directly to human organization. "Man only becomes man," Bakunin wrote, "amidst society, and thanks only to the collective collaboration of all men, whether present or past."[64] Born into the world as a "ferocious beast,"[65] the human being was initially a "speechless and unreasoning animal."[66] Thought, speech, and rational will were exclusively the products of society, of the collective accomplishment of prior generations, and could be attained by the individual only within and from human society as a whole. Society even determined both the onset and the destruction of "free thought" within the individual.[67] Bakunin therefore concluded that "in view of the fact that society shapes and determines his essence, man is dependent upon it as completely as upon physical Nature."[68] As a result, man could no more supersede his social than his physical nature: "radical rebellion against society would therefore be as impossible as rebellion against nature."[69]

Bakunin argued that man's freedom could only be attained within the context of natural authority. Although the individual was completely formed by this context and unable to escape from it, the individual need never perceive natural laws as limitations upon his personal freedom. "These laws are not outside of us," Bakunin wrote, "they are inherent within us; they constitute our being, our whole being . . .: we live, we breathe, we act, we think, we wish only through these laws. Without them we are nothing, *we are not*."[70] Instead the individual finds himself "wholly identical" with the basic structure of nature and society in every instance and is consequently unable to "feel himself a slave" to it.[71]

On the contrary, since these "restrictions" had been laid down by "the laws of our own Nature," Bakunin argued that they were in actuality the real conditions required by man to achieve his freedom.[72] Consequently, Bakunin insisted that man could be liberated only if he consciously acknowledged and respected the free and full application within human society of the same principle of mutual interaction through which natural authority ordered the relations of all other living entities. Bakunin made this point implicitly in the passage cited above that referred to each individual as formed by the "collective collaboration" of all human beings. This argument became more direct in a statement which referred to human society as itself the ever-changing product as well as the producer of mankind. "Every individual," Bakunin wrote, "even the most insignificant one, is the product of centuries of development: the history of causes working toward the formation of such an individual has no beginning."[73] Bakunin's position was most clearly stated, however, with his direct assertion that each individual stood in the same mutually interactive relationship with society as did each living entity with the natural world as a whole: "all individuals. . . are at each instant of their lives, simultaneously the producers and the products of the volition and action of the masses."[74] Bakunin thus established the process of mutual interaction or "natural influence" as a natural law central to the structure of human society. "As for the natural influence which men exert on one another," he argued, "it is again one of those conditions of social life against which revolt would be as futile as impossible."[75] In fact, Bakunin argued that this structure of natural influence not only framed society's character but was itself essential to the survival of society:

In Nature as in human society, which is itself nothing but Nature, everything that lives does so only under the supreme condition of intervening in the most positive manner in the life of others— intervening in as powerful a manner as the particular nature of a given individual permits it to do so. To do away with this reciprocal influence would spell death in the full sense of the word.[76]

It was this conception of mutual influence as necessary for both the original emergence as well as the subsequent survival of the individual which led Bakunin to refer to the "natural and social law of human solidarity."[77] Indeed he argued that such influence was "the very basis" of human solidarity.[78] Through the application, then, of Nature's central principle to human society, Bakunin believed he had generated a firm natural-law foundation for his conception of solidarity. Human solidarity, in turn, became the cornerstone of Bakunin's understanding of human freedom. Solidarity, objectively produced because it was objectively necessary, served as the opening through which Bakunin integrated the needs and desires of the single individual into the previously seamless structure of a dominant natural authority. The individual, in accordance with the objective requirements upon which he depended for self-definition and survival, could pursue his freedom only in and through the social collective.

Bakunin supported this argument with three linked arguments about the consequences of mutual influence. On the directly physical level, Bakunin noted the proverb that "no two leaves [are] alike on one and the same tree" to justify his contention about the interrelationship between the individual and society. Mutual interaction, he argued, produced a similarly complete structural dependence of each individual upon all other members of his society. "This diversity," he wrote, "constitutes the wealth of humanity. Thanks to this diversity, humanity is a collective unit in which every individual member completes all the others and himself needs all the rest."[79] Thus dependent upon his relationship with all others within the social collective, an individual's liberty depends on the existence of the liberty of his fellows: the "individual freedom of every man becomes actual and possible only through the collective freedom of society of which man constitutes a part by virture of a natural and immutable law."[80]

In a parallel argument concerning education, Bakunin contended that the "education and training" which each individual required to attain his own freedom—of which more will be said shortly—was clearly a social product.[81] Thus again, the freedom of the individual could only be attained through the action of the group. "Man realizes his individual freedom," Bakunin argued, "only by rounding out his personality with the aid of other individuals belonging to the same social environment."[82]

And lastly, Bakunin argued that in its ultimate sense an individual's perception of his freedom existed only when that freedom was recognized and accepted by those with whom he interacted. True freedom, Bakunin argued, was a socially defined status: "being free for man means being acknowledged, considered, and treated as such by all the men around him."[83] Therefore each individual could attain his own sense of personal freedom only through the equal freedom of those who surrounded him, and the effective existence of his freedom was fundamentally tied to the effective existence of theirs. Bakunin described this linkage as follows:

> No individual human being can recognize his own humanity, nor, consequently, realize it in his life, except by recognizing it in others and in cooperating for its realization in others. No one can emancipate himself except by emancipating with him all the men who surround him. My liberty is the liberty of everybody; for I am really free, free not only in idea but in fact, only when my liberty and my rights find their confirmation, their sanction, in the liberty and in the rights of all men, my equals.[84]

Inherent within this third, last defense of Bakunin's collective notion of individual freedom were the conclusions produced by the first two arguments. In all three cases, the individual's capacity to achieve personal freedom was inextricably bound to the fulfillment of that same potential within all his fellows. As Bakunin explained in a passage which mustered his notion of freedom against that argued by Lockean individualists,

> I mean that freedom of the individual which, far from stopping as if before a boundary in face of the freedom of others, on the contrary finds in that freedom its own confirmation and extension to infinity; the unlimited freedom of each in the freedom of all, freedom in solidarity, freedom in equality.[85]

It was upon this conception of a collective social liberty, predicated on perpetual mutual interaction, that Bakunin conducted his fervent campaign for individual freedom. Certainly, only this theoretical framework could endow his pursuit of individual freedom through collective solidarity with a logical rather than a contradictory character. Bakunin summarized this argument about the nature of freedom in the following often cited but rarely understood passage.

> Social solidarity is the first human law; freedom is the second law. Both laws interpenetrate and are inseparable from each other, thus constituting the very essence of humanity. Thus freedom is not the negation of solidarity; on the contrary it represents the development of, and so to speak, the humanization of the latter.[86]

Bakunin's basic argument on the relationship between freedom and solidarity led him to two further related conclusions. First, if, as implied above, the infusion of freedom into solidarity was necessarily a gradual process, then the general development of human history must be in a positive progressive direction. Bakunin argued that since "the last phase and supreme goal of all human development is *liberty*,"[87] history must eventually result in the liberation of mankind. "Society is the root, the tree of freedom, and liberty is its fruit," he concluded. "Consequently, in every epoch man has to seek his liberty not at the beginning but at the end of history, and we may say that the real and complete emancipation of every individual is the true, great objective, the supreme purpose of history."[88]

Second, and similarly integral to his conception of freedom through solidarity, was the importance which Bakunin placed upon economic and social equality within that solidarity. Having postulated that the free development of each is the condition for the free development of all, Bakunin had to require that each individual be equal to all others. "Since freedom is the result and clearest expression of solidarity, that is, of mutuality of interests, it can be realized only under conditions of equality."[89] Bakunin stressed that without such an assumption of equality, his conception of freedom was disengaged summarily from the conditions which defined it, and the term reverted to its prior bourgeois meaning of license. His position, he argued, "admits freedom only after equality, in equality, and through equality, because freedom outside of equality can only create privilege."[90]

It is important to note that this economic and social equality was never intended to level all personal potentials to a single common social denominator. Exactly opposite to claims that he had presented "an assertion and a demand that, on the whole, each individual is not and cannot be different,"[91] Bakunin explicitly insisted that only the differences within individuals that were artificially induced by unequal access to society's economic and social resources would be affected. His goal, he wrote, was "equality for all, from birth until entry into adult life, as far as such equality depends on the economic and political organization of society, in order for every individual—natural differences apart—to be the true offspring of his own efforts."[92] Bakunin also recognized that some apparent "natural differences" among people were themselves the product of past social inequalities, but he believed that beyond these there were in fact fundamental "differences of talent, ability, and productive energy" which a just society could diminish but not completely eliminate.[93] Indeed, Bakunin argued that these basic natural differences helped maintain the resilience of the society as a whole. "Equality," he concluded this argument, does not mean the leveling down of individual differences, nor intellectual, moral and physical uniformity among individuals. This diversity of ability and strengths, and these differences of race, nation, sex, age, and character, far from being a social evil constitute the treasure house of mankind.[94]

Bakunin's argument about the naturally mandated linkage between individual freedom and collective solidarity provided the context for his discussion of the individual's education. As noted above, Bakunin argued that a proper human freedom required the establishment within each individual of a "rational will," within which that individual's reasoning ability and his acquired knowledge of natural law would be fused into his "animal will." We need to consider each of these concepts in turn.

Bakunin believed that a good working knowledge of Nature's laws was an essential prerequisite to human liberty. "It is only by studying," he argued in a key passage,

> and by making use, by means of his thought, of the external laws of this Nature—laws which manifest themselves equally in everything constituting his external world as well as his own individual development . . .—that he succeeds in gradually shaking off the yoke of external nature, of his own natural imperfections, and . . . the yoke of an authoritarian social organization.[95]

Bakunin suggested that the individual acquired this knowledge through a complex two-stage process of intellectual development in which the critical point of differentiation between these stages occurred with what might be termed the quickening of the rational will. The first phase of this process involved the individual's involuntary socialization into both the physical and social worlds of his birth. Each child uncritically and unconsciously internalized the established assumptions of his society and was thus "inculcated" with the "intellectual and moral qualities"[96] or rather the "collective prejudices of the religious, political, and economic institutions of the society to which he belongs."[97] Throughout this period of socialization the individual remained simply "the product of Nature and his education," and as such was not responsible for his thoughts or beliefs.[98] "All these ideas are imprinted upon the mind of the individual and conditioned by the education and training he receives even before he becomes fully aware of himself as an entity."[99]

Bakunin noted further that the attitudes and information with which the individual was thusly endowed—whether heritage or baggage—would be his "point of departure" when his own processes of thought took hold. Even the decision to seize control over one's own intellectual development, "this resolution to work upon himself,"[100] was still the effect or immediate consequence of one's original and involuntary socialization. "At that moment," Bakunin contended, "he is nothing else but the product of external influences which led him to that point."[101]

The second stage of intellectual development, in which the individual gained the capacity for rational thought, required him to perceive, internalize, re-integrate, and then implement to his own advantage the natural laws which controlled him. Bakunin believed that this complex process would give the individual a subjective sense of self-control within what remained a dominant objective environment. In one passage Bakunin explained man's false sense of freedom from the natural world as follows:

> Man apprehends and is clearly aware of natural necessities which, being reflected in his brain, are reborn through a little known physiological process as the logical succession of his own thoughts. This comprehension in the midst of his absolute and unbroken dependence gives him the feeling of self-determination, of conscious spontaneous will and liberty.[102]

In another passage, similarly allusive to Feuerbach, Bakunin argued that after discerning these natural laws the individual then "appropriated them, so to say, by transforming them into ideas—almost spontaneous creations of our own brains. While continuing to obey these laws man in reality simply obeyed his own thoughts."[103] Through the psychological process of the brain the individual absorbed the principles of his natural environment within himself, and then redirected or recombined these fixed natural laws in order to satisfy his own needs. In "recognizing and assimilating" Nature's laws, Bakunin concluded, "man rises above the immediate pressures of his external world, and then, becoming a creator, henceforth obeying only his own ideas, he more or less transforms the latter in accordance with his progressive needs, impressing upon it to some extent the image of his own humanity."[104]

One should note that Bakunin consistently acknowledged the control which these natural structures exerted over the individual's range of choice. Qualifications like "more or less" and "to some extent" indicated the difficulty with which man intervened in the natural world and the level of restriction upon individual efforts to alter the course of natural events. Addressing this point directly, Bakunin concluded that

> up to a certain point man can become his own educator, his own instructor as well as creator. But it is to be seen that what he acquires is only a relative independence and that in no way is he released from the inevitable dependence, or the absolute solidarity by which he, as a living being, is irrevocably chained to the natural and social world.[105]

Concurrent with this two-phase accumulation of information about the external world around him, the individual underwent a parallel development of his personal will. Bakunin postulated that the "animal will" with which the individual was born was first subjected to social controls, and after intellectual quickening was subsequently transformed through rational reflection into a mature "rational will."

Bakunin defined man's animal will as the unconscious and "altogether formal power" through which all living creatures attempted to maintain their own existence.[106] Working from a directly Lamarckian frame of reference, Bakunin argued that this will was generated by "an irresistable force inherent in all living creatures. This force is the universal current of life, the same one we call universal causality."[107] This force, which he also referred to as Nature itself, was expressed in "the urge of every individual to realize for himself the conditions necessary for the life of its species," and provided the essential foundation for man's conscious or rational will: "this urge, this essential and supreme manifestation of life, constitutes the basis of what we call *will.*"[108]

The transformation of animal will into rational will was to be effected through the injection of knowledge about Nature's laws. Initially each child had to be induced by various agents of socialization to develop a measure of self-control over the first of Bakunin's three natural "yokes" which he would encounter: his own inner nature. Such socialization was essential since "no one can shake off the yoke of his own nature, subordinate the instincts and drives of his body to the guidance of his ever-developing mind, except through upbringing and education."[109] Moreover, only with the gradual development of control over his own inner nature would the individual become able after intellectual quickening to overcome the two remaining but external yokes that oppressed him.

Bakunin argued that the development of self-control through a strong personal will required that the individual's will be continually "exercised, at first, of course, through compulsory exercises, in the process of checking instinctive drives and cravings, and with this accumulation and concentration of inner power in the child there gradually comes concentration of attention, memory, and independent thought.[110] Bakunin condoned this reliance upon coercive authority as "legitimate, necessary" when it was being "applied to children of a tender age," but he immediately noted that the only purpose of this authority was to produce its own dissolution. "This principle," he wrote, "must diminish as fast as education and instruction advance," for "all rational education is at bottom nothing but this progressive immolation of authority for the benefit of liberty."[111] As the child's self-control advanced, he would internalize within his own consciousness the same selection process which had been imposed initially upon him from outside. He "undergoes an inner bifurcation," Bakunin contended, in which he becomes capable of "rising above his own drives, instincts, and urges, insofar as these are of a passing and particular nature."[112] This bifurcation enabled the child to "compare these inner drives" and then to "side with some against others" in accordance with his developing sense of a social "ideal."[113] With the internalization of this decision-making procedure the foundation for intellectual quickening was complete, and the individual had been properly prepared for the "awakening" of his rational will. Thus for Bakunin an increasing and eventually self-generating capacity to comprehend the natural laws that ordered his own inner nature would enable the individual to develop a strong personal will with which to regulate those urges. The individual would acquire both a progressive freedom from his own personal compulsions and the central tool with which to interpose his evolving social and physical needs upon the external world.

Bakunin believed that an individual's developed rational will was the only force that could reduce his bondage to the natural world. Man could "gradually free himself," Bakunin argued, only through the consistent "application of thought to the conative instinct, that is, with the aid of his rational will."[114] Man's rational will facilitated both the discovery of relevant natural laws and the redirection of those laws where tenable to man's own purposes. However, Bakunin recognized that the generation and application of this knowledge was far too vast a project for the separate individual. In fact such an undertaking required "the combination of the labor of past generations and the present generation."[115] Mankind required not just the development of individual rational wills to achieve control over its physical world but also the "collective physical and intellectual labor of society as a whole."[116]

Bakunin believed that man's release from his third yoke, from social impediments to his freedom, required a collective effort similar to that directed against the physical world. But man's complex and idiosyncratic system of social order reduced the degree of direct correspondence between the two efforts, and this last naturally produced yoke would be the most difficult for man to throw off. Since Bakunin's entire social theory, however, was an effort to explain how man was to achieve this final stage of his freedom, a full consideration of his argument here must be held in abeyance.

Bakunin's understanding of the broad determinative context that defined the limits of man's freedom, and of the structure of the educational process by which Bakunin believed the individual would come to intellectual consciousness within that context, have now been described. This fundamental framework of forces and processes formed the theoretical backdrop against which Bakunin discussed the practical components of each individual's personal liberty. Again, it is important to remember that these individual freedoms were understood by Bakunin to be fully dependent upon the conditions produced by the society as a whole, attainable only within an equitably structured society, and contingent upon the existence of similar freedoms for all other individuals within that society.

The first aspect of a practical human freedom was the individual's ability to cultivate fully his innate creative capacities. Liberty for Bakunin demanded conditions which not only allowed but induced "the full development of all the material, intellectual, and moral powers which are found in the form of latent capabilities in every individual."[117] He considered this component of an individual's freedom to be "eminently positive and social" in both focus and consequence.[118]

In contrast, Bakunin presented the second component of individual liberty as a negative element. It required the "absolute rejection" of every form of externally imposed authority "whether divine or human, collective or individual."[119] However, when restated as a theory of individual self-determination, Bakunin described this aspect as a highly positive and thoroughly social factor. "There should be an independence," he argued, "as absolute as possible, of each individual in relation to all human wills, collective as well as individual, which would desire to impose not their natural influence but their law, their despotism."[120] Such an independence was essential to any valid conception of liberty, Bakunin believed, because it "signifies man's right to dispose of himself and to act in conformity with his own views and convictions."[121] He elaborated upon this argument in the following passage, which itself clearly presumed an established structure of natural influence and the prior quickening of the individual's rational will:

> To be free personally means for every man living in a social milieu not to surrender his thought or will to any authority but his own reason and his own understanding of justice; in a word, not to recognize any other truth but the one which he himself has arrived at, and not to submit to any other truth but the one accepted by his own conscience.[122]

In short, as Bakunin argued in a different passage, individual freedom required "the entire independence of the will of each in relation to the will of others."[123]

This strict emphasis upon the uncoerced individual led Bakunin to two further, corollary arguments about human freedom. First, through his insistence that not the content but rather the process by which a social decision was reached conferred legitimacy upon it, Bakunin framed his definition of social morality in terms of individual liberty. A decision which on some other value scale might be a social good would for Bakunin be a moral evil if it was implemented through external coercion. "Good becomes evil," Bakunin argued, "once it is made subject to command,"[124] since by resorting to external authority that putative good "imposes itself on the individual as the negation, rather than itself the product, of liberty."[125] And second, by predicating all social morality upon individual liberty, Bakunin concluded that human liberty could defend itself only by and through its own free processes. It would be a dangerous misconception, he argued, to believe that a partial limitation of an individual's freedom could successfully secure the protection of that freedom. "Since morality has no other source, incentive, cause, and object than liberty, and is itself inseparable from liberty, all restrictions imposed on the latter with the intention of safeguarding the former have always turned against it."[126] Thus Bakunin's emphasis upon individual freedom brought him to conclude that social morality both precluded external coercion and could not be set in opposition to liberty.

Having now explored both Bakunin's concept of individual liberty and his notion of natural authority, the central theoretical proposition that bound these two seemingly contradictory ideas together can be seen more clearly. On the one hand, Bakunin believed that the individual human being was strictly confined by the immutable relationships of the natural world, and by the incessant process of mutual interaction which defined those relationships. The individual's personality and beliefs were initially the direct product of these forces, and his intellectual and physical development remained dependent upon them even after he had undergone intellectual quickening. The full personal liberty toward which the individual might legitimately aspire was itself completely formed and determined by natural laws. However, on the other hand, Bakunin argued with equal intensity that within this rigidly delimited natural context, each individual's freedom must pervade and dominate all aspects of daily life. Bakunin particularly relied upon this principle to fashion a practical procedure through which the will of the individual could be integrated into an effective collective form of social authority. Thus from Bakunin's perspective it was entirely logical to seek the fullest human liberty within a completely determined natural universe.

Bakunin's concept of a properly structured system of social authority can best be described as a system of collective self-discipline. It was designed to create within the society as a whole the sense of self-restraint and focussed application which rational will developed within the separate individual. However, quite unlike most notions of social authority, Bakunin's system was to produce this result through a voluntary process of mutual influence, and its decisions would therefore represent not the restriction of but the logical culmination and fulfillment of each individual's separate will. Collective self-discipline, as Bakunin understood it, was the system of social organization through which his notion of freedom through solidarity could be realized.

Collective self-discipline was constructed directly upon Bakunin's central Lamarckian notion of incessant mutual interdependence. As already noted, he believed that this notion's equivalent expression within human society could be found in the "natural influence which men exercise upon one another," and that this pattern of mutual influence was essential to the character and the very survival of mankind. By basing collective self-discipline upon this pre-existent structure of natural influence, Bakunin could incorporate the strength of natural law into his system of social authority. Additionally, its foundation in mutual interaction enabled collective self-discipline to establish the strict social equality as well as the process of reciprocal authority required if the will of each individual was to be freely merged into a collective authority. And lastly, the centrality of natural influence of collective self-discipline sharply distinguished this system of social authority from that found in traditional and bourgeois social institutions. Traditional authority, Bakunin argued, froze this natural process of mutual interaction among individuals into a fixed hierarchy of command, and thereby always induced "the transformation of natural influence, and, as such, the perfectly legitimate influence over man, into a right."[127] Collective self-discipline's emphasis upon the fluid processes of natural influence, consequently, set it apart from other systems of social decision-making.

Formally described, collective self-discipline contained two more or less sequential stages of decision making. In the first phase the individual, possessed of a rational will, considered the various analyses of a given situation put forward by his peers. He was expected to weigh both the substantive merits of each proposal, as well as the wisdom and accrued personal respect of its proponent, but ultimately he was to decide the issue according to his own best judgement. Through this process, Bakunin believed, the individual could incorporate the knowledge and experience of his fellows into what remained the decisions of his own uncoerced will. As Bakunin summarized this argument, "we are far from denying the natural and beneficial influence of knowledge and experience upon the masses, provided that that influence exerts itself very simply, by way of the natural incidence of higher intellects upon the lower intellects."[128]

Bakunin illustrated the mechanics of this first stage with a set of worst-case examples involving scientific expertise. By carefully distinguishing the "absolute authority" of the scientific fact from the personal fallibility of the "representatives of science," Bakunin suggested, the individual would have little difficulty in evaluating scientifically generated knowledge exactly as he would any other type of information. Bakunin detailed this procedure in the following passage:

> In the matter of boots, I defer to the authority of the bootmaker. When it is a question of houses, canals, or railroads, I consult the authority of the architect and the engineer. For each special branch of knowledge I apply to the scientist of that respective branch. . . . I consult several of them. I compare their opinions and I choose the one which seems to me the soundest.[129]

Moreover, within this choice among presented expertise, Bakunin argued that the individual could readily disengage specifically technical data from the social implications that policies derived from those data might entail. In effect, Bakunin believed that the individual would be able to exert full political control over the social deployment of technical expertise.

Bakunin seized upon the latter aspect of this first stage to introduce two structural consequences of individual decision making. First, Bakunin noted that the individual could always elect to "follow, to a certain extent" the directions of a given specialist without sacrificing his autonomy, since that decision would have been imposed only by that individual's "own reason."[130] And second, Bakunin pointed out that, when one individual decided in some situation to defer to the expertise of another, he did so only upon the presumption that in some future situation their relationship might be reversed. This conception of reciprocal authority was spelled out in such passages as:

> We willingly bow before the respectable, although relative, temporary, and closely restricted authority of the representatives of special sciences, asking for nothing better than to consult them by turns . . .—on condition, however, that they be willing to receive similar counsel from us on occasions when, and concerning matters about which, we are more learned than they.[131]

These two corollary propositions of the first stage of collective self-discipline occupied an intermediate, essentially transitional zone between the two phases of this system of social authority. Their logical source lay in the individual's autonomous decision-making, while their logical consequences opened out onto the arena of collective social authority. Further, the process of reciprocal authority reflected Bakunin's philosophical belief in the diffuse character of social knowledge. Bakunin had argued in another context that this diversity of knowledge and experience among individuals could confer extraordinary strength upon their combined efforts. By incorporating all available information into its decision-making process Bakunin hoped to establish a more capable and flexible system of social authority.

Bakunin carefully stipulated, however, that the primary function of reciprocal authority was to facilitate the individual's autonomous decision-making rather than simply to integrate information. Any conflict which might arise between these two roles was quite clearly to be resolved in favor of the former. Bakunin argued that, for example, if one individual should somehow become omniscient— perhaps a philosopher-king—the self-sufficiency of that individual's knowledge would have satisfied reciprocal authority's information function but at the same time it would have effectively destroyed the decision-making role of the autonomous individual. Consequently, Bakunin argued, despite that individual's great learning, the threat that he posed to the individual aspect of reciprocal authority would make it "necessary to drive that man out of society."[132] In a different but similarly reasoned passage, addressed to the need to distribute scientific expertise among the working classes, Bakunin argued that, rather than submitting themselves to a tutelary government of "men of science," the working classes would do better to "dispense with science altogether."[133]

The second stage of collective self-discipline integrated the individual's first-phase judgement into an effective yet collectively exercised system of social authority. This voluntary fusion was to be produced by a second, more or less discreet round of mutual interaction, in which the decision of each individual would itself be "evaluated and judged by the whole collective."[134] Bakunin believed that through this process a social group could arrive at policy and administrative determinations that would be internally coherent, would incorporate the best available knowledge, and would simultaneously be predicated upon the personal will and judgement of each individual within that group.

Collective self-discipline's second round of decision making was premised upon the pattern of reciprocal authority that had emerged from its first stage. The same temporary deference that had enabled the individual to build the knowledge of his peers into his own decision was here extended to secure the individual's acceptance of specific decisions taken by the whole collective. When it was properly structured, Bakunin argued, collective decision making was "simply the voluntary and thoughtful coordination of all individual efforts toward a common goal."[135] Within this second phase of decision making, reciprocity connoted the willingness of an individual, after having made his own judgement, presented it to his peers, and weighed the other opinions similarly presented, to cede his personal preference to that of the whole collective. Bakunin argued that in so doing the individual would be submitting only to a "voluntary and thoughtful discipline" which both "harmonizes perfectly with the freedom of individuals" and yet provided the basic organizational framework which was always "necessary when a great number of individuals freely united undertake any kind of collective work or action."[136] Through this process of conscious individual cession, Bakunin believed, the collective could attain a level of external application and internal restraint that would equal the self-discipline produced within each individual by his rational will.

Bakunin developed the practical political mechanisms of this second stage of decision making almost entirely within the context of his theory of revolutionary authority, and thus a consideration of those mechanisms is best left for discussion in chapter 4. He did, however, detail the basic procedure through which reciprocal authority could be infused into the implementation of collective decisions, and thereby provided us with a general theory of administrative if not policy reciprocity.

Having reached a collectively agreed upon decision, a group had to devise an equally collective procedure by which to implement that decision. Bakunin proposed that, through a process of mutual interaction similar to the second stage of collective self-discipline, the collective establish a series of informal ad hoc positions appropriate to each immediate task at hand. Quite unlike the traditional structure of state bureaucracy, then, this administrative authority would never be lodged in permanent offices. Additionally, and in part as a consequence of this structural fluidity, the daily supervision of administrative activity would not be vested in a class of career professionals. In an administrative authority based on collective self-discipline, Bakunin wrote, "no function remains fixed and petrified, nothing is irrevocably attached to one person."[137]

This absence of permanent offices and career personnel, Bakunin believed, would render all aspects of administrative behavior fully accountable to the collective as a whole. Structural positions would be both subject to continual collective reconsideration, as well as regularly reassigned among its members, "naturally distributed in accordance with everyone's attitudes, evaluated and judged by the whole collective."[138] Rather than becoming a routinized and reified obstacle to popular accountability, this administrative framework was to produce and maintain a functional reciprocity of executive responsibility, and thus an effective equality of individual position. Within such a system, Bakunin argued,

> hierarchic order and advancement do not exist, so that the executive of yesterday may become the subordinate of today. No one is raised above the others, or if he does rise for some time, it is only to drop back at a later time into his former position, like the sea wave ever dropping back to the salutary level of equality.[139]

As Bakunin conceived it, then, the administration as well as the formulation of collective policy would be predicated upon his principle of natural influence and upon a concomitant reciprocity of executive responsibility. Both forms of social authority exercised "no fixed or constant authority" but were instead strictly rooted in "a continual exchange of mutual, temporary, and, above all, voluntary authority and sub-ordination."[140] Bakunin's conception of administrative reciprocity paralleled the broader structure of collective self-discipline as a whole, since within each framework the will of the individual was to be fully integrated into and indeed become the will of the collective.

In sum, then, Bakunin's proposal for a new system of social authority was bound together by his notion of natural influence and the structure of natural authority that derived from that influence. Collective self-discipline's decision-making procedures were based upon those present within the existing natural and social worlds, and this new system of social authority could consequently tap and incorporate into itself the several strengths that inhered in this natural framework. In an important sense, collective self-discipline would reproduce within its man-made constructs the "spontaneous and living order" that Bakunin believed was the dominant form of organization within the natural world, and which he argued had been deformed by traditional and bourgeois systems of fixed hierarchical authority.[141] Through its relationship to natural authority, Bakunin contended, his system of collective self-discipline would generate the "greatest possible development of all local, collective and individual liberties,"[142] and would make it possible to "proclaim . . . individual and collective freedom as the only source of order in society."[143]

Additionally, Bakunin believed that his system of social authority could never confront the individual with an alien and obdurate force that might trigger off his instinct to revolt (see chapter 4). Collective self-discipline would instead "arrange matters" so that the individual would be forced to respect the equal liberty and rights of his fellowman through "the actual organization of the social environment—which is to say by the consciously engineered confluence of natural and social authority.[144] And lastly, Bakunin believed that collective self-discipline's foundation in natural influence would enable it to evade the sterile uniformity that inevitably accompanied an "automatic, routine-like, blind" structure of externally imposed discipline.[145] Rooted on the contrary in the "fertile, living, real unity" which would emerge from individual and collective freedom, Bakunin believed that his system of social authority was "the only true human discipline, the discipline necessary for the organization of freedom."[146]

Bakunin concluded that collective self-discipline, by successfully harnessing the pattern of natural authority into a conscious system of social authority, would create a human society within which "power, properly speaking, no longer exists."[147] Through this formal or "proper" definition of power Bakunin intended to convey (as elsewhere) the conception of domination found within traditional and bourgeois institutions, in which the individual's rational will was subordinated to fixed and arbitrary social privileges. Within a fully formed system of collective self-discipline as within all systems of natural influence, he argued, such arbitrary authority based on privilege could not exist. Social decision making and administration would not disappear but would be systematically decentralized and redistributed throughout the collective by its very organizational form. "Power is diffused," Bakunin summarized, "and becomes the sincere expression of the liberty of everyone, the faithful and serious realization of the will of all; everyone obeys because the executive-for-the-day dictates only what he himself, that is, every individual, wants."[148]

As Bakunin presented it within his manuscripts, then, his system of collective self-discipline was designed to integrate what might well on initial encounter appear to be two contradictory perceptions of man's relationship to the natural and social worlds. He believed that his approach alone could secure to the individual the freedom to control the conditions of his own existence within what remained a strictly determined physical and social environment. Thus there was nothing inconsistent in Bakunin's insistence on the one hand that "my liberty" required "my dignity as a man, and my human right, which consists in not obeying any other man and behaving only in accordance with my own convictions,"[149] while he argued elsewhere with equal intensity that

> with all the self-consciousness produced within him by the mirage of a sham spontaneity, and not withstanding his will or intelligence—which are indispensible conditions for building up his liberty against the external world, including the men which surround him—man like all animals on this earth remains nevertheless in absolute subjection to the universal inevitability governing the world.[150]

Through the mediation of collective self-discipline Bakunin could conclude that the "first and last condition of [man's] liberty rests then in absolute submission to the omnipotence of Nature, and the observation and the most rigid application of its laws,"[151] without ever contravening his demand for the utmost individual and collective liberty.

3 *Three Critiques*

Bakunin's analysis of modern society was constructed upon three central critiques. Based on his own philosophical notions of mutual interaction and collective self-discipline, Bakunin attacked the concept of the state as such, the concept of science as presently practiced, and the structure of capitalist economic and political systems. Each of these concepts or institutions, he argued, necessarily reduced man to a constricted relationship with himself, with his fellows, and with the outside physical world. First, consistent with his grounding in Lamarck and Feuerbach, Bakunin criticized all three frameworks as artificial and man-made abstractions which by their very existence interfered with man's ability to realize his social and political potential. And second, working from his theory of social authority, Bakunin contended that each of these frameworks would be imposed or manipulated so as to reinforce the class character of human society: each concept or institution inevitably fostered a rigid distinction between those groups who could control its content and use, and those groups that were excluded from such control. Viewed both from a philosophical and practical political perspective, Bakunin concluded, the fundamental structure of the state, of contemporary science, and of capitalist economic and political systems was intrinsically oppressive for the broad mass of mankind in general, and for the working classes in particular. Bakunin consequently argued that this common structural problem could only be resolved satisfactorily by a social revolution.

Critique of the State

Bakunin's critique of the state was framed on the basis of both theoretical and political criteria. He conjoined these two approaches in his definition of the state as "authority, force."[1] Theoretically, the state was an abstract entity, a man-made contrivance that withdrew all political authority from man's immediate environment and hypostatized it in an arbitrary structure that was completely inaccessible to the general population. Moreover, this process of abstraction was always justified as in the best interests of precisely those sectors of the populace that had been stripped of their powers of self-determination: for Bakunin the concept of authority necessarily implied a corresponding structure of imposed "tutelage." "Any logical and straightforward theory of the state," Bakunin wrote, "is essentially founded upon the principle of *authority*, that is, the eminently theological, metaphysical, and political idea that the masses, *always* incapable of governing themselves, must at all times submit to the beneficial yoke of a wisdom and a justice imposed upon them, in some way or another, from above."[2]

In practical political terms, Bakunin viewed the state as simply an instrument of political force. Physical coercion had always been the backbone of the state, Bakunin argued. Despite their moralistic pretensions, "all states were founded by violence, by conquest," and subsequently physical force had not so much disappeared as it had been submerged into the state's day-to-day functions.[3] In the Europe of the 1870's, Bakunin contended, coercion had been subsumed into a set of "well-regulated and systematized" institutions that centralized the state's control over all administrative, financial, and internal and external military behavior.[4] He described the contemporary state as a "military, police, and bureaucratic centralization."[5] And he argued that the process of centralizing physical coercion within the contemporary state was being accelerated by the particular economic and political requirements of "capitalist monopoly," and that as a consequence the specifically capitalist version of the state would, if left to itself, ultimately end in a military dictatorship.[6]

For Bakunin, the contradiction between the state's claim to moral authority on the one hand, and its actual foundation in physical coercion on the other, was compounded by what he believed was the class-specific character with which state force was always exercised. Hidden behind the state's moral posturing about the best interests of the population, Bakunin insisted, lay the reality of the state as an instrument of class rule. Once an initial conqueror had transformed the state's moral claim to authority into state institutions based ultimately in physical force, one or another group within society would inevitably control that administrative structure and utilize it for their own class benefit. In effect, then, the abstract moral basis of the state served only as an ideological cover for the class-based coercion that would be exercised in its name.

Bakunin emphasized the class character of the institutionalized state in at least three related points. First, he argued that there could not be an actual state unless there was a ruling class to run it. As he wrote in another context, "abstractions have no legs on which to walk."[7] Bakunin believed that if a state as such existed, the appropriate question wasn't whether there was a ruling class, but only which class filled that role. "The State has always been," Bakunin argued, "the patrimony of some privileged class: a priestly class, an aristocratic class, a bourgeois class."[8] Bakunin contended further that by the structure of the state as such, when all other classes external to the state apparatus were no longer able to control the state, the administrative class within the state itself would become the ruling class. In what pointed toward a major contribution to the theory of the modern state, Bakunin continued the logic of the sentence above by insisting that "finally, when all the other classes have exhausted themselves, the State becomes the patrimony of the bureaucratic class."[9] In a sense, Bakunin believed that the very existence of centralized institutions of state coercion would induce some group to seize control and utilize that state force to their own benefit. Once initially established, the simple presence of state coercion would ensure its perpetuation.

A second aspect of the state's class character, Bakunin argued, was that any class in control of state power would attempt to perpetuate its political control. "The chief and avowed aim" of any government, he contended, "consists in preserving and strengthening the State, civilization, and civil order, that is, the systematic and legalized dominance of the ruling class over the exploited people."[10] More particularly, a ruling class had a direct interest in retaining the economic privileges that they had either acquired or augmented through their political control of the state. These economic benefits were, moreover, not just the spoils of political power but the very means by which a ruling class could maintain its political position. As Bakunin saw it, the extraction of economic tribute from the general population was a politically essential as well as a financially remunerative practice of a ruling class. "Exploitation and Government are two inseparable expressions of that which is called politics, the first furnishing the means with which the process of governing is carried on, and also constituting the necessary base as well as the goal of all government, which in turn guarantees and legalizes the power to exploit."[11] Thus for Bakunin the basic desire of a ruling class to perpetuate its rule required that class, regardless of its original economic position, to consolidate a firm economic foundation from which to extract sufficient value to sustain itself. This fixed relation of political control of the state to economic exploitation thereby transcended the particular form of bourgeois exploitation within a capitalist state to comprehend any ruling class within any political state: for Bakunin the relation was inherent within the very nature of the state as such.

Bakunin's third point about the class nature of the state concerned the specific political and economic consequences which the state would have for those groups within it which *weren't* within the ruling classes. Having postulated that every state would by definition have a ruling class, and that every ruling class would direct its primary efforts toward self-perpetuation through an involved process of economic exploitation, Bakunin could conclude that the real interests of the subject classes could never be served either within or by the political state. This again, Bakunin argued, was an inevitable result not only of a medieval state or of a bourgeois state, as Marx believed, but rather of any and every state. The obstacles to human freedom weren't localized within the politically oppressive or economically exploitative activities of one particular state or one given ruling class, but they existed within the structure of the state as such.

Juxtaposed to this three-pronged argument about the inevitable class character of the state was Bakunin's insistence that the state wasn't an inherent aspect of human society. Viewed through his Lamarckian conception of mutual interaction as the universal process of development, the state was a specifically man-made device that interfered with the natural and necessary course of human life. The state, Bakunin wrote, lacked the "necessary and immutable character of society."[12] "The State is not a direct product of nature, it does not precede, as society does, the awakening of thought in man."[13] Rather, the state was a transitional construct which, while it performed an historically essential task in man's development from his animal origins into a moral human being, would ultimately be discarded in a later historical stage. "The State is evil," Bakunin argued, "but an historically necessary evil, as necessary in the past as its utter destruction will eventually become in the future. . . . The State is not society, but one of its historical forms."[14] Thus the state was, according to Bakunin, not only the patrimony of a privileged class which would inevitably engage in political oppression and economic exploitation, but also a transitory human construct which was, historically speaking, expendable.

Bakunin described two further aspects of the state which he argued were inherent in its nature and structure. The first concerned the reliance of the ruling class upon physical coercion both externally against other states and internally against its subject classes. And the second sketched out what Bakunin believed would be the inevitable tendency of the state's administrative apparatus to develop a bureaucratic form.

The state's dependence upon physical force, as Bakunin saw it, developed from the initial act of conquest with which the state was founded. Out of that act grew the concern of the new state's ruling class both to defend their possession against the predations of other states and to preserve their political position within the state from domestic challenge. In effect, once the institutions of state force had been established, the ruling class which created and now controlled those institutions could retain its privileged position only by using the state's coercive powers against various de facto external and internal enemies. Moreover, external and internal forces were directly linked each to the other: the deployment of state force externally always called forth a need for internal action, and vice versa. In Bakunin's analysis, then, once the state was founded its basic structure was such that external and internal coercion required and reinforced each other: external wars and internal repression were the two inevitable sides of the same state coin.

The state's relation to external violence began with the fear of its ruling class that some other state might attempt to invade it: that having itself been a product of violent conquest, their state could become a victim of that process as well. "Founded essentially upon an original act of violence, conquest," Bakunin wrote, "every centralist State automatically constitutes an absolute denial of the rights of every other State."[15] Faced with total physical insecurity, every state had no choice but to develop sufficient military power not simply to defend itself, but to turn itself into an impregnable "universal State."[16] As Bakunin presented the strategic relation of offensive to defensive capabilities, "every State, under pain of destruction, and fearing to be devoured by its neighbor States, must reach out toward omnipotence, and having become powerful, must conquer."[17] In this unstable situation, Bakunin contended, with every state arming to overwhelm its neighbors before being overwhelmed itself, there was little likelihood of peace. Indeed Bakunin was adamant about the linkage between the nature of the state and war. "So long as States exist, there will be no peace. There will only be more or less prolonged respites, armistices concluded by the perpetually belligerent States."[18] Thus the formal structure of the state, both in its founding and in its relationship with its neighbor states, demanded war. For Bakunin, war was a natural, inevitable, and perpetual aspect of the state as such:

> dynastic wars, wars of honor, wars of conquest or of natural frontiers, balance-of-power wars, destruction and permanent ingestion of State by State, rivers of human blood, burning countryside and ruined towns, whole provinces laid waste. . .[19]

The state's dependence upon the physical coercion internally, to maintain the political and economic power of its ruling class, was similarly predicated upon the state's violent origin. In many ways, the regularized physical coercion built into the state's daily operations was just a more systematic continuation of the initial conquest by which the first ruling class established the state and their own privileged position within it. In this initial process the ruling class seized both political and economic control over an excluded population, and was thus from the first dependent upon state force to prevent rebellion. "The State," Bakunin argued, "cannot be sure of its own self-preservation without an armed force to defend it against its own *internal enemies*, against the discontent of its people."[20] Moreover, the repercussions of the state's military adventures against other states would serve to reinforce the ruling class's need to rely upon state force against its own citizenry. First, as Bakunin saw it, large-scale military activity required a level of economic production which only an extremely "busy and disciplined" workforce could achieve.[21] Second, the danger of defeat would lead the state to crush any internal dissension that might threaten its war effort. And third, the territorial expansion which came with victory would force the state to increase the impersonal character of its administrative apparatus. In a comment about the linkage between a bureaucratic division of labor and social alienation which anticipated both Weber and Michels, Bakunin noted that "theoretically, it is quite evident that the larger the state, the more complex its organism, and the more alien it becomes to the people."[22]

Finally, not only does the state's external use of force generate a need for its internal application, but the exercise of state force internally against the general population would also induce external military activity as well. Bakunin's presentation of this point was anecdotal. The French bourgeoisie, after the revolt of 1848, were so petrified of the "looming threat of popular emancipation" that they installed a military regime, hoping by this sacrifice to have "at least purchased the peace and quiet necessary to the success of its commercial and industrial transactions."[23] However, Bakunin observed, this military regime was able to suppress France's working classes only at great economic cost, and the subsequent combination of economic deterioration and military predilection led not to peace but to war. The French bourgeoisie "had reckoned without the high cost of military rule, which paralyzes, unsettles, and ruins nations by the very fact of its internal organization, and whose inevitable consequence, obedient to an inherent logic which has never failed, is *war*."[24]

Bakunin also described what he argued was the inevitable tendency for the state's administrative apparatus to assume a bureaucratic form. He was one of the earliest social thinkers to propose a structural connection between the state and bureaucracy, and to contend that bureaucratic practices were essential to the operation of every state's administrative apparatus, that such practices were intrinsic to the nature of the state, and that a new bureaucratic class would arise that would administer the state simultaneously in its own class interest as well as in the interest of the state's formal ruling class. In effect, Bakunin developed a theory of bureaucracy that anticipated not only Weber's conclusion that there could not be a central state without legal-rational bureaucratic administration, but also Michels' belief that such bureaucratic administrations would inevitably combine if not replace the state's formal goals with their own.

Bakunin's argument about bureaucracy was derived from his two essential premises about the structure of the state in general: that it was an arbitrary man-made abstraction which was separate from the natural world, and that this abstraction acquired institutional form at the hands of a ruling class, which then employed the state's powers of physical coercion for their own benefit. He contended that ruling-class controls over state coercion required the state's administrative apparatus to be organized along rigidly hierarchical lines, and imparted an artificial and machinelike character to its decision-making procedure. And he believed that the state's fundamental structure as a man-made abstraction gave a similarly machine-like texture to the administrative apparatus' external relationships with the state's citizenry.

The initial impetus toward the transformation of the state's administrative apparatus into a rigidly hierarchical or bureaucratic form came from the political requirements of its ruling class. Faced with an environment that was both internally and externally hostile to its continued control over the state, the ruling class had no alternative but to centralize all political and economic decision making under its direct command. In order to exercise the continuous operational control over this decision-making process that their antagonistic class position required, the ruling class was forced to structure this centralized apparatus along strict hierarchical lines. Thus, internally, this state apparatus would be organized as a primitive machine, in which efficiency was defined as the short-term linear product of a maximal division of labor.

Bakunin argued further that the state would have machine-like characteristics in its overall relationship to the state's population. Based both on its rigidly mechanical internal arrangements as well as its inherently abstracted relation to ongoing daily life, the state's administrative apparatus would appear as an alien and artificial structure, simultaneously removed from and ignorant of life in the "real world." Bakunin referred caustically to "pneumatic machines called governments"[25] that instead of having "a natural organic, popular force" on human activity were "on the contrary entirely mechanical and artificial."[26] Moreover, inasmuch as the state's mechanical relationship to society was intrinsic to its nature as a state, even the most progressive or popularly elected state governments would still be "in their essence only machines governing the masses from above."[27]

Bakunin's analysis of a bureaucratic administration as the inevitable result of the state's class-specific and abstracted nature underscored his discussion of morality and corruption in the state's bureaucratic apparatus. As he viewed it, the bureaucratic structure of state administration encouraged two basic forms of corruption: the personal financial corruption of the individual functionary, and the political corruption involved both in imposing the orders of the state's ruling class upon its population, and in exercising political authority within an insular and permanent administrative structure.

Bakunin dealt only cursorily with the problem of personal financial corruption. He noted that the interests of the individual bureaucrat periodically coincided with those of the ruling class he was serving, and that as a result the bureaucrat could regularly pursue two sets of satisfactions at the same time. "In the monarchy," Bakunin wrote, "the bureaucrats oppress and rob the people for the benefit of the privileged in the name of the king, as well as in their own interest; in a republic, they oppress and rob the people in the same manner, for the same pockets, and the same classes, but, by contrast, in the name of the will of the people."[28]

As the above citation demonstrates, however, Bakunin was substantially more forthright in his discussion of the politically corrupt character of the state policy decisions. His basic definition of policy corruption—imposing the ruling class' will upon the state's citizenry—branded all state administrative edicts as immoral, for he had argued that the sole formal purpose of any state bureaucracy was to serve its ruling class. The "science of bureaucracy," Bakunin insisted, consisted of nothing more than actions "to maintain public order and the servility of subjects, and to take from them as much money as possible for the State treasury, without ruining them completely, and without pushing them through despair to revolt."[29]

Additionally, Bakunin argued that this class-based form of policy corruption would be compounded by the tendency of state functionaries to become self-impressed as well as politically self-serving. In contrast to these inevitable consequences of the bureaucrat's permanent career position, Bakunin counterposed his own notion of collective self-discipline, which he contended was the only popularly accountable form of public administration and which therefore could restrain public executives from becoming overly impressed with their political authority. Setting out this general criticism of state bureaucracy, Bakunin argued that "lack of permanent opposition and continuous control become a source of moral depravity for all the individuals who find themselves invested with some social power."[30] In another passage, he detailed what such popular accountability entailed, suggesting that the very structure of state bureaucracy prevented its functionaries from meeting these political conditions:

> unless that person is frequently reinvigorated by contacts with the life of the people; unless he is compelled to act openly under conditions of full publicity; unless he is subjected to a salutary and uninterrupted regime of popular control and criticism,. . .he runs the risk of becoming utterly spoiled by dealing only with aristocrats like himself.[31]

These two forms of policy corruption, Bakunin believed, were endemic to the structure of the state bureaucracy—the first due to ruling-class control and the second to its permanent character. It wasn't possible for an individual to enter state service without shortly thereafter becoming acclimated to these two parallel policy patterns: "it suffices for anyone, even the most liberal and popular man, to become part of a government machine in order to undergo a complete change in outlook and attitude."[32] There was little difference, in Bakunin's view, between the average state official and the prototypical Prussian bureaucrat, of whom he wrote, "Brutus reincarnate, in a cotton hat and with a pipe dangling from his mouth, each German functionary was capable of sacrificing his own children to that which he called reason, justice, the supreme right of the State."[33] Bakunin concluded that, in the process of serving the policy goals of both his ruling-class employer as well as his own sense of self-importance, the state functionary was engaged in imposing an artificial and class-based political structure upon the state's citizenry, "destroying for the benefit of the government and the governing classes the life and spontaneous action of the population."[34]

Bakunin illustrated his theory about the relationship between the state and bureaucracy with two examples from Turkish Serbia (the facts for which were evidently supplied by a Serbian student who visited Bakunin in Switzerland). Bakunin argued that in Serbia the bureaucratic class had in fact become the ruling class. No longer simply a managerial conduit for some other elite, the Serbian bureaucracy now operated that state in its own class interest. "In Turkish Serbia," Bakunin wrote, "only the bureaucratic class exists. As a result, the Serbian State will oppress the people solely in order that its functionaries might live more handsomely."[35] Thus Bakunin contended that his argument that the state would always have a ruling class, and that ultimately when no other class remained the bureaucratic class would fill that role, had been historically confirmed.

Bakunin's second Serbian example concerned the ability of the state bureaucracy to transform new personnel into supporters of the appropriate class-based state policies. Despite prior liberal inclinations—probably acquired in European universities—these inductees soon adopted the political biases and internally self-impressed forms of policy corruption that they had formerly abhorred. "Once integrated into this class," Bakunin observed,

> they become enemies of the people whether they like it or not. Perhaps they would wish—and it's no doubt true, particularly at the beginning—to liberate the people, or at least to improve their situation, but they are constrained to oppress them. It suffices to pass two or three years in this environment to adapt oneself

to it and, finally, to accept it.... Once resigned to this necessity, against which they no longer have the strength to struggle, they then become arrogant scoundrels, all the more dangerous for the people as their published declarations are liberal and democratic.[36]

This example, Bakunin believed, confirmed his arguments about both the capacity of the state's bureaucratic apparatus to impose its policy requirements upon its personnel and the intrinsically anti-popular character of those requirements.

Overall, Bakunin argued that one must look to the very structure of the state if one wished to understand its behavior. He argued that the state as such was a man-made abstraction which had no necessary relationship to the natural world, and which when institutionalized exercised its coercive powers for the benefit of a ruling class. He insisted that by its inherent nature a state must have not only a ruling class, but a bureaucratic form of administration that would serve both the needs of its ruling-class employers as well as its own distinct class interest. And lastly, he argued that the state policy and state administration by definition could never be popularly accountable. All of this, Bakunin believed, would occur within every centralized political state: it was the necessary consequence of the state's structure, of the intrinsic character of the state as such. "It would be impossible to make the State change its nature," Bakunin concluded, "for it is only because of this nature, and in foregoing the latter it would cease to be a State."[37]

Bakunin believed that the state's true nature was consistently and systematically obscured by the ideological defenses that most ruling classes had erected around it. Appeals to the public interest, to religious principles or to national patriotism were for Bakunin simply attempts to develop a theoretical cover with which to legitimate the state's abstract yet class-specific character. In his schema, each of these appeals functioned primarily as an agent of ideological integration for the state.

The concept of the public interest, as Bakunin understood it, posited that within human societies there was a general interest that summed up all separate group or individual interests, and that consequently superseded those separate interests both morally and politically. This summation usually was arrived at within the confines of the state—indeed in certain versions of this concept the state embodied the public interest by definition. While Bakunin did share the fundamental notion that there was a broadly defined common good that undergirded society, his conception of the general interest was bound up in his arguments about mutual interaction and collective self-discipline. He contended that the common social good could be served only by the continual, natural, and unofficial process of mutual influence among individuals and groups of equal stature, and therefore could never exist within the abstracted yet class-specific institutions of the political state. The only form of public interest possible within the state, Bakunin argued, was not the summation but the mutual neutralization of all individual and community interests that conflicted with the goals of the state's ruling and administrative classes. The state, he wrote, "is an arbitrary being, in whose breast all the positive, living, individual or local interests of the people mingle, clash, destroy, and absorb each other into the abstraction known as the common interest, the *public good* or the *public welfare*."[38]

This process of neutralization had two related consequences for the relationship between the state's policies and its citizenry, both of which paralleled the two central points of Bakunin's overall critique. First, in its capacity as an artificial and non-organic structure which nonetheless had a monopoly on physical coercion, the state always sought to achieve this public interest by crushing out all "spontaneous life and action" from everyday popular life.

> It is clear that all the so-called general interests of society...constitute an abstraction, a fiction, a lie, and that the State is like one great slaughterhouse, and like an immense graveyard where, in the shadow and under the pretext of this abstraction there come all the real aspirations, all the living initiatives of a nation, to let themselves be generously and sanctimoniously sacrificed and buried.[39]

And second, hidden within its pretensions to universal concern, the same state actions always maximized the economic and political interests of its ruling and administrative classes. The above passage continues,

> And since no abstraction ever exists by itself or for itself, since it has neither legs to walk on, nor arms to create with, nor stomach to digest this mass of victims which it is driven to devour, it is plain that, in exactly the same way the religious or heavenly abstraction, God, represents in reality the very positive and very real counterparts of a privileged caste, the clergy (its terrestrial counterpart), so the political abstraction, the State, represents the no less real and positive interests of the class which is principally if not exclusively exploiting people today...the bourgeoisie.[40]

Thus for Bakunin the notion of the public interest simply served as a convenient ideological mask behind which the state could realize its true nature and satisfy its real masters.

The above passage also included a strong attack upon a second ideological defense of the state, religion. Bakunin argued that a major historical function of religion had been to provide an abstract doctrine that could justify the concrete material interests of its administering priesthood. Religion's contribution to the protection and legitimation of the state was similarly derived, based in its capacity to deflect the general population from material concerns. Religion, Bakunin argued, is the eternal mirage which leads away the masses in the search for divine treasures, while, much more reserved, the governing class contents itself with dividing among its members. . . the miserable goods of the earth taken from the people, including their political and social liberty. There is not, there cannot be, a State without religion.[41]

Or, as Bakunin wrote in a more sardonic vein, "whenever a chief of State speaks of God. . . be sure that he is getting ready to shear once more his people-flock."[42] Given the importance of religion in obscuring the actual purposes of state action, Bakunin continued, those ruling classes that cannot find a suitable vehicle among existing religions inevitably set out to invent a new one. In *God and the State*, Bakunin rather acidly recounted how the French bourgeoisie in 1830, freshly invested with state control, proceeded to develop an "official religion."

The third vehicle of ideological mystification which Bakunin discussed was patriotism. This concept had two distinct meanings for Bakunin, each related to a historical period, and only the second of which concerned the defense of the state. The first form of patriotism signified the "purely natural feelings" of "social solidarity" which primitive man felt for his tribe or village. "Natural patriotism," Bakunin wrote, "is an instinctive, mechanical, uncritical attachment to the socially accepted, hereditary, or traditional pattern of life—and the same kind of an instinctive, automatic hostility toward any other kind of life."[43] This essentially Lamarckian form of "animal patriotism," however, was a "purely local feeling." As such it was a "serious obstacle to the formation of States," for states had a broader scope and a class basis that directly opposed the interests of the common man in the small village.[44] Consequently, Bakunin argued, the national state destroyed this indigenous form of patriotism and replaced it with a new, second form that more directly reflected the material interests of the state's ruling class. "The very existence of the State demands that there be some privileged class vitally interested in maintaining that existence. And it is precisely the group interests of this privileged class which are called patriotism."[45]

Bakunin illustrated his point by suggesting that among the states of 1870 Europe, national patriotism had become a rather transparent euphemism for bourgeois class interest, and served only to preserve and protect the class structure within those states. "Bourgeois patriotism," he argued, "is only a very shabby, very narrow, especially mercenary and deeply anti-human passion, having for its object the preservation and maintenance of the power of the national State—that is, the mainstay of all the privileges of the exploiters throughout the nation."[46] Thus, in Bakunin's view, the concept of patriotism—much like that of the public interest and of religion—served primarily to legitimate the simultaneously abstract and class-specific character of the state. From the perspective of the state's general population, he believed, all three were simply ideological weapons by which the state maintained its oppressive authority.

Bakunin argued further that, within the specifically liberal state, the ruling bourgeois class utilized social contract theory as an additional source of ideological legitimation. He didn't really differentiate among the various contract theorists, but instead lumped together all those who had either put forward a contract theory or who, in their practical political activities or statements, had employed contract theory in defense of the centralized state. Bakunin contended that although Rousseau had been "sorely mistaken" in his contract approach to social institutions, he hadn't been alone in this error: "the majority of modern jurists and publicists, whether of the Kantian or any other individualist liberal school" were equally culpable.[47] For Bakunin, the issue wasn't so much the particular form which one writer's contract theory took but what Bakunin believed were the fundamental assumptions about man and society that lay behind all contract theory, and more importantly, the role that contract theory had in legitimizing what Bakunin argued was by definition illegitimate: "the implications of the social contract are in fact fatal, because they culminate in the absolute domination of the State."[48]

Bakunin's basic argument against contract theory focussed on what he believed was its core assumption: that prior to his entrance into society, man had existed in a "natural, wild state" of "absolute individual isolation" in which he had been "totally free" and enjoyed "absolute liberty."[49] This central presumption contained a number of implications about man's nature and about the character of a contract state that, in Bakunin's eyes, proved that a contract state was equally as oppressive a state as every other form of state, and that consequently reduced claims that a contract state was different from other states to the level of ideological defense.

Since the individualist theory that sat at the core of contract theory presumed man to be totally free only when he was completely solitary, Bakunin inferred that contract theory had to consider the freedom of any one man to be an obstacle to the freedom of all other men. "Since each individual's liberty is sufficient in itself, each man's liberty necessarily involved denial of every other man's, and when all these liberties encounter one another they are bound to be mutually limited and diminished and to contradict and destroy one another."[50] Among such individually defined men, Bakunin argued, "egotism was the supreme law, the only right."[51] Therefore, Bakunin concluded that contract theory clearly assumed both human freedom as such and man's basic nature to be prone toward violence and inherently evil: "by this reasoning, human liberty produces not *good* but *evil*; man is by nature *evil*."[52]

Based on these assumptions, Bakunin argued, contract theory then posited a "free, deliberate decision of men" to band together so as to provide themselves with physical protection.[53] To preserve all other aspects of their liberty, those who were parties to the contract voluntarily surrendered their right to unilateral physical violence. "They relinquish," as Bakunin phrased it, "a part of themselves so as to safeguard the rest."[54] It was on this point that Bakunin took particularly strong issue with contract theory. He himself believed firmly that by its very character "liberty is indivisible," and that therefore "no part can be removed without killing the whole."[55] He based this disagreement upon his philosophical argument that the liberty of any one individual could be meaningful only if it reflected the similar liberty of all those around him: that by the collective character of human society, liberty was a collective attribute. Consequently, from Bakunin's perspective, the surrender of liberty which contract theory required would be complete rather than partial, for if human freedom was indivisible then contract theory dictated that "men cannot unite... except on condition that they repudiate their freedom, their natural independence" which they had before entering into the contract.[56] This unity of the contract state would be based not on an affirmation of human freedom but on its complete repudiation. "The State itself, by this reasoning, is not the product of liberty," Bakunin argued, "it is on the contrary the product of the voluntary sacrifice and negation of liberty. Natural men... to the extent that they have sacrificed liberty for security and have thus become citizens,... become the *slaves of the state*."[57] In short, from the perspective of the contract state like any other state, "the good is born not of liberty but rather the negation of liberty."[58]

Bakunin believed that the contract state would resemble all other states because contract theory lacked any effective conception of human society separate from the state. It insisted on treating human beings as if they were autonomous individuals, separately nurtured and developed, until such time as they consciously decided to establish "a mechanical aggregate of individuals of a purely artificial kind"—a state—which was their first and only acquaintance with social organization.[59] Contract theory therefore failed either to recognize or to incorporate into itself what Bakunin argued was the dominant social structure in man's existence and the primary source of each human being's individuality. "What emerges from this theory," he concluded,

> is that society proper does not exist; it utterly ignores natural human society, the real starting point of all human civilization and the only medium in which the personality and liberty of man can really be born and grow. All it acknowledges is, at one extreme, the individual, a being who exists in himself and is free in himself, and at the other that conventional society arbitrarily formed by these individuals and based on a formal or tacit contract—the State.[60]

Bakunin insisted that the state as posited in contract theory would be similar to all other states not only in its basic repudiation of human freedom, but also in its predilection for warfare. Based on an exclusive and exclusionary social contract, the contract state would soon spawn a host of other contract states established by groups left out of the first contract. This multiplicity of independent contract states, however, would find itself with the same set of security concerns as any other group of states, and the same scramble for military omnipotence would ensue. If one followed the logic of contract theory, Bakunin contended, "we thus have humanity divided into an indefinite number of foreign states, all hostile and threatened by each other. There is no common right, no social contract of any kind between them; otherwise they would cease to be independent states and become the federated members of one great state."[61] Consequently, for the contract state as for any other state, "war would still remain the supreme law, an unavoidable condition of human survival."[62]

From these and other related arguments, Bakunin concluded that contract theory would produce a state like every other state, with all the tendencies and liabilities that were intrinsic to the state's nature. There was no logical foundation for the variety of special claims that implied that the contract state was somehow more legitimate in its acts or intentions. On the contrary, Bakunin argued, the contract state was equally as abstracted and class-based in its structure, and equally as oppressive of its population, as any other state. He therefore considered those who relied upon contract theory to justify the liberal state to be sophists who were simply erecting an ideological defense for the ruling bourgeois class.

As noted above, Bakunin adamantly and insistently argued that his analysis of the state's nature was equally applicable to Marx's proposed proletarian dictatorship. Although the full structure of Bakunin's critique of the Marxist state goes beyond the framework of this chapter, it is important to point out that Bakunin explicitly contended that this supposed workers' state would soon evidence all the destructive characteristics of every other centralized state. Such a new socialist state would still have an abstract and arbitrary structure, it would still have a specific ruling class, it would still develop a bureaucratic system internally and a belligerent posture externally, and it would still exercise coercive force against its own citizenry in order to sustain the position and privileges of its ruling class. In fact, Bakunin suggested that the highly centralized structure of a Marxist state would encourage some of the worst abuses of state power, for although the capitalist would no longer exist, the capitalists' economic function would be incorporated into the new state's administrative tasks and would massively increase the scope and range of that state's repressive activities.

Bakunin believed, in sum, that the state was an inherently abstract and arbitrary institution that employed its monopoly on coercive force exclusively for the benefit of its ruling and administrative classes. Further, as an instrument of class domination, the state acquired from its controlling classes an obligation to maintain and expand its power indefinitely, and by whatever means necessary. "The supreme law of the State," Bakunin wrote, "is self-preservation at any cost."[63] Constrained, therefore, both by its inability as a man-made abstraction to comprehend daily life, and its requirement as a class-based organ to satisfy its privileged classes, the state routinely exploited and oppressed its domestic population and continuously provoked wars with its neighbors.

Bakunin concluded from this analysis that the state had an intrinsically immoral nature. Morality, in his view, required a pervasive respect for the essential dignity and integrity of human beings. "All human morality," he argued, "all collective and individual morality rests essentially upon *respect for humanity*. . . the recognition of human right and human dignity in every man."[64] The structure of the state, however, forced it to act in direct opposition to the basic economic and political rights of its general population, and to suppress physically any untoward expression of its citizens' personal sense of dignity and self-respect. Based on its own requirements for survival and expansion, the state's perception of "good" and "evil" was precisely the opposite of what Bakunin had designated as the basis of "human morality":

> everything which serves to the conservation, grandeur, and power of the State, however revolting it might appear to human morality—that is *the good*, and vice versa, all that is contrary, be it the thing most sacred and in human terms the most just—that is *the bad*. Such is in its truth the secular morality and practice of all States.[65]

In short, he argued, "the morality of the State. . . is the reversal of human justice and human morality."[66]

This conclusion set the context for Bakunin's powerful and well-known polemic against the fundamental immorality of the state. He attacked the inevitable human consequences of the state's basic structure, and effectively capsulized the reasoning behind his adamant opposition to the state as such.

> This explains to us why all the history of ancient and modern States is nothing more than a series of revolting crimes; why present and past kings and ministers of all times and all countries—statesmen, diplomats, bureaucrats, and warriors—if judged from the point of view of simple morality and human justice, deserve a thousand times the gallows or penal servitude.
>
> For there is no terror, cruelty, sacrilege, perjury, imposture, infamous transaction, cynical theft, brazen robbery, or foul treason which has not been committed and all are still being committed daily by representatives of the State, with no

other excuse than this elastic, at times so convenient and terrible phrase *reason of State*. A terrible phrase indeed!...As soon as it is uttered everything becomes silent and drops out of sight: honesty, honor, justice, right, pity itself vanishes and with it logic and sound sense; black becomes white and white becomes black, the horrible becomes humane, and the most dastardly felonies and atrocious crimes become meritorious acts.[67]

Bakunin had clearly structured his analysis of the state along substantively different lines from that of Marxian socialism. The Marxist interpretation of the state was embedded in the historical development of the dialectic, and consequently stressed the class rather than the institutional character of the state. According to Marx, the bourgeois state was the last partial or oppressive state, inasmuch as the rise of the bourgeois class necessarily created a new "universal class" which would not only overthrow the bourgeois variant of the partial state but would make it historically impossible for such a partial state to arise ever again. Within this overarching historical framework, the particular forms of exploitation and repression practiced by the bourgeois state were derived exclusively from the subordinated relationship of the bourgeois state to the production of surplus value and to capitalism's consequent commodity fetishism. Therefore, from a Marxist perspective, the seizure and formal control of the state apparatus by this new universal class—by the proletariat—would by definition place the state in the employ of man's broadest social interest, and by stripping the state of its partial character also strip it of its oppressive and exploitative character. In this analysis, the bourgeois state acts in an oppressive and exploitative manner because it is subservient to the partial concerns of the bourgeois class: simply put, the bourgeois state is oppressive because it is bourgeois. And conversely, the new workers' state will be socially and economically liberatory because it will represent the universal concerns of the universal class: in effect, the proletarian state will be liberatory because it will be proletarian.

Bakunin's analytic emphasis was almost exactly opposite. Based on his evolutionary rather than dialectical reading of history, Bakunin considered the bourgeois state to be oppressive and exploitative first and foremost because it was a state, and only secondarily oppressive, in its specific refinements, because it was bourgeois. Further, this analysis led Bakunin to argue strenuously that Marx's proposed workers' state— precisely because it was to be a state—would be a similarly oppressive and exploitative institution. For Bakunin the fact that such a new state would be a workers' state was only a formal and incidental consideration to the fact that it would nonetheless remain a political state, and he contended that underneath its particular proletarian veneer this new state would have the traditional liabilities of character and attitude found in every other state.

His substantially different understanding of the relationship between the institution of the state and its ruling class led Bakunin to propose a substantially different replacement for the bourgeois state. While Marx advocated a working class seizure of the bourgeois state and its subsequent remodeling into a new socialist state, Bakunin insisted that the state as such—as a form of social organization—had to be completely dismembered. "The revolution as we understand it," Bakunin argued, "will have to destroy the State and all the institutions of the State, radically and completely, from its very first day."[68] It should be stressed that Bakunin never considered the destruction of the state to be tantamount to the elimination of all social authority from human society. He argued on the contrary that the removal of the state's abstract yet class-based authority was the essential pre-condition for the emergence of the only legitimate form of popular social authority. Only with the destruction of the state as such, and with it the principle of arbitrary social authority which it embodied, could the general population establish a system of collective self-discipline based on the dominant natural principle of mutual interaction and mutual influence. Bakunin intended to replace the state not with Hobbesian chaos but with a "free federation" of local collectives, which he believed was the sole form of social organization that could nurture and sustain the free collective yet classless life of the popular masses. In 1867 Bakunin described this transition explicitly:

> We conclude today the absolute necessity of the destruction of the State, or, if one would rather (*si l'on veut*), their radical and complete transformation, in the sense that, ceasing to be centralized powers organized from top to bottom, they reorganize themselves—with absolute liberty for all parties to unite or not to unite, and with each always retaining the freedom to withdraw from a union, even if it had been freely consented to—from bottom to top according to the real needs and natural tendencies of the parties, through the free federation of the individuals and the associations, the communes, the districts, the provinces, and the nations within humanity.[69]

Bakunin's analysis presents us with a stripped down or barebones interpretation of the state, in which all state behavior is ultimately determined by two overriding factors: the state's structure as an artificial man-made entity abstracted from and ignorant of daily life, and the relationship between the state's use of physical coercion and its ruling class. This approach intentionally ignores the multitude of short-term idiosyncracies that can be observed within the particular behavior of specific states—the tendency of a given ruling class to factionalize over certain policy problems, for instance, or the efforts within various liberal states to broaden their political bases through astute manipulation of the franchise—in order to concentrate upon what Bakunin believed was the underlying structural thread that both connected and neutralized the value of these minor distinctions. With this choice of focus, Bakunin could lucidly explain some of the more unfortunate aspects of bourgeois and Marxist states alike: their tendencies toward perpetual warfare, their internal dynamic toward increasingly extensive and onerous bureaucratization, the potential of their administrative classes to develop into new ruling classes, and their sanctimonious justification of morally unjustifiable behavior. Further, Bakunin's analysis placed these developments within a materialist frame of reference, and spawned a post-industrial alternative that he believed was theoretically free of these destructive tendencies. Indeed, Bakunin formulated a socialist alternative that has been thrown up against the centralist model of socialism at every historical turn in the twentieth century.

In an important sense, Bakunin's ultimate criticism of the state as a form of social organization was that it inevitably functioned as a political trap. Undergirding his entire analysis was an image of the state as an extremely deceptive social institution. In its appearance, the state was a physically powerful entity—it had a monopoly over both the internal and external exercise of coercive force— yet it seemed to lack any inherent values or direction. It gave the impression of being simply a medium, a neutral vehicle through which any one group or class could acquire control over the economic and social behavior of its fellows. Extremely powerful yet entirely undirected, without internal personality or character, the state was thereby the perfect faceless ally in the struggle for class supremacy. In reality, Bakunin argued, exactly the opposite was true. Far from being a neutral and uninterested ally, or a powerful but directionless shell, the state's very capacity to exert physical force would inexorably alter the perspectives and goals of the class that seized control over it. Once committed to establishing its control over the state, any given class would discover that its major decisions would have to be made in accordance with the state's needs, in accordance with the needs of the institutions of political power. Their supposedly faceless ally would thus in reality impose upon them an entire set of values and behaviors. In effect, the dynamics of exercising physical force within a material context—the constraints of power, so to speak—would overwhelm all other concerns of the new ruling class, and rather than ruling the state they would themselves be ruled by it.

In a certain sense, this argument represents the application of materialist theory to the problem of the state: objective conditions bound up in the exercise of political power dictate the behavior and ultimately the moral outlook of any class that wields such power. Regardless of its original material basis, Bakunin was suggesting, once a class assumed control over the state it was in a new objective situation, in a new material context, and its old values and goals would give way to attitudes and beliefs more appropriate to its new situation.

In brief, Bakunin argued that although the state had the initial appearance of being a neutral and value-free weapon, wholly subject to the commands of its ruling class, in reality the state was a highly value-laden form of social organization, with a particular inherent nature that inevitably swallows up all conflicting values and goals. Thus, the real issue posed by Bakunin's critique of the state is the contention that the state as such rules and manipulates its ruling class, and that therefore whichever class holds the putative reins of state power the result will ultimately be the same.

Critique of Science

Bakunin's critique of science was, in its broad structure, similar to his critique of the state. Science was an artificial entity, created by man for his own use but incapable of fully comprehending either the sensuous living character or the true complexity of human society and of the natural world in general. Additionally, due to its abstract structure, science like the state could readily become the captive of a ruling class and be transformed into a weapon of both social oppression and ideological legitimation. Despite these parallels to the state, however, the basic character of science differed from that of the state in one crucial aspect: there was nothing inherent within science as such which required it to be a class tool. On the contrary, Bakunin argued that if science were freed of its class character—something which by definition was impossible for the state—science could fulfill its true potential as an agent of social liberation. Therefore, while he believed that the state was an abstraction that had to be destroyed, science was an abstraction which instead had to be retrieved from ruling-class control and reformed.

Bakunin considered the concept of science, correctly understood, to be a method of intellectual explanation, through which man could comprehend the workings of the physical or natural world as well as those of human society within that world. Drawing upon his Lamarckian conceptions of mutual interaction and natural authority as the determinant natural forces, Bakunin presented the proper role of science as the discovery and codification of "the natural and permanent laws" that governed each natural environment.[70] Elsewhere, he referred to science as "simply universal experience clearly expressed, systematically and properly explained."[71] Bakunin believed there was a fixed set of natural laws and principles that were determined within the natural world, preordained by the processes of animal development, and which man could uncover by diligent search.

These laws and principles, however, could only be discovered through a rigorously inductive process. Bakunin argued that the only way in which man could ever find these pre-existing natural laws was to begin with clear and observable facts—with the "things, phenomena and facts" of the known world—which, having been "verified" as real, could then be integrated into a useful theoretical conclusion.[72] Science, he wrote,

> proceeds from the details to the whole, and from the confirmation and study of the facts to their understanding, to ideas which are no other than faithful accounts of the successive related connections and mutual interaction and causality which really exist among real things and phenomena; its logic is none other than the logic of things.[73]

Bakunin emphasized that it was only their grounding in observable concrete facts that gave scientific conclusions any validity, and he caustically contrasted the conclusions of science properly performed against what he argued were the bloodless results fabricated by "theologians and metaphysicians."[74] Science for Bakunin employed a strictly inductive approach to arrive at a fixed and immutable conclusion. "To understand a phenomenon or fact," he wrote, "means discovering and establishing its successive phases of real development, recognizing its *natural law*."[75]

Bakunin argued that despite its universal scope and natural basis, science had an innately abstract character which severely limited its social usefulness. Science wasn't abstract in the same chimerical or fantastic sense that the state had been, for its conclusions embodied and reflected the natural laws of the physical world. These conclusions were nonetheless abstractions for Bakunin in that they were summatory and remote from the immediate reality of daily life, structurally unable to comprehend the full dimensions of the natural world. Bakunin had defined science as a systematic process of inductive thought, the purpose of which was to discern a general pattern of information—a natural law—within a heterogeneous set of specific facts and events. In order to perform this task, science had to be functionally incapable of appropriating or representing the sensuous reality, the actual existence of the objects and individuals involved in these situations. On the contrary, science could only arrive at effective conclusions if it ignored the concrete individual elements which gave objects and individuals their own unique character: by definition science abstracted an entity's form from its living content. "Thought and science," Bakunin argued, "can grasp that which is permanent in the continued transmutations of things, but never their material and individual aspect."[76] The difficulty with science's exclusive concentration on form, then, was that it completely neglected those material and individual elements of human life that Bakunin, with his philosophical roots in Feuerbach and Lamarck, believed gave existence its meaning and value. Bakunin therefore insisted that the "real or practical organization of society," that the human living content had to be given priority over scientific conclusions if the actual evolutionary development of the natural world was to continue, and if the actual existence of the sensate human individual was to retain its meaning.[77] "Life is fleeting and transitory," he wrote, "but it also palpitates with reality and individuality, with sensibility, sufferings, joys, aspirations, needs, and passions. It alone spontaneously creates real things and beings. Science creates nothing; it only recognizes and establishes the creations of life."[78]

For Bakunin, both science's social strengths and social weaknesses were directly derived from its fundamentally abstract nature: the positive as well as disastrous consequences of science grew out of its general or universal perspective upon the natural world. The positive characteristics, Bakunin argued, were bound up in science's capacity to educate man about the physical and social environment in which he lived. And the negative realities and potential future disasters developed from science's inability, as an abstraction, either to sustain the complex physical and social conditions necessary for human development on the one hand, or to prevent its merely intellectual conclusions from being manipulated and distorted by various privileged social classes on the other.

Science's potential as an indispensable tool for social liberation grew out of its ability to systematize and regularize man's knowledge of his world. By informing man about the natural and social worlds, Bakunin believed, scientific data made it possible for man not only to comprehend his environment but to act effectively on and in it. Science alone, Bakunin wrote, "can give us a clear and precise idea" of the structure of man's natural and social worlds.[79] And the central importance of such an understanding, or the "mission of science," lay in its capacity to instruct man's future actions within those worlds. Science for Bakunin "fixes, so to speak, the unchangeable landmarks of humanity's progressive march by indicating the general conditions which it is necessary to rigorously observe and always fatal to ignore or forget. In a word, science is the compass of life."[80] In Bakunin's view, science had no prescriptive or determinative power over the future shape of human society, as it did within the rigid formulations of Saint-Simon and Comte. Rather, here science was only a critical intellectual capacity turned on the past "to light the road" that men themselves would seek and define.[81] "The most rational and profound science cannot predict the forms which social life will take in the future. It can only define the negative factors which logically flow from a rigorous critique of the existent society."[82]

Science's abstract nature was also responsible, however, for a series of characteristics that distorted science's liberatory potential into either a source for, or adjunct to, popular oppression by privileged social classes. Science would necessarily become a source of popular oppression, Bakunin argued, if its conclusions were ever to become the sole basis for social decision making. Since it was only capable of comprehending human life at its most general and unspecific level, it was structurally unable to acknowledge the immediate concrete concerns of those individuals its decisions would affect. Moreover, in its position as a commentator upon rather than a creator of daily life, a solely scientific determination of social decisions would put the abstracted form in control of the actual living content from which it was taken. "Positive science," Bakunin wrote, "recognizing its absolute inability to conceive real individuals and interest itself in their lot, must definitely and absolutely renounce all claim to the government of societies; for if it should meddle therein, it would only sacrifice continually the living men it ignores to the abstractions which constitute the sole object of its legitimate pre-occupations."[83] Bakunin explicitly described what a wholly science-based form of social decision making would entail for mankind. Complex human society would be reduced to a one-dimensional static image of scientific abstraction, and would become capable only of a servile obedience to that disembodied authority:

> It would be sad for mankind if at any time theoretical speculation became the only source of guidance for society, if science alone were in charge of all social administration. Life would wither, and human society would turn into a voiceless and servile herd. The domination of life by science can have no other result than the brutalization of mankind.[84]

Bakunin presented an additional argument against allowing science free rein over social decision making: at any given historical stage, man's scientific knowledge was always incomplete and inadequate.[85] Science lacked a finished picture of the physical and human environment, and was therefore unable even within its limited abstract range to comprehend fully the world it was to rule.

Science had and would again become an adjunct to class-based oppression, Bakunin contended, whenever its theoretical conclusions could be manipulated by a privileged social class to their own advantage. As an abstract entity, science had no existence beyond that given to it by men. Consequently, in a class-based state or society, science would necessarily be bound up with the class interest of those men who developed science—the scientists— or more generally with the state's ruling and administrative classes. These three classes would inevitably exercise their potential to distort the conclusions or even the process of scientific investigation to their separate or mutual benefit.

Bakunin paid particular attention to the social consequences of allowing a separate scientific class to have monopolistic access and control over scientific knowledge. Once scientists were no longer held accountable to the general population for their acts, he argued, they too would develop the same set of self-impressed and self-interested attitudes that grew up among state administrators, and that Bakunin believed would inevitably emerge from a privileged status. In such situations arguments about the public advancement of scientific inquiry would soon cloak the unrelenting pursuit of private class prerogatives. The "licensed representatives" of science, Bakunin contended,

> men not at all abstract, but on the contrary in very active life and having very substantial interests, yielding to the pernicious influence which privilege inevitably exercises on men, would finally fleece other men in the name of science, just as they have been fleeced hitherto by priests, politicians of all shades, and lawyers in the name of God, of the State, of judicial Right.[86]

Additionally, a scientific class would seek to maintain its privileged access to scientific knowledge by preventing other classes from ever acquiring it. Bakunin argued that a socially unaccountable scientific class would as a matter of self-preservation attempt to keep the general population in a state of perpetual ignorance and "tutelage." Far from educating other people, or making their findings available to those who might benefit from them, a scientific class would attempt to make itself indispensable to society by withholding their knowledge. In fact, Bakunin suggested, a well-situated scientific class would try to consolidate its political position "by rendering the society confided to its care ever more stupid and consequently more in need of its government and direction."[87] The ultimate consequence of an unrestrained scientific class would be the reduction of the general populace to the level of simply research animals. Given both the abstract and individually unconcerned character of scientific inquiry in general, and the particular political concerns of a privileged class of scientists, Bakunin forecast that "left free to act after their own fashion, they will subject human society to the same experiments that, in the name of science, they carry out today on rabbits, cats, and dogs."[88]

Bakunin also argued that science had been and would continue to be manipulated by the political state's ruling and administrative classes. Basing himself on the relationship between science and the ruling classes up until his own period, Bakunin argued that a ruling class exerted two separate forms of control over scientific inquiry. With regard to the natural or physical sciences, which Bakunin believed were still predicated upon a "conscious analysis of the facts," state controls would be directed not at the internal integrity of their conclusions but rather upon limiting their application to areas that would be helpful to the state's ruling class. This sort of state selectivity, Bakunin argued, had become normal in past relations between the physical sciences and state power: "all the inventions of the mind, all the great applications of science to industry, to commerce, and generally to social life, have benefited up to now only the privileged classes and the power of the States."[89]

In contrast to their external control over the physical sciences, Bakunin believed, was these ruling classes' direct internal interference within the structure and content of the social sciences. Seeking to legitimate their own economic and political status, ruling classes force social scientific research into an ideological straitjacket in order to mask the class character of their decisions. Thus within capitalist states, Bakunin contended, the social sciences' proper foundation in the natural authority of mutual interaction was deliberately obscured by a set of idealist and individualist notions which were more congenial to the capitalist ruling class. This process of distorting social science content for ideological advantage could be observed in "such science as history, philosophy, politics, and economic science, which are falsified by being deprived of their true basis, natural science, and are based to an equal extent on theology, metaphysics, and jurisprudence."[90] Indeed, Bakunin argued that the social sciences performed a function within the capitalist state quite similar to that served by Catholic doctrine within medieval states: each set of abstract conclusions provided a theoretical justification for what was in reality the class-based exercise of state power. "Just as Catholicism once sanctioned the violence perpetrated by the nobility upon the people, so does the university, this church of bourgeois science, explain and legitimize the exploitation of the same people by bourgeois capital."[91]

Bakunin realized that the theoretical and practical political liabilities created by science's abstract nature would tend to recreate and reinforce each other within the political state. Science's structural inability to deal with every individual in his immediate environment would inevitably be compounded by the efforts of the state's ruling class to manipulate to its own class advantage whatever general conclusions science could provide. Bakunin believed that these interrelations between state and science would only consolidate the simultaneously abstract inability of the state to comprehend the complexity of daily life and its class-based and oppressive utilization of physical force. In an attack upon what he argued were the authoritarian implications of science's dominant role within both Marxist and Comtist states, Bakunin wrote that "the government of science and of men of science, even be they positivist disciples of Auguste Comte or, again, disciples of the *doctrinaire* school of German Communism, cannot fail to be impotent, ridiculous, inhuman, cruel, oppressive, exploiting, maleficient."[92] In short, Bakunin believed that within a class-based state, bound as it was to exercise state force for the benefit of its ruling and administrative classes, abstract science would inevitably become suffused and controlled by the state's class-specific goals. This manipulation of both natural and social science had occurred within all prior states, and Bakunin argued that it would continue to exist as long as man was governed by states.

The fundamental problem of integrating science into human society, according to Bakunin, thus revolved around the implications of its necessarily abstract nature. The positive advantages which scientific knowledge could bring to the general population had to be harnessed while simultaneously preventing science from either dominating the processes of social decision making or being appropriated by some privileged or ruling class. As Bakunin summarized this dilemma, "it is in this nature of thought that the indisputable rights and the great mission of science are grounded, as well as its impotence in respect to life and even its pernicious action whenever it arrogates to itself, through its official representatives, the right to govern life."[93] Science could thus overcome its structural limitations only if it were freed of the political consequences of its own abstract nature. An effective solution would have to establish rigid guidelines to restrict science from becoming a political force within society. "What I preach," Bakunin concluded, "is to a certain extent the revolt of life against science, or rather against the *government of science*, not to destroy science—that would be high treason to humanity—but to remand it to its place so that it can never leave it again."[94]

The mechanism which Bakunin relied upon to reassert this control over science was simply to "liquidate" science as a body of knowledge separate from the general populace. He proposed to "spread" science "among the masses," making as much knowledge as possible accessible to all, and instituting his system of collective self-discipline to determine the application of the remainder.[95] With this approach, Bakunin argued, science would no longer be a separate process of theoretical abstraction isolated from the immediate workings of the real world:

> without losing anything of its universal character, of which it can never divest itself without ceasing to be science, and while continuing to concern itself exclusively with general causes, the conditions and fixed relations of individuals and things, it will become one in fact with the immediate and real life of all individuals.[96]

Further, science would no longer be under the political authority of a particular class—capitalist, scientific, or bureaucratic—and consequently would no longer be distorted or manipulated to the exclusive benefit of those classes.

The primary obstacle to such a solution, of course, was that it could be implemented only within a stateless and classless structure of social authority, which in turn could be achieved only through a social revolution. Bakunin argued that the resolution of the problem of abstract science would be the same as that required to solve the problem of the abstract state. Both science and the state had fixed structural liabilities which could be remedied solely by a popular seizure of social control over them. The only substantive distinction between these two problems, as noted at the beginning of this section, was that while the difficulties posed by abstract science were to be handled by reforming its social structure, the problem of the abstract state required its complete physical elimination from human society.

Bakunin also provided, in his critique of science, a rare insight into life in a post-revolutionary collectivist-anarchist society. In an effort to highlight the oppressive consequences of contemporary scientific applications, he gave a short description of how a redistributed science would function. His illustrations suggested that there would be a shifting combination of direct popular distribution of basic knowledge with collective popular authority over more technical information, which would together make science popularly accountable.

Bakunin realized that the amount of scientific knowledge that could be digested by the general population, while it might increase over time, would never comprise the full body of available information within an industrialized society. His goal, then, wasn't to attempt to distribute all scientific knowledge among the populace, but only enough fundamental information to enable most individuals to participate intelligently in efforts to exercise popular control over science's more esoteric pursuits. "It seems to us," Bakunin wrote,

> that those who imagine that after the social revolution everyone will be equally learned are severely mistaken. Then, as now, science as science will remain one of the numerous social specializations. . . .
>
> Only general scientific education will become common property, and particularly a familiarity with scientific method, the habit of thinking scientifically, i.e., of generalizing facts and drawing more or less correct conclusions from them.[97]

The process of collective popular control over more technical information was to be based on Bakunin's concept of mutual interaction, and on the specific notions about mutual influence among free and equal beings, which Bakunin considered to be the foundation of human freedom. As he presented it, an individual with only a general scientific education would weigh such factors as the "character," the "mental cast," and the "method" of a particular scientist, would compare the proffered data or application with his own personal experience and observations, and finally would consult with "other reliable scientific observers" so that together they might mutually arrive at a proper decision.[98] Politically speaking, the central element here was that the final decision was to be made by the general populace both individually and then collectively—not by scientists and state administrators. In this manner, the social applications of scientific knowledge would buttress rather than challenge the overall collective authority of the general population: it would become possible for society to exercise political control over science.

Moreover, Bakunin argued that such a post-revolutionary system would free scientists from the restrictive political controls that had been imposed in the past by various privileged classes—including their own. The practitioners of science would finally be able to concentrate their full attention upon the discovery and codification of scientific knowledge and to tap science's real potential to assist in the development of human society. Making science popularly accountable, Bakunin wrote,

> will not prevent men of genius, better organized for scientific speculation than the majority of their fellows, from devoting themselves exclusively to the cultivation of the sciences, and rendering great services to humanity. Only, they will be ambitious for no other social influence than the natural influence exercised upon its surroundings by every superior intelligence, and for no other reward than the high delight which a noble mind always finds in the satisfaction of a noble passion.[99]

In short, the great advances which this post-revolutionary system would achieve in political accountability wouldn't come at the cost of a loss in the quality or scope of scientific endeavor. As Bakunin viewed it, both could be attained simultaneously.

This, then, was the possible solution that a social revolution could provide to the problem of science. By separating what Bakunin argued was science's positive potential to instruct mankind from its negative tendencies toward political oppressiveness, science could become popularly accessible, popularly accountable, and more productive. Lastly, science would acquire a sense of dignity that it had lacked previously. "Science," Bakunin concluded, "in becoming the patrimony of everybody, will wed itself in a certain sense to the immediate and real life of each. It will gain in utility and grace what it loses in pride, ambition, and doctrinaire pedantry."[100]

Critique of Capitalism

Bakunin's critique of capitalism had a substantially different emphasis from either his critique of the state or of science. These two critiques had been directly predicated on his philosophical notions of mutual interaction and collective self-discipline, and they focussed upon what Bakunin argued was the inevitable translation of abstract structure into practical class consequences within all political states. With his critique of capitalism, however, Bakunin moved to an analysis of the specific economic and political structure that dominated his own period, and which was essentially the most recent expression of a more general historical pattern. Bakunin's critique of capitalism thus represents a kind of case study, in that it demonstrates how his basic understanding of the relationships among economic, political, and social factors fits together in this one contemporary example. While his discussion emphasized the particular economic and political characteristics of capitalism, and as a result appears to be primarily a dialogue with Marx, his argument was nonetheless premised upon the same broad set of philosophical conceptions that he had acquired from Lamarck and Feuerbach, and that were more directly visible in his analysis of social authority within the structure of the state and of science.

There are a number of analytic advantages to be gained by concentrating specifically on the economic and political aspects of Bakunin's critique of capitalism. This approach provides a concrete illustration of how Bakunin perceived the linkage between the political and economic components of social authority and of the particular form which his materialism took. It gives a vantage point from which to compare Bakunin with Marx, in that Bakunin adopted most of Marx's economic analysis of capitalism but differed as to the political conclusions that Marx then extrapolated from that analysis. It presents the particular concrete economic and political framework within which Bakunin developed his analysis of social classes, and from which he argued that a social revolution would be required to make all men free. And lastly, it demonstrates the fundamentally socialist character of Bakunin's theory of collectivist anarchism, for Bakunin's absolute rejection of capitalist political and economic systems drives a long wedge between his own understanding of anarchism and that of various French utopian and present-day libertarian theorists.

Bakunin's understanding of the economics of capitalism was distinctly and quite consciously based on his reading of Marx. Bakunin openly acknowledged this debt both before and after The Hague Congress of 1872, and, as noted in chapter 1, always considered himself to be a disciple of Marxist economics. He wrote of Marx's general materialist approach to history that Marx had

> demonstrated the uncontestable truth, confirmed by all ancient and modern history of human society, of nations and States, that the economic fact always preceded and continues to precede political and juridical right. One of the principal scientific merits of M. Marx was to have stated and demonstrated this truth.[101]

More particularly, Bakunin lauded the critique of capitalism presented in *Capital* as "magnificent," "profound," and "decisive," and wrote that "it is based on a very detailed and extensive knowledge and analysis in depth of that system and its conditions. Herr Marx is a mine of statistical and economic information."[102] And although he criticized *Capital* as "far too metaphysical and abstract" in its style, and thus "inaccessible" to the popular classes, Bakunin considered Marx's analysis to be sufficiently important that he himself began the first translation of it into Russian.[103]

Acknowledging the inclusive and encyclopedic character of Marx's economic critique, Bakunin clearly didn't feel that it was necessary to undertake anything similar himself. What he did attempt to do was to render Marxian economic theory in a more popularly understandable form. Additionally, Bakunin modified several minor points in Marx about the forms of economic appropriation that should be considered to be objective exploitation, and which in turn determined which social classes within capitalist society ought to be defined as objectively revolutionary. The major purpose in delineating Bakunin's economic analysis of capitalism, however, isn't to distinguish Bakunin's approach from Marx as much as it is to tie them together.

Bakunin's basic economic analysis took as its touchstone the value and importance of human labor. In an argument which drew upon Bakunin's philosophical fusion of Lamarck and Feuerbach, he contended that labor alone was the foundation of all moral and material human values, being both the "fundamental basis of dignity and human rights" as well as the "sole producer of wealth."[104] "It is only by means of his own free intelligent work," Bakunin insisted, "that man . . . wins from the surrounding world and his own animal nature his humanity and rights." [105] Further, man's relation to labor, and particularly to the creative labor which was to come with the socialist future, was forged not only by economic necessity but by man's own internal need to "fashion his world."[106] Labor was "a vital need for every person who is in full possession of his faculties. . . . Man, by his very nature, is compelled to work, just as he is compelled to eat."[107]

The primary problem with the economic structure of capitalism, in Bakunin's view, was that it prevented man from engaging in such morally and materially rewarding labor. Bakunin described the individual worker as "forced" by "threat of hunger" to sell "the sole commodity which he possesses" to capital.[108] Bakunin regularly referred to that commodity as the worker's "productive force" and clearly understood it to be the source of all surplus value—a concept which he employed but for which he substituted the more commonly recognized term "profit." In one passage, for instance, having noted that capitalist competition resulted in "the lowest possible price," Bakunin argued that industrial profit couldn't come from artificially high prices but must represent the differential between the value of the worker's labor and the amount he was paid for it: "because of the competition of employers and capitalists, the source of real profits of both is the comparatively low wages and the long hours imposed upon workers."[109] Elsewhere, Bakunin alluded to Marx's argument that surplus labor was created by living labor power when it revalorized previous labor stored in the form of fixed capital, but again Bakunin translated this argument into popularly comprehendable language. "Neither property nor capital," he wrote, "produce anything at all, when they are not fertilized by labor."[110]

Bakunin, like Marx, used this argument about surplus value to explain the process by which capital built itself upon exploited labor while it progressively widened the chasm between its own wealth and that of the working classes. Bakunin accepted Marx's conclusion that capital was intrinsically exploitative, representing nothing but (as Marx once described it) "the theft of others' labor time" which was then opposed to those others (the working classes) as an alien yet controlling power.[111] Bakunin railed continually against the domination of capital and property, arguing that although "only collective labor creates wealth," that wealth was appropriated in a capitalist economy for private and antisocial purposes.

Bakunin also recognized the intrinsically expansionist nature of capital, and noted the further miseries that capitalist growth would inflict upon the working classes. Again paralleling Marx, he believed that the structure of competition built into "capitalist production and banking speculation" forced them to expand "ceaselessly" under "penalty of failure."[112] In turn, the increasingly monopolistic character of this expansion would force "an ever-growing number" of petty bourgeois and peasant freeholders into an already overflowing labor pool, compounding the existent competition competition among workers for jobs.[113] Thus the maturation of capital would simply reinforce the existent subsistence level of market-determined wages:

> This tendency of the workers [to compete], or rather the necessity to which they are condemned by their own poverty, combined with the tendency of employers to sell the products of their workers, and consequently to buy their labor, *at the lowest price*, constantly reproduces and consolidates the poverty of the proletariat.[114]

Bakunin argued further that capitalist competition would necessarily prevent either trade-specific unions or producer's cooperatives from improving the working classes' economic position. Concerning trade-specific unions, Bakunin relied upon the commodity character of wages to argue that if such a union actually succeeded in raising wages above the market-determined level within its industry, capital's profits would decrease, and capital would necessarily withdraw from that industry and reinvest in other, non-union, higher profit enterprises. If, then, the unionized workers were to retain their jobs— "in order not to die of hunger"—they would have no choice but to satisfy capital and once again accept the market-determined price for their labor.[115]

Bakunin presented a similar argument against the potential benefits claimed for producer cooperatives. He contended that such workers' collectives if "left to their own resources" could never accumulate enough of their own capital to compete successfully with bourgeois capital.[116]

Moreover, if a producer cooperative did survive capitalist competition, the surrounding capitalist economy would force that cooperative to become a "new collective bourgeoisie," which, like the Rochdale workers, would become systematically exploitative of the "mass of workers" who were outside the successful cooperative.[117]

In the basic structure of the economic analysis of capitalism, in short, Bakunin was decidedly a student of Marx. He accepted most of the fundamental arguments that Marx had advanced about the behavior of capital: that it was based on the surplus labor value created by the working classes, that wages for labor would stay at the subsistence level, that capitalist enterprises had to expand and consolidate their operations, and that producer collectives could not escape capitalist requirements. Some distinctions between Bakunin and Marx do emerge, however, in the conclusions that they draw from their respective applications of this economic analysis to the structure of social classes within capitalist society.

Marx's definition of economic class was tied not just to the process of material production per se, but to participation within a rigidly defined structure of capital formation within production. He categorized human labor on that basis alone: "only labor that produces capital is productive, so that labor which does not do this, however useful it may be (it could be harmful) is not productive for capitalization, and hence unproductive work."[118] Thus for Marx, only labor that directly created surplus value was "productive," and consequently industrial laborers—Marx's proletariat—were the principal productive class. This analysis cut across traditional social-class lines, in that segments of both upper and lower status groups performed labor that didn't "directly augment" capital: "state employees, doctors, lawyers" on the one hand, and small-holding peasants and farm wage-labor on the other.[119]

Bakunin, by contrast, built his analysis of economic class upon the individual's relationship to the capitalist process as a whole, to a concept of capital formation that included the appropriation of commercially generated exchange value as well as industrially produced surplus value. He argued that economic class was determined by the connection one's labor had to these processes of capital formation: labor either created new material value or it only consolidated the appropriation of that new value from those who had produced it. "There is productive labor and there is the labor of exploitation," Bakunin wrote.

> The first is the labor of the proletariat; the second that of the property owners. He who turns to good account lands cultivated by someone else, simply exploits someone else's labor. And he who increases the value of his capital, whether in industry or in commerce, exploits the labor of others.[120]

The key element in the definition of economic class for Bakunin, then, concerned the creation or addition of fixed material value to an object, and he believed that this transformation took place within the agricultural and commercial sectors of a capitalist economy as well as in industrial manufacture. These three different economic sectors were predicated on the same basically exploitative relationship between labor and capital, in that those who produced this new value were themselves structurally excluded from sharing in its benefits. "Productive labor creates wealth and yields the producers only misery....it is only non-productive, exploiting labor that yields property."[121]

This determination of economic class, through the objective relation of one's labor to an expanded notion of capital formation, served as the basis for Bakunin's definition of social class. He argued that the distinction between "the work of production" and that of "administration and exploitation" led directly to the distinction between the "muscular work" of "artisans, factory workers, and farm laborers" including small freeholders, and the "mental" or "nervous" work of the owners of capital.[122] Despite the "many intermediary and imperceptible shadings" that could be observed between various groups and individuals, the economic structure of capitalist society generated only two fundamental categories of social class—the working classes and the privileged classes.[123] Through his approach to the structure of capital formation and of economic classes within capitalism, then, Bakunin could conclude that not just Marx's industrial proletariat but also most peasants and commercial service employees were objectively exploited, and ought therefore to be considered part of the objectively revolutionary class.

Bakunin's approach to the structure of social class within capitalist society stretched not just Marx's definition of productive labor, but his definition of capital as well. Bakunin argued that Marx's strictly economic category of a fixed store of social value had to be broadened to include intellectual knowledge, or what Bakunin termed "mental capital." He described this intellectual form of capital as "the sum of the mental labor of all past generations," and believed that it reflected the "collective mental power produced by centuries of development."[124] This mental form of collective labor was not appropriated through conquest or contract, like fixed economic capital, but through controls over the structure of education. Within capitalist society, Bakunin argued, access to this mental capital was available exclusively to the privileged classes, and it consequently served to reinforce their economic and political power over the working classes. And while bourgeois education was delivered in an intellectually distorted and psychologically enervating form, it nonetheless provided the central organized form of mental capital in capitalist society, transforming man's collective mental labor into an important component of economic capital: "education is a force, and however bad, superficial or distorted the education of the higher classes may be, there is no doubt that...it contributes mightily toward the retaining of power in the hands of a privileged minority."[125] In terms of the structure of social classes within capitalist society, Bakunin's expansion of the concept of capital to include accumulated mental labor provided two further insights. It established a fixed objective basis upon which to incorporate the academic or intellectual class—the guardian of mental capital—into the orbit of the privileged classes. And, when coupled with Bakunin's argument about the inevitable bureaucratization of the state, the notion of mental capital suggested an objective foundation for the transformation of a state administrative class into a state ruling class.

Having tied the structure of social classes within capitalist society to a divergent but still materialist analysis, Bakunin was able to approach questions about the social conditions within these classes, and particularly questions about the degree of personal liberty within each, from a similarly materialist perspective. Marx, of course, had rooted his critique of individual freedom within capitalism in the fundamental economic characteristics of market competition. Unless an individual's economic interest directly paralleled the immediate interest of capital itself, he would find the "free competition" of capital to be a constrictive and ruinous rather than a liberating force: "This kind of individual liberty is thus at the same time the most complete suppression of all individual liberty and the total subjugation of individuality to social conditions which take the form of material forces."[126] Thus for Marx all economic freedom was only a secondary reflection of capital movements, and as a result it was only an "illusion" which would dissipate as capital developed.[127]

Bakunin accepted Marx's approach, and concentrated on applying it to the specific character of individual economic freedom and social conditions generally within the working and privileged classes. Of the working classes, Bakunin argued that the commodity nature of wage labor reduced the so-called free contract between worker and owner to "the meeting of wealth and hunger, of master and slave," in which the worker was forced to accept "a sort of voluntary and transitory serfdom."[128] The formal economic liberty of the working classes to contract at will thus became "a completely fictitious liberty, a lie."[129] "The truth," Bakunin wrote, "is that the whole life of the worker presents nothing else than a desolating continuity of temporary servitudes, juridically voluntary, but economically enforced, therefore a permanence of servitudes, momentarily interrupted by liberty accompanied by hunger, and consequently a real slavery."[130] Bakunin noted further that within the production process itself, the division of labor had stripped the "rational elements" from the working classes' tasks, and had as a result intensified the "stupifying" nature of the work which the working classes were required to perform.[131]

Moving from the working classes' lack of economic freedom, Bakunin argued that perhaps the central component of social freedom was also missing from working-class life within capitalist society. This was leisure, which Bakunin believed was essential for both personal self-development in general and "the development of the mind" in particular.[132] Deprived of leisure by the prevailing economic conditions of their survival, the working classes were unable to pursue either formal or informal education, and were forced to remain ignorant of whatever they had not themselves personally experienced. "Poverty, hunger, exhausting toil, and continuous oppression are sufficient to break down the strongest and most intelligent man," Bakunin argued.[133] Only in one rather narrow sense was this enforced ignorance an advantage: they had not been subjected to the "corrupted and distorted" version of mental capital which passed for formal education within capitalist society.[134] Spared the debilitating personal consequences of the "doctrinaire, classical, idealistic, and metaphysical education which poisons the minds of bourgeois youth,"[135] the working classes had both "preserved a freshness of spirit and heart,"[136] as well as retained their "highly practical and positive minds."[137] In the long run, however, Bakunin believed that the natural advantage maintained in their mental and social attitudes would pale in significance before the increasing scientific knowledge accumulated through formal education by the privileged classes, despite the tainted character of that educational process. Surveying the overall situation of the working classes, Bakunin concluded that "in view of the advancing education of the dominant classes, the natural vigor of the people's minds loses its significance."[138]

Bakunin summarized his analysis of the general social conditions under which the working classes lived in capitalist society by contrasting the positive, fulfilling, and even liberatory character of labor which he had taken as the touchstone of all human existence, with the crushing and degrading nature of labor within the economic and social structures of capitalism:

> If work is an accursed thing nowadays, it is because it is excessive, brutalizing, and forced in character, because it leaves no room for leisure and deprives men of the possibility of enjoying life in a humane way, and because everyone, or nearly everyone, is compelled to apply his productive powers to a kind of work which is the least suitable for his natural aptitudes.[139]

Bakunin restricted his comments about the social conditions of the privileged classes within capitalist society to references to their long-term psychological and sociological debilitation. Approaching his argument about the centrality of human labor from the opposite tack, Bakunin contended that the limited and specialized character of their labor left the privileged classes with extensive but "unearned" leisure. This "privileged leisure," unconnected to regular productive labor, served not to reinvigorate these classes but instead "enfeebles, demoralizes, and chokes" them.[140] Additionally, they were subjected to the disconcerting influence of bourgeois education, which tended, in Bakunin's view, to distort their sense of values and to weaken their will. In effect, although the privileged classes had access to the advantages of "existing civilization," the bourgeois character of those benefits left these classes prey to "all the poisons of a humanity perverted by privilege."[141] Bakunin concluded that over time, the destructive form of these advantages would overwhelm their benefits, and the moral and social character of these privileged classes would disintegrate. Since "inactivity and the enjoyment of all sorts of privileges weaken the body, dry up one's affections, and misdirect the mind," Bakunin concluded, "it is evident that sooner or later the privileged classes are bound to sink into corruption, mental torpor and servility."[142] In a sense, Bakunin argued that the very advantages of the privileged classes were their disadvantages, and that a proper understanding of the economic and social class structure of capitalist society would lead one to argue for social revolution in the best interests of the privileged as well as the working classes.

Bakunin's central argument for the necessity of social revolution, however, was rooted in a clearly materialist understanding of the relations between capital and the working classes. Adopting Marx's analysis of the inner workings of capital, Bakunin argued both that capitalism was internally contradictory, and that the social consequences of its economic contradictions would lead inevitably to its overthrow. Concerning capital's internal structure, Bakunin suggested that capital's increasing reliance upon the division of labor would impede rather than improve productivity due to the destructive consequences of separating mental from physical labor: "mind cut off from physical activity weakens, withers, and fades, whereas the physical vigor of humanity cut off from intelligence is brutalized, and in this state of artificial divorce neither produces the half of what could and should be produced."[143] And with regard to the social consequences of its internal structure, Bakunin argued that capital had created an irreversible "abyss" between its owning and working classes, and that the social conflict that this economic pressure generated would end in the triumph of the working classes.[144] Bakunin underscored the materialist character of his overall social argument, and at the same time acknowledged his direct debt to Marx, when he concluded that the owning or bourgeois classes had been "condemned to death by history itself."[145]

Bakunin's analysis of the structure of capitalist society took a fundamentally materialist approach which was drawn more or less directly from his reading of Marx. While he stretched or modified several of Marx's basic definitions, Bakunin did so only to broaden the social applicability of Marx's argument so that it might more closely reflect what Bakunin felt was the actual structure of capitalist society; he never tampered with the core character of Marx's materialist conclusions. Bakunin's adoption of a Marxist form of economic analysis demonstrates a key element in his conception of collectivist anarchism, one which has been undervalued if not ignored in most contemporary discussions of his thought: Bakunin's system was predicated upon a socialist rather than a capitalist economic framework. His thinking was sufficiently steeped in economic materialism that he recognized the historical and functional impossibility of either returning to some pre-industrial or yeoman version of a market economy (as individualist anarchists desire), or of simply liberating the industrial capitalist economy from the distortionary authority of the liberal state (as libertarians desire). Moreover, his Lamarckian belief in the progressive character of historical development enabled Bakunin to dismiss these quick but ahistorical economic fixes as insufficient and unnecessary as well as unattainable.

Bakunin's perception of the nature of the state, coupled with his largely Marxist understanding of capitalism, provided the theoretical foundation for his analysis of the specifically bourgeois state and of its typically parliamentary political system. Since the bourgeois state's political structure was an expression of its overall character, Bakunin believed that the bourgeois state's capitalist and statist roots would inevitably have a critical impact upon its political system. As a result, he dismissed the various instruments of formal political participation within bourgeois parliamentary systems—such basic aspects as periodic elections and universal suffrage—as structurally incapable of providing substantive political self-determination for the working classes. Indeed, parliamentary forms were on the contrary only strategic devices through which the working classes were given the illusion of real political self-determination precisely as they ratified the policies of the ruling bourgeois classes. From Bakunin's twin theoretical perspectives upon the state and capitalism, a parliamentary system was inherently a bourgeois shell game at which the working classes could never win. Parliamentary process and democratic self-determination, in Bakunin's analysis, were by definition autonyms rather than synonyms.

Bakunin presented his perspective upon parliamentary systems in three related but essentially distinct arguments. In the first, he described the inherent theoretical liabilities of the bourgeois state's capitalist and statist foundations. The second argument was directed against reformist notions that either universal suffrage or issue referenda could alter the inherently bourgeois equilibrium within these parliamentary systems. And the third detailed the dangers of tactical alliances between the socialist movement and radical bourgeois parties within such parliamentary systems.

Bakunin's general theory of classes within the state led him to argue that, in a parliamentary political system, even a truly representative election of a state official couldn't overcome the structural change from subject to governor that would take place in the "perspective and position"[146] of the newly elected individual. Indeed Bakunin insisted that precisely the periodic character of these elections would serve to remove that official from the "continuous control" of the electorate.[147] Even the worthiest individual would find that, once elected, his prior informal political participation—his "natural influence"—had calcified into self-interested right.[148] As a result, Bakunin argued that members of the working classes who were elected to a representative assembly would immediately become "former workers" who "no longer represented the people, but themselves and their pretensions to govern."[149] Despite all prior intentions, he concluded, the essential class character of any state was such that "if there should be established tomorrow a government or a legislative council, a Parliament made up exclusively of workers, those very workers who are now staunch democrats and Socialists will . . . become oppressors and exploiters."[150]

Bakunin also attacked the consequences which the bourgeois state's capitalist underpinnings would have for a bourgeois parliamentary political system. Effective participation within a parliamentary system, he noted, was directly dependent upon various economic and social resources which the popular classes were structurally precluded from acquiring. Forced to perform exhausting labor for subsistance wages, they lacked the leisure, the political experience, and the financial resources required to engage in "serious" regional or national political activity.[151] Further, they were largely dependent upon the bourgeois press for information about specific issues and candidates. Consequently, Bakunin concluded, the popular classes were exceptionally vulnerable to bourgeois political manipulation, and he found it not at all surprising that the popular classes were regularly convinced to vote down their own class interest.[152] The only perceptible exception occurred in local elections, in which the issues and candidates were often personally familiar to all, the resources required for participation were minimal, and the informal mechanisms of popular control over elected officials were the strongest.[153]

In brief, Bakunin argued that a bourgeois parliamentary system could never be democratic because of its statist and capitalist foundation. For the popular classes within a bourgeois state, he concluded, "the system of democratic representation is a system of hypocrisy and perpetual lies."[154]

Bakunin's second argument against bourgeois parliamentary systems focussed on the two specific reforms that were most often put forward as sufficient to redress the system's class imbalance: universal suffrage and direct issue referenda. From Bakunin's perspective, universal suffrage simply expanded what remained a politically worthless franchise and was inherently incapable of improving the popular classes' long-term economic and social situation. He thus rejected what was put forward by many Marxian socialists as a clearly progressive reform, condemning it as an "illusionary" device which enabled the popular classes only to ratify their own continuing disappropriation. "Universal suffrage," Bakunin wrote, was "a dangerous instrument without doubt, and demanding a great deal of skill and competance by those who make use of it," but at the same time "the surest means of making the masses cooperate in the building of their own prison."[155]

Bakunin dismissed the concept of direct issue referenda, or "direct legislation," with equal contempt. In a referendum, he argued, the popular classes lacked even the traditional parliamentary prerogative of amending a proposal. They could only adopt or reject the language that was arbitrarily put before them—language that was generally drafted by one sector or another of the bourgeois state.[156] Moreover, as in other regional and national elections, the popular classes lacked "the time and the education needed to study these proposals, to reflect upon them, to discuss them."[157] Except in rare cases of overwhelming popular concern, therefore, referenda could never be more than the "vote of the blind," and they were intrinsically incapable of threatening the bourgeois character of the parliamentary system. "Even in a representative system corrected by the referendum," Bakunin concluded, "popular control doesn't exist."[158]

From Bakunin's perspective upon bourgeois parliamentary systems, then, neither universal suffrage nor issue referenda could substantially alter these system's fundamental character. The politics of the bourgeois state, exactly like its economics, had a fundamental class structure that was not amenable to piecemeal reform.

This second part of Bakunin's analysis of bourgeois parliamentary systems leads directly to his third argument. Since parliamentary systems were structurally incapable of satisfying the political interests of the popular classes, then the already common socialist strategy of forming short-term tactical political alliances with the radical bourgeoisie was by definition futile and self-defeating. Such alliances, Bakunin argued, obscured the real economic and social problems facing the popular classes, misdirected these classes' attempts to correct their real problems, and thus had the inevitable consequence of reducing the popular classes to the role of an unwitting instrument of bourgeois class power.[159]

Bakunin based this argument against political alliances on his economic analysis of classes within capitalist society, and upon what he believed was the "insoluble internal contradiction" that their fundamentally bourgeois or privileged class status raised for these radical bourgeois. "They are," Bakunin scoffed, "revolutionaries in their dreams and reactionaries by the real conditions of their existence as individuals and as a class."[160] Any bourgeois would destroy "the very base of his own existence" if he seriously assisted direct economic action against capitalism, and such "suicidal" behavior required the denial of both Nature and logic.[161] Ultimately a radical bourgeois was still a bourgeois, Bakunin argued, and would come to defend both bourgeois economic supremacy and the working-class exploitation upon which that supremacy was based.

Consequently, the radical bourgeois was interested exclusively in internal political changes within the capitalist state structure that wouldn't seriously alter the existing distribution of economic and political power. Bakunin contended that the definitive characteristic of the radical bourgeois was an intransigent insistence that "the political must *precede* the social and economic transformation."[162] The bourgeoisie strenuously opposed strikes and other direct economic action, preferring to "concentrate on inciting the political and patriotic passions of the workers": demanding formal political rights, provoking violent physical attacks on leading political figures, promoting nationalistic wars.[163] The radical bourgeoisie even contended that a proper bourgeois education was essential for effective working-class action—a proposition which Bakunin, with his sharp distinction between legitimate mental capital and the distortions of bourgeois education, found particularly repugnant:

> But you do not teach them, you poison them by trying to inculcate all the religious, historical, political, juridical, and economic prejudices which guarantee your existence, but which at the same time destroy their intelligence, take the mettle out of their legitimate indignation, and debilitate their will.[164]

In short, Bakunin argued that the radical bourgeois, in order to preserve his own class foundation, must demand that all working-class efforts toward change remain channeled within the existent capitalist state framework, and that in any alliance with the working classes the radical bourgeois would be obligated to deflect direct economic action into less threatening attempts at political reform.

Bakunin presented a second structural argument against political alliances with the radical bourgeoisie: the intrinsic advantages and resources which each class could bring to an alliance were strongly skewed in favor of the radical bourgeoisie, and consequently their class background greatly increased the probability that the radical bourgeoisie would prevail within the alliance itself. As a member of the privileged classes, the radical bourgeois had far superior access to leisure and to mental capital, which were two important prerequisites to effective political activity. In addition, Bakunin argued that the fundamental process of defending bourgeois class interests was "neither new nor . . . immensely large in scope," and that as a result most bourgeois had a well-developed sense of how to best protect their situation.[165] In a related note, Bakunin contended that this type of tactical political alliance had historically proved to be more beneficial to its less progressive faction, since the muddled compromises which inevitably emerged from it had severely damaged the spirit and direction of the more militant party. "The more advanced party," he argued, "is inevitably weakened because the alliance diminishes and distorts its programme and destroys its moral strength and self-confidence."[166]

By their essential status as bourgeois, and by the not-so-secondary fact that their class dominated the existing political state, the radical bourgeoisie could outmaneuver the working classes within any joint organization or undertaking. Bakunin's argument against these alliances leads to the more general conclusion that, in his view, the structural situation within the capitalist state precluded any and all attempts to build political bridges between the working and the privileged classes. The disparity of position and interest was so great between these classes that every mutually organized endeavor was condemned simply to reproduce the oppressive relation between capital and labor in a new form. The radical bourgeoisie were no more than "the siren voices of the bourgeoisie,"[167] the most palatable faction of a class "which has nothing in common with the goals of the proletariat,"[168] and with whom alliance in any form could never be productive for working-class interests.

Bakunin argued that Lassalle's German Social Democratic Party well illustrated the long-term consequences of attempting to establish effective working-class social authority through the political structure of the capitalist state. Having selected as its central goal the seizure of state power, the SDP sought to achieve it both peacefully and gradually from within the political apparatus of the state, and in alliance with as many radical bourgeois elements as possible. From Bakunin's perspective, Lassalle's program read like a catalogue of inadequate and inappropriate policies for any organization committed to serious social change:

> As the first and foremost aim of the party he put peaceful agitation by all peoples for the universal rights of electing government representatives and authorities. Having won this right by way of legal reform, the people would have to send only their representatives to the national parliament which would turn a bourgeois government into a people's government by a series of decrees and laws. The first business of a people's government would be to allow unlimited credit to producers' and consumers' workers associations, which would only then be in a position to compete with bourgeois capital and would, in a short time, conquer it and swallow it up. When the swallowing-up process is over, there will then come a period in which society will be radically reorganized.[169]

In reality, Bakunin argued, the practical political consequence of this program would be to deliver up the German working classes into the waiting hands of the bourgeoisie and their state. Based both on his argument about the inherent class character of the state and on his economic analysis of classes within a capitalist system, Bakunin insisted the SDP's decision to organize politically within the state would force it to defer and finally to forego the more potent working-class weapon of direct economic action: "it will sooner or later be forced to oppose economic action—the tactic of strikes."[170] Faced, then, with the political requirements set by its chosen organizational strategy, which were also essential to its continued alliance with radical bourgeois groups, the SDP would cease to be a revolutionary working-class organization at all. In what was a concise summation of the same process of goal inversion—in the same political party—that led Michels to his iron law some forty years later, Bakunin concluded acidly that "the German SDP has to sacrifice the economic emancipation and consequently the political emancipation of the proletariat...to the ambition and the triumph of bourgeois democracy."[171]

Moreover, Bakunin argued that Lassalle's program was taken directly from Marx, and cited passages from the 1848 *Manifesto* and Marx's 1864 Address to the International in support of this assertion. It is useful to note here that Bakunin considered Marx's reformist political approach through alliances with bourgeois elements and within the bourgeois state to be a particularly dangerous strategy. "I have no hesitation," he wrote, "in saying that all the Marxist flirtations with bourgeois radicalism—reformist or revolutionary—can have no other outcome than the demoralization and disorganization of the nascent power of the proletariat, and therefore the further consolidation of the established power of the bourgeois."[172]

As is evident within Bakunin's critique of the politics of capitalist society, and of the capitalist state in general, Bakunin believed that a correct analysis of the overall structure of capitalist society had to combine two highly compatible but nonetheless distinct theoretical perspectives. On the one hand, this analysis had to reflect Marx's materialist critique of capitalist economic systems, with all its subsequent social and political implications about the structure of capitalist society. Yet it must also include Bakunin's more broadly based analysis of the nature of social authority within all societies, which was predicated on his philosophical notion about natural influence and mutual interaction. Bakunin recognized the importance of understanding the internal economic character of capitalism, and of comprehending how that character formed and produced the particular social and political structures observed within capitalist society. But he also believed that it was equally if not more important to recognize that the entire economic, political, and social network spun by capitalism was only the present form of what was in reality a much broader structure of oppression and exploitation which was inherent within any state and any class-based society.

This dual analytic focus explains why Bakunin so readily adopted the major elements of Marx's economic critique of capital, yet disagreed so demonstrably with the political solution that Marx proposed as the appropriate remedy. From Bakunin's perspective, Marx could suggest, first, the political seizure of the state and, second, doing so by peaceful parliamentary means because Marx didn't recognize the state as such as a self-extending and self-perpetuating form of oppression, which would always and under every circumstance recreate political domination and economic exploitation.

4 *Bakunin's Theory of Social Revolution*

Bakunin's general theory of social revolution, like his critique of bourgeois society, strongly reflected the central principles of his basic collectivist-anarchist argument. His conception of the historical process by which a social revolution unfolded, and of the "revolutionary association" that would guide it, was largely ordered by his notions of mutual interaction and collective self-discipline. Certainly, his emphasis upon the revolutionary as well as the analytic implications of collectivist anarchism isn't surprising, for Bakunin regularly noted his intention not only to criticize the bourgeois world but to overthrow it. At this point, one arrives, then, at the practical purpose for which the theoretical structure of collectivist anarchism was erected: to comprehend the contemporary condition of the working classes and to facilitate a liberatory socialist revolution.

On the Nature of Social Revolution

For Bakunin, the nature and necessity of social revolution lay in the objective condition of the "urban and rural proletariat." Working within a materialist framework of history, he understood questions of political and social justice to be determined by economic structures, and he consequently believed that any substantive change in the working classes' social condition could only follow a prior economic transformation. "The question of bread," he insisted, "is the question of intellectual emancipation, of liberty, and of humanity."[1] Bakunin bluntly argued, further, that conditions in 1870 Europe were such that the economic question concerned not only the working classes' long-term intellectual development but their immediate survival: "in the miserable circumstances in which the worker now finds himself, the main problem he faces is most likely bread for himself and his family."[2] Thus for Bakunin as for all materialists, the primary and most pressing difficulty facing the European working classes was the economic question.

Bakunin believed that the working classes' economic privation was, in turn, an inevitable by-product of a capitalist economy. Capital necessarily impoverished those classes by systematically appropriating for itself the value which their labor had generated. Almost by definition, any substantial improvement in the working classes' economic condition was "a sheer impossibility" within a capitalist economy.[3] Bakunin therefore concluded that only the "immediate economic emancipation" of the working classes could produce the needed improvement in their economic situation.[4] In a passage which was consistent with his argument that both urban and rural workers were objectively revolutionary, he called for "the general emancipation of all those who, earning with difficulty their miserable livelihood by any productive labor whatever, are economically exploited and politically oppressed by capital, or rather by the owners and the privileged brokers of capital."[5]

Bakunin recognized, though, that capital was not a solitary factor operating in a social vacuum. It had long since entered into a symbiotic relationship with other institutions of more formal social authority, and particularly with the state, with which it bartered wealth for physical security. Further, Bakunin argued that the state itself, beyond its specific relation to capital, was built upon a highly oppressive form of authority which recreated and reinforced the working classes' economic exploitation in other sectors of social life, and which would necessarily have to be replaced in a "free"—that is, economically, politically, and socially emancipated—society. In effect, Bakunin believed that any serious economic liberation inherently required the "complete liquidation" not only of the capitalist economic apparatus but of all its related social institutions and of the class-based authoritarian principles upon which the internal structures of those institutions were based.[6]

Bakunin further realized that, historically, no "privileged and dominant class" had ever relinquished its economic or social prerogatives unless "driven by force or fear" to do so.[7] The privileged classes which controlled economic and social power within the nineteenth-century capitalist state were no more willing than their predecessors to commit class suicide.[8] Therefore Bakunin further concluded that "reasoning and agitation" or other proposed "peaceful means" would be insufficient to overthrow either capitalist institutions or the classes which dominated them. Only "action"—physical force—could obtain the necessary change.[9] "The people," Bakunin wrote, "longing for emancipation, cannot expect it from the theoretical triumph of abstract right; they must win liberty by force."[10] In effect, Bakunin's objective analysis of capitalist institutions led him to insist upon the necessity of a coercive social revolution.

This same analysis simultaneously determined which classes within capitalist society could carry out that revolution. Bakunin, like Marx before him, believed that material exploitation alone could generate and sustain socialist activity. Thus the designation of those classes who were directly expropriated by capital was for Bakunin equally a definition of the only army of the revolution. That Bakunin extended Marx's concept of economic exploitation to include farm and service as well as industrial labor only broadened the scope of this argument rather than altering its content.

This materialist analysis, however, was only a general critique of capitalist society rather than a focused theory of revolutionary change. It indicated the structural potential for social revolution, but was unable to either delineate or evaluate the actual process by which revolutionary capacity would become revolutionary force. Bakunin consequently sought to develop these materialist tenets into a detailed analysis of the revolutionary process itself.

Bakunin began by examining the structure and composition of the working classes' objective revolutionary potential. He probed the general notion that these classes were an objectively engendered agent of revolution to try to discover exactly how that broad principle found expression within their daily lives. He came to argue that in its contemporary form this potential rested in two closely related, objectively based yet subjectively held attitudes that he labeled the working classes' "socialist instinct" and their "instinct to revolt." The working classes' socialist instinct, despite the clear implication of the term "instinct," was understood by Bakunin to be a historically created set of social attitudes. For Bakunin, history's passage had generated within the working classes an intense desire for social and political justice. "What every worker aspires to deep down in his heart is a fully human existence with respect to his material well-being and intellectual development, an existence based upon justice."[11] This desire had become so deeply internalized within these classes, and had so completely contextualized their entire political outlook, that in Bakunin's view it had acquired the practical characteristics of innate instinct. He thereby considered it appropriate to popularize it as such. Moreover, he contended that both historical experience and current concern had combined to fuse an unavoidably socialist content into this instinct's core. In short, while his notion of a socialist instinct relied upon the language of Lamarckian biology, the substance which Bakunin intended to convey seems to be derived more from a materialist approach to history than from evolutionary theory.

The objective foundation of this socialist instinct can be seen in almost every comment Bakunin made about it. He argued that, in his own time, all the conditions of its material existence conspired to reawaken within the working classes "the century-long instinct" for an economic and social revolution.[12] Similarly, he began another passage "instinctively, by virtue of its social position, it is socialistic."[13] Bakunin also explained the anticipated reversion of bourgeois socialists to their objective class position by a reference to an opposite but parallel economic experience: "it is instinctive. It comes from the fact that the conditions and habits of life. . .always exercise upon men a more powerful influence than their ideas."[14]

Moreover, Bakunin linked the working classes' "socialist instinct" to material history through a corollary concept, their socialist "ideal," which reformulated socialist instinct into a more directly historical entity. This "ideal," he wrote, was "necessarily the product of the people's historical experience."[15] It had been developed through "a natural accumulation of experience and thought, transmitted from generation to generation and necessarily broadened, deepened, perfected, and given form very slowly. It is achieved by an unending succession of painful and bitter experience."[16] This historically determined "ideal" served to establish the explicit connection between Bakunin's conception of a present-day socialist "instinct" and the materialist processes of history.

An additional confirmation of these two concepts' joint historical grounding can be observed in Bakunin's insistence that neither working-class attitude was amenable to short-term human manipulation. Noting that both Mazzini and Gambetta had failed in such attempts, Bakunin argued that the "tendencies, passions, and thoughts"[17] that comprised their socialist instinct or ideal must be so completely "the product of their own history" that the working classes "carry them naturally, instinctively in their own breasts."[18] In sum, although Bakunin considered the working classes' socialist instinct to be subjective and psychological in its immediate form, he believed that their subjective attitude was directly rooted in the objective processes of these classes' material history.

In comparison, Bakunin's second component of revolutionary potential, the working classes' "instinct to revolt," has a somewhat more involved relationship to these classes' material development. Bakunin presented it as a psychological tendency that was innate within all human beings. He described it as a "spirit of contrariness" that "awakens. . .almost at infancy,"[19] generating what he termed an "irresistable urge" to oppose arbitrary external authority.[20]

Bakunin appears to have used this notion of "contrariness" as a summary, probably verbal, vehicle for what was in fact a rather complicated philosophical argument. For although he doesn't refer to the issue of volition explicitly, his argument about contrariness subsumes Bakunin's belief that personal volition was the source of self-respect and dignity in all living creatures. This relationship can be clearly seen in Bakunin's linkage of volition to revolt and dignity in order to illustrate the meaning of contrariness. "Revolt is an instinct of life," Bakunin argued. "Even the worm revolts against the foot which crushes it, and one can say in general that the vital energy and comparative dignity of all animals is measured by the intensity of this instinct of revolt which it carries in itself."[21]

The relationship of volition to this instinct to revolt can be further clarified when one recalls Bakunin's definition of collective self-discipline. The fundamental political power of that definition was the capacity of collective self-discipline, negatively construed, to eliminate those forms of domination that Bakunin believed were inherent in externally based authority. If the individual's "instinct to revolt" emerges in reaction to precisely the type of external authority which collective self-discipline is designed to eradicate, then that instinct must be an inverse expression of the same desire for individual and collective social authority that formed the basis of collective self-discipline itself. Thus in Bakunin's mind the "instinct to revolt" clearly translated into the desire to control the conditions of one's own life, or a notion of personal volition.

Here again, while he used the language of Lamarckian evolutionary theory to describe it, he clearly recognized that this instinct to revolt would be molded by objective historical forces, and that the strength or tenacity that it demonstrated within a given social class would directly reflect that class's historical experiences. This argument that personal volition would of necessity be historically determined was derived from Bakunin's basic contention that the modern state, by definition, was predicated upon the "forced enslavement of the masses."[22] Since the state's structural requirements directly contradicted the working classes' innate desire to control the conditions of their own lives, these classes could assert that desire—and thereby preserve their own sense of self-respect and dignity—only through continuous rebellion against the institution which had dispossessed them. "But for the masses," Bakunin asked, ". . . what constitutes political will? They can only be certain of one thing, the sainted revolt, that mother of all tradition, the tradition of revolt, the traditional art of organizing and making the revolt succeed, these historical conditions essential to all real practice of liberty."[23] Thus the instinct to revolt was intrinsic to the working classes' historical struggle with the state, and would itself ultimately be shaped by that conflict.

In turn, since this instinct was historically conditioned it could also be historically extinguished. Of course Bakunin, like most nineteenth-century materialists, believed that in the long run history was a positive progressive force, and that the form of personal volition which this instinct to revolt and collective self-discipline represented would inevitably triumph. Yet he nonetheless realized that, in some countries for some working classes, historical conditions had or would become sufficiently severe to crush out personal volition:

> A people which suffers tyranny, necessarily loses over the long term the salutary habit of revolting, and even the instinct of revolt. It loses the sentiment of liberty, and the will (la volunté) and habit of being free, and once a people loses all that, they become necessarily, not only through external conditions but internally in the very essence of their being, a slave people.[24]

For Bakunin, then, though he believed that the working-classes' desire to control the conditions of their own existence would ultimately emerge triumphant, he recognized that cross-pressures within the historical process had the potential to eliminate that desire in some situations. Thus his notion of an "instinct to revolt," like his notion of a "socialist instinct," was an objective product of a given working class's material history.

One should note that Bakunin's concept of volition and his instinct to revolt, being historically determined and thus historically vulnerable, were quite different from the ethereal, immutable volition of Fichtean and Kantean metaphysics, or from the exclusively psychological interpretation advanced by commentators like Pyziur.[25] Additionally, Bakunin's uncertain prognosis for the historical fate of this instinct contradicts any assertion that with this discussion of instinct he had reduced history to the progressive revelation of a one-dimensional tautology.

When one takes a broad view of Bakunin's two instincts, they appear to be rather similarly structured. Both the instinct to revolt and the working classes' specifically socialist instinct embody a combination of a basic human desire for self-determination and a set of historical experiences acquired in the attempt to attain self-determination. The working classes' socialist instinct becomes only a particular class-specific variant of the more generalized notions about human volition and self-respect that underlie the instinct to revolt. These two instincts retain certain distinctions that were useful to Bakunin in constructing a materialist theory of revolution, and were put forward separately. Taken together, however, they represent Bakunin's assessment of how the broad materialist principle that the working classes were objectively revolutionary appeared within these classes' daily lives.

Bakunin believed that these two instincts indicated only the presence of a revolutionary potential, not of an active and effective revolutionary force. The working classes' instinct to revolt and their socialist instinct could do little more than favorably dispose these classes to revolutionary pursuits, for these instincts were themselves inadequate for the serious preparation of an actual revolutionary movement. A serious revolutionary effort, Bakunin argued, required that the working classes be both "educated and organized"—a refrain which in certain senses summarized Bakunin's basic approach to social revolution. And certainly, Bakunin concluded, a brief glance at the political situation of the European working classes in 1870 would suffice to demonstrate that these two instincts had neither educated nor organized the working classes in the required manner.

Clearly, Bakunin contended, neither instinct had remedied the working classes' vast and debilitating ignorance about the shape of social reality. If they were to seize control of their own lives, he began, the working masses must first become conscious of their own collective strength and capacity. They must "conceive of themselves as an all-powerful mass bound by ties of solidarity."[26] In fact, however, they remained "disunited" in their self-conception as well as in their actual lives.[27] They continued to perceive their difficulties as particular and individual rather than social and general in origin. Moreover, being ignorant of the social character of their misfortunes, they were unable to identify the forces and classes which were responsible for them. Far from recognizing the "principal sources of their misery," the working classes hated "only the manifestation of the cause and not the cause itself."[28] With their social atomization compounded by their analytic ignorance, they were left "completely powerless."[29] In such circumstances, Bakunin argued, it was "impossible" for the working classes to achieve the requisite level of "self-awareness" and knowledge without "the aid of education, of science."[30] The two instincts that comprised the working classes' revolutionary potential had clearly been inadequate to the task of properly educating them.

In fact, Bakunin argued, these two instincts had not only failed to educate the working classes, but the instinct to revolt was itself on occasion responsible for leading these uninformed classes off in the wrong direction. The instinct to revolt generated an extremely powerful, emotion-laden vehicle which these classes were as yet unprepared to control, and the working classes' innate but undirected tendency to resist external authority often left them vulnerable to ulterior manipulation. "Ignorant of the real causes of their woes," Bakunin wrote, this instinct reduced the working classes to a volatile but unprotected "instrument" that was "at the disposition of the first artist who condescends to use it."[31] He concluded, therefore, that

> instinct as a weapon is not sufficient to safeguard the proletariat against the reactionary machinations of the privileged classes. Instinct left to itself, and inasmuch as it has not been transformed into consciously reflected, clearly determined thought, lends itself easily to falsification, distortion, and deceit.[32]

Bakunin believed that this untutored instinct to revolt bore primary responsibility for the false directions and lost opportunities that had plagued recent working-class movements. In Germany and France in 1848, in Lyon in 1870, and in Paris in 1871, he argued, the general populace had been "rich in instinct and negative theoretical ideas" but had not been able to support these essentially reactive concepts with the "positive and practical ideas" based on considered convictions that were necessary to the construction of a "new system."[33] They had consequently failed to transform their initial expressive dissent into the sustained instrumental actions required for a permanent solution. Instead, divided, ignorant, and misled, their instinct to revolt had led them only to sporadic, localized, and therefore futile acts of violence.

In a similar vein, Bakunin noted that this instinct to revolt could not be properly channeled by miserable social conditions alone. If the entire passage of history as a whole had been unable to instruct this instinct, one derivative by-product of that vast process would by itself be quite helpless. Throughout history, Bakunin observed, the broad masses had always been "poverty-stricken and discontented," yet even when they had been "reduced to the utmost misery" they rarely evinced "any signs of stirring."[34] Moreover, when the masses had on occasion risen against their situation, poverty alone had been incapable of guiding their visceral but still uneducated instinct to revolt. Poverty, Bakunin wrote, could "provoke a limited number of local revolts" but these would by necessity be only expressive, undirected "fits of indignation."[35]

In sum, Bakunin argued that the instinct to revolt, as it presented itself in the working classes of 1870 Europe, had been unable either to educate these classes adequately as to their true situation, or itself become adequately educated by historical experience. Its tutelage was thus limited to the painfully slow expansion of working-class awareness which had accumulated in the form of the working classes' socialist ideal. Consequently, while on the one hand ensuring that "the process of real advancement had never altogether stopped,"[36] the instinct to revolt was, on the other hand, unable to generate the broad-based and conscious educational transformation that the working classes required.

Even if this instinct could have somehow "awakened" within the working classes an "intelligence which rises to the level of their instinct,"[37] however, Bakunin argued that it would still have been unable to satisfy the second half of his revolutionary maxim: the instinct to revolt could never have organized these classs into an effective and directed revolutionary force. This instinct's inability to organize the working classes was in Bakunin's mind equally as important a failing as was its inability to educate them. To recognize the magnitude of this failure, though, one needs first to describe the centrality of this notion of revolutionary organization for Bakunin's overall theory of social revolution.

Bakunin's insistence upon the importance of preparatory organization was derived from Bakunin's basic philosophical notion of mutual interaction. This notion, consistent with Bakunin's reading of both Feuerbach and Lamarck, was in turn premised upon the ability of the human consciousness to impose its will upon the external physical environment. In this context, the question of social revolution involved the realignment of the existent pattern of mutual interaction among men so as to modify the distribution of material and social forces within the society as a whole. "The present order," Bakunin wrote,

is the final summary, or rather the result of the clash, struggle, worsting and mutual annihilation of one another, and also the combination and interaction of all the heterogeneous forces, both inward and outward, operating within and acting upon a country.... It follows that a change in the prevailing order is possible and that it can take place only as a result of a change in the equilibrium of forces operating in a given society.[38]

The conscious human force that could alter the current "equilibrium" was that of human solidarity. Bakunin argued that just as in the natural world everything that "lives" or "exists in a mechanical, physical, or chemical sense" must "invariably influence" the surrounding world, in human society each individual, as a separate actor, also "embodies a modicum of the social force."[39] Although this individual's share was "insignificant and almost nil" when contrasted with "the vast totality of all social forces," the common action of "a few dozen persons" joined together could dramatically affect that larger composite. Such a union, Bakunin wrote, produced not simply the numerical sum of the group's separate individual forces but rather "gives birth to a new force which far exceeds the simple arithmetical sum of their isolated individual efforts."[40]

Bakunin proceeded to argue that in Europe in 1870 the overall sum of social forces could be divided into two main categories. One was that of the working classes—"the sum of unconscious, instinctive, traditional, and as if elemental forces, which were totally unorganized"—and the other represented the privileged classes and their vehicle of social control, the state—"an incomparably smaller sum of conscious, concerted, purposefully combined forces which act according to a given plan and which are mechanically organized in keeping with the latter."[41] Bakunin contended that it was upon the "incontestable advantage" of "organized force over the elemental force of the people" that the power of the state presently rested, and that consequently the working classes could only overthrow that state by organizing their own social force into a physically stronger political instrument. In the relationship between social force and political authority, Bakunin concluded, "numbers mean nothing if forces aren't organized."[42]

One should note that Bakunin's insistence upon adequate prerevolutionary organization had a further, specifically practical genesis. In his own revolutionary activities, Bakunin had observed the bloody consequences of insufficient preparation, and indeed he himself spent twelve years in prison and exile as the result of a poorly organized revolt in Dresden in 1849. Less personally, Bakunin also argued that the absence of effective organization had in the last century doomed most working-class insurrections before they began. On a practical as well as a theoretical basis, then, Bakunin concluded that the two working-class instincts which defined these classes' revolutionary potential had been distinctly unable to translate that potential into an adequately educated and effectively organized revolutionary movement. In sum, the working classes required a higher level of education and organization than they could acquire through their own historical development.

Before one can follow this argument to its next stage, in which a revolutionary association enters to provide the necessary educational and organizational impetus, there are two remaining aspects of Bakunin's revolutionary theory that require our attention. The first is Bakunin's notion of an adequate pre-revolutionary working-class education, and the role that propaganda and/or social theory could play in that process. And the second is the relationship in Bakunin's mind between spontaneity and historical materialism in the revolutionary process as a whole.

Bakunin construed the education that the working classes still required as a routinized human intervention into an ongoing historical process. It represented the injection of nineteenth-century materialist knowledge into the "sort of traditional science" that these classes had already accumulated in the form of their "socialist ideal."[43] Bakunin believed this additional information would focus that essentially abstract ideal upon the contemporary source of the working classes' difficulties, and that as a result the working classes would finally acquire a level of political awareness which Bakunin alternately termed "rational consciousness"[44] or "socialist thought."[45]

Once armed with this refocussed intellectual capability, the working classes would be prepared to rectify their impoverished condition. All that remained was to animate this knowledge, to transform "rational consciousness" into an active "revolutionary consciousness" which would set the working classes to organizing a social revolution.[46] This final stage would arrive, Bakunin argued, when the working classes came to trust and believe in both the fundamental justice of their demands and the historical inevitability of success. They must, he wrote, "have faith in the real efficacy and certainty of this means of salvation."[47]

As Bakunin understood this process, then, the role of education in translating the working classes' revolutionary potential into revolutionary action would be twofold. First, education would induce an awareness of these classes' actual historical situation—"rational consciousness." And second, education would assist the working classes in acquiring some psychological certainty that their new analysis was correct and that their efforts could be successful. One should note that while Bakunin's notions of rational and revolutionary consciousness are clearly subjective psychological attitudes, they are both grounded in the material process of history. Education was objectively based, in his account, both in its content—the explanation of historical development—and in the "instinctual" preparation that it presumed of its students. And Bakunin's concept of trust or faith was similarly constrained:

> This faith is a matter of temperament, collective disposition, and mental state. Temperament is given to various peoples by nature, but it is subject to historical development. The collective disposition of the proletarian is always a two-fold product: first, of all preceding events, and then, especially, of his present economic and social situation.[48]

In effect, by integrating these psychological attitudes into a materialist framework, Bakunin was able to acknowledge their immediate legitimacy for the working classes yet simultaneously give these subjective attitudes an objective historical foundation.

Bakunin made two additional points about the integral relation of objective material history to any effort to educate the working classes. First, he argued that the specific content of the program had to reflect directly the true historical situation of the classes it was to educate. Although he regularly referred to the substantive aspects of education as propaganda, Bakunin clearly indicated that he understood this term to carry an applied or operational rather than a deceptive connotation. Propaganda, Bakunin argued, would push the working classes toward social revolution only insofar as it clarified certain disparate but real aspects of their current situation. Propaganda could be effective only if it sought to focus the historically developed "socialist instinct" of the working classes—it ought never attempt to fabricate new or artificial revolutionary demands. Bakunin developed these points in passages such as the following.

> What can propaganda do, then? In bringing a more just general expression, a new and more congenial form to the existent instincts of the proletariat, it can sometimes facilitate and precipitate development, always from the point of view of their transformation into the consciousness and the reflected will of the masses themselves. It can give them an awareness of what they have, of what they feel, of what they already instinctively desire, but never can it give to them what they don't have, nor awaken in their breasts passions which by their own history are foreign to them.[49]

Bakunin noted further that propaganda, as an operational concept, need not mimic the pattern and structure of traditional education. Bakunin recognized that actions often had a more direct impact than verbal discussion, and that they can better convey the personal commitment of the propagandist. Therefore, he argued, the necessary education of the working class should take place not just through discussion but also "through actions, for that is the most popular, the most potent, and the most irresistable form of propaganda."[50]

The second point Bakunin made about the relation of material history to revolutionary education detailed the proper role for social theory in the development of effective propaganda. Bakunin recognized that theory had the capacity to extract a clear and comprehensive picture from apparently unrelated phenomena and could thereby provide useful guidance to those involved in framing the content of revolutionary education. For theory to perform this function, however, it had to be correctly formulated, and consequently social theory must reflect the same historical limitations as the propaganda that it was to instruct. Bakunin argued that theory must be restricted to the recombination of already existent information, and its function limited to representing fairly the full meaning of that information. By so severely limiting the purview of social theory, Bakunin apparently hoped to transfer the inductive naturalistic approach he believed proper to the physical sciences into the social realm:

> The living, concretely rational manner of forging ahead is, in the domain of science, to go from the real fact to the idea which embraces, expresses, and by this explains it; and, in the applied domain, to go from the social life to the most rational manner of organizing it in conformity with the indications, conditions, necessities, and the more or less passionate exigencies of life itself.[51]

Bakunin explicitly condemned all efforts at deductive social theory as futile attempts to force life into conformity with invalid and artificial models. As previously noted, he regularly criticized other revolutionary figures like Gambetta for relying upon theoretical notions which Bakunin argued lacked a material foundation. In short, as with physical science, Bakunin insisted that social theory must reflect the objective world: "natural and social life always come before theory, which is only one of its manifestations but never its creator."[52]

In both their form and content, then, Bakunin's proposals for educating the working classes acknowledged the central importance of material history to the success of that endeavor. Here Bakunin's argument about pre-revolutionary working class education paralleled his conception of those classes' fundamental revolutionary potential as well as his explanation of those classes' inability to yet realize their potential. In each instance, the material forces of history had first generated the potential for development within those classes but had subsequently precluded them from fulfilling that potential on their own. It was this rather Lamarckian pattern of simultaneous preparation yet constraint that led Bakunin to argue that only external intervention could "educate and organize" the working classes for social revolution.

One last point needs to be made here concerning Bakunin's conception of the basic relationship of the material forces of history to the process of social revolution. Bakunin always argued that in the final analysis every revolution was the product of objective factors—of "events and facts"[53]—that were rooted in the material framework of the entire society. Bakunin's intellectual debt to Lamarckian evolutionary theory (and perhaps to his Young Hegelian background as well) was evident in passages such as the following, in which Bakunin noted that "in history as in physical nature, nothing is made by a single blow. Even the most sudden revolutions, the most unexpected and the most radical, have always been prepared by a long labor of decomposition and new formation."[54] Thus a social revolution could not be "improvised or made arbitrarily" through only the "deliberate will" of human beings, nor could it be "artificially accelerated" by such intervention.[55] Rather, in this analysis a revolution always developed over an extended period of time, carefully cultivated by history, and made itself apparent only when fully grown. "They come about of themselves, produced by the force of things, the tide of events and facts. They ferment for a long time in the depths of the instinctive consciousness of the popular masses—then they explode, often triggered by apparently trivial causes."[56]

Bakunin didn't insist, however, that each specific aspect of a revolution was historically predetermined. Only the overall thrust and direction was inevitable. Within those broad confines, the precise configuration of events was uncertain and would emerge through the complex ongoing processes of daily human existence. There was within his conception of social revolution, therefore, an historically bounded but fluid instrument of popular participation which mediated abstract historical pressure into concrete objective form. And it was this process to which Bakunin referred as the "spontaneous" component in the development of a revolution.

His conception of revolutionary spontaneity paralleled closely Bakunin's understanding of anarchy itself. He linked them through descriptions of the "new social world" that would follow a successful social revolution as "resting only upon emancipated labor and spontaneously created upon the ruins of the old world, by the organization and free federation of workers' associations."[57] In effect, the spontaneous element in a social revolution embodied the broad-scale human creativity which the initial revolutionary explosion would unleash, and which would then flow back into political life. However, consistent with Bakunin's notion of anarchism in general, these spontaneous acts would always occur within a historically determined context.

Bakunin's effort to subsume revolutionary spontaneity within an objective material framework went unnoticed by Paradox commentators like Carr and Pyziur. They preferred to attribute Bakunin's references to spontaneity as proof that his concept of a working-class revolution was ahistorical and purely volitional, possible both at any time and under any social or historical conditions. These Paradox conclusions, however, not only misinterpreted Bakunin's general notion of anarchy, but ignored specific statements in which Bakunin argued that "there are periods in history when revolutions are quite simply impossible; there are other periods when they are inevitable."[58] Thus when Bakunin referred to the continual potential for social revolution in contemporary France, Italy, and Spain, his arguments weren't based on the wild-eyed ahistorical pan-revolutionism attributed to him by these commentators. Rather, they derived from Bakunin's belief that the historical pre-conditions for social revolution were "already widespread in practically all the countries of Europe, and that their fusion into an effective force is purely a matter of mediation and concentration."[59]

In sum, Bakunin believed that every contributory component of a social revolution, even the seemingly uncontrolled "spontaneous" outbreak of revolution itself, had to be historically prepared. Yet Bakunin also recognized that such preparation could not of itself produce a social revolution: the material forces of history could create the necessary preconditions for a working-class revolution, but these forces were of themselves insufficient to "educate and organize" the working classes into an effective revolutionary movement. Consequently, if those classes were to achieve the liberatory promise of their historical potential, if they were to become sufficiently well educated to both apprehend the direction of historical pressure and then to develop an organization capable of providing strategic direction within it, they would require the external assistance of a revolutionary association.

On the Role of the Revolutionary Association

The central function for which the working class needed to organize was to concentrate their overwhelming social force into a parallel power capable of confronting the bourgeois state. Only through such political organization, Bakunin argued, could the newly acquired education which the working class was to receive be translated into effective political fact. As he explained their historical situation,

> the mere consciousness of the justice of its own cause is not sufficient. It is necessary that the proletariat add to it the organization of its own forces, for the time is passed when the walls of Jericho would crumble at the blowing of trumpets; now force is necessary to vanquish and repulse other force.[60]

The only real question therefore became that of how the working classes could best overcome the historically generated constraints that had precluded them from developing an adequate revolutionary organization in the past. The only viable solution, Bakunin argued, was the introduction of an outside agent which could catalyze the working classes into seizing control of their own revolutionary potential. This non-working class agent would perform the limited and short-term task of educating and organizing the working classes so that they might themselves, by their own acts, then translate their historically prepared "socialist instinct" into social revolution. Bakunin believed that this could be accomplished in a non-coercive and educational fashion, without either distorting the original revolutionary ideals of the working classes or supplanting those classes' control over their own destiny with a permanent Leninist elite.

Bakunin referred to this outside, non-working class agent as a "revolutionary association." The nucleus of this association was to be composed primarily of bourgeois intellectuals and students who had effectively and fully declassed themselves. Bakunin recognized that such voluntary transformations were rare and difficult, but he believed they were nonetheless possible if an individual was able to move beyond just subjective sympathy for the working classes to a real and substantive merging of his identity and future with theirs. Bakunin described these bourgeois as having "come to hate with all their souls the present political, economic, and social order, who have turned their backs upon the class from which they sprang, and who have devoted their energies to the cause of the people."[61] This declassé nucleus was essential, Bakunin believed, because, in the strict class structure of nineteenth-century Europe, only the bourgeoisie had access to formal education and thus to the knowledge and skills that the working classes lacked: "positive knowledge, the power of abstraction and generalization, and organizational abilities."[62]

Bakunin provided this revolutionary association with a fully detailed strategy with which to conduct its activities. In its external relations with the working classes as well as within itself, both before and after a successful social revolution, the association was to adhere strictly to the central principles of Bakunin's general social theory. In particular, the association was to integrate into its operational framework, as a kind of guiding beacon, Bakunin's conceptions of mutual interaction and collective self-discipline. One should note that here, as before, Bakunin's reliance upon this notion of mutual interaction as his primary analytic tool indicates the theoretical consistency of his overall political argument. For Bakunin's theory of social revolution specifically, however, his understanding of mutual interaction led to several important conclusions about the proper structure of a revolutionary association.

As Bakunin perceived it, the broad fundamental goal of a social revolution, and consequently of a revolutionary association before it, was to "institute anarchy," to overthrow completely the restrictive economic, social, and political apparatus of the bourgeois state so as to attain the "full affirmation of unfettered popular life."[63] Bakunin argued that it would be simply impossible for such an egalitarian society to spring forth full-grown, Medusa-like, from a theretofore authoritarian organization. It must be prepared in and through the revolutionary process itself if it was ever to emerge from that revolution in a mature, self-determining form. This central Bakuninist premise was summed up some hundred years after Bakunin by Murray Bookchin, who posited that "there can be no separation of the revolutionary process from the revolutionary goal. . . . Self-administration . . . can be achieved only by Self-activity."[64] This fundamental requirement for a liberatory social revolution led Bakunin to insist that the principles of collective self-discipline must permeate every aspect both of a social revolution and of the revolutionary association which was to be its precipitant.

Bakunin's basic approach to social revolution was in consequence not at all compatible with the hierarchical, centralized, and more or less putschist notions held by many of his contemporaries. Quite the contrary, Bakunin argued directly that if a revolutionary association first seized the bourgeois state and then set out to liberate the working classes by arbitrary revolutionary decree, that association would itself necessarily succumb to the dynamic of hierarchical authority, and its new so-called Revolutionary State would unerringly recreate the same supposedly bourgeois relations that it had just interred. Bakunin recast his general critique of the state into three major criticisms of the new state to which he believed a revolutionary putsch would inevitably lead.

First, Bakunin argued, in a revolutionary state as in all states, the intellectual capacity of the revolutionary authorities could never encompass the "infinite multiplicity and diversity" of daily human existence. Therefore the dimensions of the new authorities' deliberations would be far more narrow, and their directives far more limiting than what was required by the complexity of the true situation.[65] Second, the very existence of such arbitrary authority would destroy the moral basis which must undergird a social revolution. Even socialist collectivity, Bakunin argued, could only be forcibly imposed upon "slaves,"[66] and furthermore that process of imposition itself would erode the moral and ethical principles of those who implemented it. Lastly, in direct consequence of the first two points, Bakunin contended that a new revolutionary state would soon come to represent only a "reaction disguised by revolutionary appearances."[67] Under the impact of its arbitrary authority, the new state would find itself re-institutionalizing precisely the restrictive and inadequate decision-making procedures that had doomed its bourgeois predecessor. Through the regeneration of social privilege which would inevitably follow these decision patterns, the revolutionary state would recreate the "sentiment of revolt" among the newly excluded working classes and thereby trigger a "legitimate counter-revolution" in which the excluded classes would desert the new state for the blandishments of bourgeois reaction.[68] Bakunin summarized this process of revolution and counter-revolution with his observation that "the Revolution ceases to be a revolution when it acts despotically, when, instead of promoting freedom among the masses, it promotes reaction."[69] All of this, Bakunin insisted, would be the integral and necessary result of an authoritarian or putschist form of revolution.

It was to forestall just such a fatal degeneration that Bakunin structured his own revolutionary association, both externally and internally, in accordance with the principles of mutual interaction and collective self-discipline. A properly conceived revolutionary association, Bakunin argued, would by definition be the "most pronounced enemy of every sort of *official power*."[70] The association was to remain "invisible" in all formal and official senses both after as well as before a social revolution. "Never," Bakunin wrote, would the "association as a whole or any of its members" seek or accept "official public office."[71]

In Bakunin's model, however, the revolutionary association's commitment to the principles of mutual interaction went beyond this essentially negative step of refusing to be institutionalized in any official form. Bakunin believed that post-revolutionary abuse of authority was the unavoidable last phase of a centralized putschist approach to revolution. Thus, if a revolutionary association was to induce a revolution without destroying precisely the self-directive, working-class capacity it intended to liberate, the association must also undertake the essential positively directed task of cultivating and coordinating the fundamentally autonomous revolutionary activities of those classes. It must understand itself as simply the "midwife" of the working classes' "self-emancipation,"[72] confining its own activities to the coherent reformulation of those interests and desires "deeply embedded in the historic instinct and the whole condition" of those classes.[73] In both its self-conception and its instrumental acts, a revolutionary association could be no more than "the intermediary between the revolutionary idea and the popular instinct."[74]

In order to implement this limited, educational approach to the exercise of revolutionary authority, Bakunin's association had to achieve a clear, theoretically consistent yet completely informal presence within local working-class organizations. This was to be accomplished, Bakunin proposed, by the association confining itself to the organization of the "natural action" of its individual members within these working-class groups.[75] The association's authority was to be predicated solely upon the "natural influence" that Bakunin believed would be "exercised . . . by individuals or groups of individuals" strictly on the basis of their knowledge and ability once the arbitrary authority of imposed institutional structures had been removed.[76] Bakunin contended that a properly constructed revolutionary association would assume no more than the "natural action of a club" in that its efforts to organize the masses will. . . never be anything but the organization of the activity—. . . completely natural—of a group of individuals inspired by the same thought and tending toward the same goal—firstly, upon the opinion of the masses, and only after that, by the intermediary of this opinion,. . . on their will, their acts.[77]

In short, in Bakunin's model, a revolutionary association "influences the people exclusively through the natural, personal influence of its members."[78]

The association's strictly informal influence was to be directed toward the strengthening of existent working-class organizations and, where such structures were absent, to the founding of new ones. Consistent with his broader theory of revolution, Bakunin believed that the pattern of working-class organizations must be based upon the "various manifestations of their actual daily life," and particularly upon the working classes' "various forms of labor."[79] Such an organizational foundation would serve three functions: it would incorporate the substantial "natural organization"[80] already in existence; it would anchor the revolutionary movement to the working classes' historical interests; and it would increase the movement's resistance to bourgeois overtures.

Bakunin believed that whether indigenous or induced, these working-class organizations had to be local in scope and autonomous in program. Moreover, they too were to be internally structured according to the principles of collective self-determination. Authority was to be distributed within each group only as short-term necessity required, with "no fixed and constant authority, but a continual exchange of mutual, temporary, and above all voluntary authority and sub-ordination."[81] This arrangement, Bakunin argued, would serve to "unleash" the working classes' "will,"[82] and, by furthering their acquaintance with economic and social "self-determination" would generate a "still closer unity" within the organization.[83] To ensure the development of collective self-discipline within these disparate local organizations, the revolutionary association was to employ its educative authority to "gain influence" over the "most intelligent and advanced" individuals "of high standing" within each group—that is, those who themselves exercised informal influence locally.[84] In effect, Bakunin was proposing a two-tier process of informal educative authority through which to secure the pre-eminence of that form of unofficial authority at the revolutionary movement's local level. It should be stressed, however, that here again Bakunin had limited his revolutionary association to a strictly advisory or educational form of authority.

The internal structure of Bakunin's association was similarly patterned on his fundamental precepts of mutual interaction and collective self-discipline. Bakunin believed that "permanent self-exercised control"[85] would be essential if the association was to avoid the debilitating effects of hierarchical command and power. Yet he also argued that a revolutionary association must have a "collective, well-organized will" built upon "common thought" and a process of "striving toward a common goal" if it was ever to "establish a certain co-ordination in action" among a geographically dispersed membership.[86] Effective coordination was critical not only to prevent members from working at cross-purposes with their fellows—in which case they would surely "neutralize one another's efforts" [87]—but more importantly to invest their combined efforts with the multiplicative impact of collectively exercised social force through what Bakunin termed the "law of collective action."[88] Thus within the internal processes of a revolutionary association, collective self-discipline must be applied so as not only to induce participatory decision making but also to facilitate the implementation of those decisions.

The association's "single will," Bakunin wrote, would be determined by "laws" that every member "helped to create," or at a minimum "equally approved" by "mutual agreement."[89] This "definite set of rules" was to be "frequently renewed" in plenary sessions wherein each member had the "duty to try to make his views prevail," but then he must accept fully the decision of the majority.[90] Thus the revolutionary association's "rigorously conceived and prescribed plan," implemented under the "strictest discipline,"[91] was in reality to be "nothing more or less than the expression and direct outcome of the reciprocal commitment contracted by each of the members toward the others."[92]

Within the context of a mutable, mutually accepted program, each member was expected to defer his personal concerns to the requirements of the collective whole. In both interactions within the association as well as activities undertaken in its name, the member was always to remember that his "primary duty" was to the revolutionary association, with his obligation to his fellow members in a close "second place."[93] However, it should be noted that Bakunin never suggested in his own works that the member would have to sacrifice or abandon his family and community—a caveat which did appear in Nechaev's early works. Bakunin presented the member's obligation to the association, rather, along the lines of adopting the goals and constraints of the revolutionary association as one's primary political commitment.

Bakunin argued that each member's personal responsibility for what was a collective goal required each member to comport himself in a manner that would be consistent with the attainment of that goal. Bakunin therefore called for an "honest, reliable revolutionary"[94] who was "hardworking and intelligent,"[95] full well capable of conducting himself with "good faith, courage, caution, discretion."[96] The revolutionary must be "filled with moral purpose"[97] and as a result be "unalterably devoted to the people."[98] And most important of all, Bakunin argued, each member must be "devoid of personal vanity and ambition," be it either collective or individual.[99] Renouncing "vainglory, love of rank and fame"[100]—all of which Bakunin believed were "temptations" which had as their "inevitable result" only internal organizational "intrigue"[101]—committed revolutionaries must instead harbor "enough worthy ambition to want only the triumph of their idea, not of their selves."[102] By so doing they would confirm that they "prefer the reality of power" to the "egocentric trappings" of "force."[103]

Contained within the phrase "reality of power" was Bakunin's belief that it wasn't the operational logic of collective self-discipline alone which required the individual member to subordinate his personal goals to those of the revolutionary association. In the contemporary context of 1870 Europe, Bakunin argued, highly impersonal historical forces had transformed the previously individual orientation of authority within social institutions into a new, collectively controlled, social framework. Therefore, the contemporary revolutionary was functioning in the "century of collective, not individual power"[104] and must be brought to recognize that henceforth "in revolutionary action as in modern labor the collective must supplant the individual."[105] This perception, of course, underscored not only Bakunin's discussion of revolutionary tactics but was a central element in his entire analysis of social change: mutual interaction is nothing if not a collective rather than an individual process.

Bakunin's emphasis upon the importance of the revolutionary collective directly paralleled an additional aspect of mutual interaction: despite his concentration on the collective, Bakunin had no intention of derogating the highly personal qualities of the individuals who participated within it. On the contrary, consistent with his conception of regular, individual contributions to policy formulation, and also with his Hegelian-derived assessment of individual development as possible only in and through the social group, Bakunin contended that the separate individual's ability and knowledge would increase within and as a result of this collective structure. As he reminded those who might join his association, "you will think, you will exist, you will act collectively which nevertheless will not prevent you in the least from the full development of the intellectual and moral faculties of each individual."[106] Thus a focus upon the collective character of the revolutionary association reflected, from Bakunin's perspective, a desire to expand simultaneously the individual's own sphere of personal development.

In brief, the sole purpose of Bakunin's revolutionary association was to impart a sense of coherence and direction to the working classes' own efforts within an already developing pre-revolutionary situation. Rather than the pursuit of either individual or separate collective benefit, the association's obligation was that of the "midwife" who assists a family at the birth of *its* child: the association was to serve as the "organ" or "agent" through which the "unity of revolutionary thought and action" could assert itself in the pursuit of goals that were fully consistent with the working classes' historically generated instincts. Bakunin's revolutionary association, in short, was never to act as a discreet political force in the Leninist sense, which the term "vanguard" has now come to imply. It was, rather, an organization dedicated to the attainment of what Marx himself had postulated as the proper goal of revolutionary education: convincing the working classes to accept and act on what they already knew. Moreover, distinctly unlike a Leninist cadre, Bakunin's association was to be internally organized in a highly democratic yet "rigorously disciplined" manner and to conduct itself externally among the working classes in an informal, educative, and strictly non-authoritarian fashion.

This was the theoretical context within which Bakunin made his controversial reference to his revolutionary association as a "collective dictatorship." Bakunin had noted elsewhere that physical action always foreclosed previous alternatives, defined the course of real events, and was therefore effectively authoritarian in its consequences: "that man is, and always will be, the dictator, not juridically but actually, who acts."[107] When Bakunin subsequently described a revolutionary association as "that invisible, collective dictatorship of those who are allied in the name of our principles,"[108] and whose impact upon the working classes was to be achieved "by a force that is invisible, that no one admits and that is not imposed upon anyone,"[109] he was consequently not engaging in either intellectual self-contradiction or self-deception. He was simply summarizing the operational strategy detailed above. Bakunin himself clearly identified the linkage between a collective dictatorship and his revolutionary strategy in a letter he wrote to Nechaev on June 2, 1870, which concerned the potential for revolutionary activities in contemporary Russia. Since this issue is of central importance to Bakunin's entire theory of social revolution, yet has rarely been properly understood, the full passage in which Bakunin used this notion of a collective dictatorship is given below:

> But imagine that in the middle of [a triumphant, spontaneous revolution] there were a secret organization, dispersing its members in small groups throughout the empire, but nevertheless firmly united and inspired with a single idea, a single aim, applicable everywhere in different ways according to the circumstances, of course, and acting everywhere along the same lines. These small groups, unknown to anyone as such, would have no officially declared power. But strong in the idea behind them, expressing the very essence of popular instincts, desires, and demands in their clear and conscious aims among a crowd of people who would be struggling without any purpose or plan, these groups would finally have the strength of that close solidarity which binds isolated groups in one organic whole, *the strength of mind and energy* of its members, who manage to create round themselves a circle of people who are more or less devoted to the same idea, and who are naturally subject to their influence. These groups would not seek anything for themselves, neither privilege nor honor nor

power, and they would be in a position to direct popular movements in opposition to all those who were ambitious but not united and fighting each other, and to lead the people toward the most complete realization of the social-economic ideal and the organization of the fullest popular freedom. This is what I call the collective dictatorship of a secret organization.[110]

Clearly, Bakunin wrote of a collective dictatorship which itself had few of the authoritarian or coercive features associated with the notion of dictatorship. On the contrary, he employed the term only to combine his previously noted recognition of physical action as foreclosure with the otherwise non-coercive and educational character of a properly structured revolutionary association.

Two further, as yet undiscussed, aspects of Bakunin's revolutionary strategy are also apparent in the above passage. The first concerned the intended physical size and operational scope of this association, and effectively highlighted the degree to which it was designed to function as a kind of local political militia or Cincinnatus League.[111] Bakunin believed that a hundred "powerfully and seriously allied" men would be an adequate force with which to organize all Western Europe.[112] This small number would suffice in that these men would not in any way be organized "apart from the people" but, having become themselves part of the working classes, they would be nurturing the "revolutionary power" of those classes as a whole.[113] Bakunin compared this relationship to that found in the military, describing the organized working classes as the revolutionary army with the revolutionary association acting as that army's "general headquarters," or, in another much misunderstood phrase, its "general staff."[114] With these terms, Bakunin was once again not contradicting his entire strategy of indirect and locally autonomous revolutionary authority. Rather, as was again evident in the full context, he was summarizing the educative and coordinative function of a revolutionary association, albeit in a somewhat ill-fitted analogy: "the [association] should only be the general headquarters of this army, and the organizer not of its own, but of the people's forces, as a link between the people's instinct and revolutionary thought."[115] Here one has an excellent example of the difficulty created by Bakunin's efforts to popularize revolutionary theory, for he developed a most curiously mixed metaphor with his description of a revolutionary association as both midwife and military general staff. It should be noted, however, that Bakunin clearly had not intended this military reference to undercut what remained the association's selfless perspective toward personal or collective authority.

The above interpretation of Bakunin's revolutionary strategy can be further confirmed in the informal, Cincinnatus-like behavior that this association was to adopt in the period after a successful social revolution. As indicated above, its membership was to remain dispersed among the local working-class organizations, both to provide guidance as those organizations struggled to implement a voluntary collective authority and to expose and defuse attempts to reimpose any form of arbitrary authority, "even one that appears to be revolutionary itself."[116] After the initial, more or less military phase, therefore, the revolutionary association would re-emerge only when it became necessary to protect the revolution's social or economic equilibrium—much like a local political militia. As Bakunin explicitly argued above, such a post-revolutionary stance could only evolve from a similarly selfless pre-revolutionary position.

The second facet of Bakunin's revolutionary strategy mentioned in the passage above has been similarly misunderstood. This was Bakunin's belief that a revolutionary association had to structure itself as a secret society, "invisible" from both the working classes as a whole and the bourgeois state. By wrenching his argument out of its historical context and by ignoring the restrictive modifications he attached to it, Paradox commentators like Pyziur and Nomad severely distorted Bakunin's logic and intentions.

Bakunin's argument about the necessity of a secret form of revolutionary organization reflected his belief that the Congress of Vienna in 1815 had effectively established a "political Holy Alliance among all states against bourgeois liberalism."[117] With the feudal monarchies of Prussia, Austria, and Russia as the prime movers, a system of joint alliances had been established through which to reinforce internationally each country's internal pattern of political repression. Consequently, throughout the first half of the nineteenth century, serious (in most cases bourgeois) political opposition on the Continent could function only by adopting the legacy of the Freemasons and Babeuf's Conspiracy of the Equals. Replete with a "pyramidal structure for security" and "secret rite and dreadful oath for motivation," such secret societies stretched from Germany to Italy—with its Carbonari and Mazzini's Young Italy—and back to France.[118] One historian concluded of the 1830's in France that

> the French had been prepared by the accumulated precedents of freemasonry, of the secret societies organized by republicans and royalists against Napoleon, by bonapartists and ultraroyalists against moderate royalism, and by republicans and bonapartists against the Bourbon line. In this context, a secret society seemed an appropriate vehicle for political action.[119]

It wasn't until Marx helped organize the Communist League in 1847 that the internal structure of the secret political society was both democratized through leadership elections and secularized by the discarding of its "time-honored rituals."[120] Political conditions on the Continent were still sufficiently repressive, however, to require the league to remain, in Engels' words, "unavoidably a secret society."[121]

The First International itself was faced with a similar series of governmental attacks. Bismarck proposed an all-European conference to coordinate efforts against the International, and Pope Leo XIII castigated it as a "criminal organization" whose socialist doctrine was a "heresy of the depraved."[122] Moreover, the Paris Commune of 1871 was brutally suppressed by just such an international alliance between the French reaction and the invading Prussians. Bakunin himself wrote of that particular alliance's consequences: "Paris—soaked in the blood of its most generous-hearted children—there indeed is mankind crucified by the international and co-ordinated reaction of all Europe."[123]

It was thus in response to the contemporary political environment, and fully consistent with the traditional response to that environment throughout the first half of the nineteenth century, that Bakunin insisted upon the necessity of structuring his revolutionary association as a secret society. As he described the problem in the same letter to Nechaev, "nothing but a secret society would want to take this on, for the interests of the government and of the government classes would be bitterly opposed to it."[124] It is important to note, though, that Bakunin never intended to have his secret society mimic or restore those archaic aspects of secret societies that Marx himself had stripped away from them. As James Guillaume observed, Bakunin's conception of a revolutionary association bore only a superficial resemblance to "the classic type of secret society." Rather, drawing upon his central theory of revolutionary authority, Bakunin's association was to combine external secrecy with internal participation, being, to quote Guillaume again, a "free association of men who were uniting for collective action, without formalities, without ceremonies or mysterious rites."[125]

Having explored Bakunin's arguments about the proper character of revolutionary authority, and having considered some of the means by which Bakunin believed this approach to revolutionary authority could be instituted, two additional points of contention about Bakunin's understanding of revolutionary strategy remain to be evaluated. The first, concerning the usefulness of a coup d'état, is quite short. However, the second point—Bakunin's relations with Nechaev—requires a rather lengthy digression into Bakunin's conception of the role of violence in a social revolution.

Bakunin's attitude toward a Blanquist style coup d'état was quite direct. Both in his broad theoretical arguments about social revolution and in his explicit statements on the subject, Bakunin indicated that he was adamantly opposed to the undertaking of any such effort. Summarizing the logic behind his flat rejection of Blanquist thinking, Bakunin argued that the realities of the political situation in Europe in 1870 were such that "any attempt which is not popular in character, but is at all artificial, and deals in secret plots, sudden assaults, surprises and blows, is bound to wreck itself against the State."[126]

The second issue, that of Bakunin's relation to Nechaev and to the disputed 1869 *Catechism*, is perhaps the most controversial aspect of Bakunin's entire revolutionary doctrine. However, before evaluating that relation Bakunin's rather well-developed theory of revolutionary violence must be examined.

Bakunin made an explicit distinction between two different forms of violent revolutionary action: those against human beings and those against "positions and things." Personal violence, he argued, was an inevitable characteristic of the first days of any popular revolution. The working classes, "raging against all the deceits, vexations, oppressions, and torture of which they are victims,...break forth like an enraged bull,"[127] and could be expected to be both "bloody and vindictive."[128] Bakunin accepted this phase of a revolution as a necessary, more or less natural occurrence, in part derived from his rather fatalistic recognition that, historically, "every step forward" had only been attained after being "baptized in blood."[129] Nonetheless, Bakunin consistently described this personal violence as a form of natural disaster, often comparing it to a "hurricane" both in its duration and its futility.[130] Bakunin argued more pointedly that such violence was "neither moral nor even useful" to the revolutionary cause,[131] and that consequently if it were left to run its full course its impact would be extremely counter-productive.

Bakunin's moral argument against personal violence derived from his effort to minimize whatever inherent contradiction might exist in his desire to achieve the "greatest individual freedom for all" through an armed rising of the working classes against an oppressor class. As he rather bluntly put it, "when one is carrying out a revolution for the liberation of humanity, one should respect the life and liberty of men...."[132]

The practical arguments that Bakunin presented against personal violence gave pragmatic confirmation of his moral position. To begin with, Bakunin contended, violence against individuals directly contradicted the fundamental philosophical foundation of historical materialism, which held that the class attitudes of all individuals were "the inevitable product of the social status created for them by society and history."[133] Since, by this argument, social oppression "stems far less from individuals than from the organization of things and from social positions,"[134] an attack against the physical individuals who momentarily wielded power would be an assault only against oppression's superficial "manifestations" and a consequent avoidance of "the causes which continually produce it anew."[135] Bakunin rather pungently summarized this line of analysis with his comment that "political butchery has never killed off any party, but has in the main proved powerless against the privileged classes."[136]

Bakunin argued further that personal violence not only left the structural roots of oppression unscathed, it also produced a sense of moral revulsion which would buttress rather than eradicate the basis of political reaction. "The guillotine," Bakunin wrote in reference to the Reign of Terror, "does not kill reaction. It only makes it revive."[137] In a related argument, Bakunin admonished his revolutionary association against using another "Jacobin instrument," that of "terrorism by the cities against the villages,"[138] for both moral and practical reasons, discussed below.

Bakunin summarized his two practical objections to personal violence in the following passage:

> It inevitably comes about that after killing many people, the revolutionaries see themselves driven to the melancholy conviction that nothing had been gained and that not a single step has been made toward the realization of their cause, but that, on the contrary,. . . they prepared with their own hands the triumph of reaction. And that is so for two reasons: first, that the causes of reaction having been left intact, the reaction is given a chance to reproduce and multiply itself in new forms; and second, that ere long all those bloody butcheries and massacres must arouse against them everything that is human in man.[139]

"History," Bakunin noted elsewhere of such violence, "is full of lessons in this connection."[140]

Given, then, the inevitability of an initial bloodletting by the working classes on the one hand, and the directly counter-productive as well as morally indefensible nature of such actions on the other, Bakunin charged his revolutionary association with the responsibility to minimize the extent and duration of personal violence. Arguing that once the revolution "begins to take on a Socialist character"—in effect, once it becomes a social revolution—it will "cease to be cruel and sanguinary,"[141] Bakunin contended that a revolutionary association must "cushion the explosion" by expediting the transformative process.[142]

In direct contrast to this insistence that a revolutionary association minimize violence against human beings, Bakunin argued that it must maximize its violence against the material basis of social oppression. It was "necessary to destroy the actual institutions,"[143] to bring about the "abolition of positions and things,"[144] in order to ensure that the privileged classes would "vanish from the face of the earth. . . not as individuals, but as classes."[145] This form of destruction was to be accomplished through the dismemberment of the bourgeois state, and of its subsidiary relationships and prerogatives, most particularly that of private ownership of property.

Bakunin's position was clear even in those passages of his written works which on first glance might seem to sanction the immolation of buildings rather than the disassembly of institutions. He concluded in one instance that "it will be necessary to destroy everything, and first and foremost property and its bedfellow the State."[146] In most contexts, however, Bakunin's meaning was difficult to misunderstand. For example, he differentiated his conception of revolution from prior theories by noting that his approach

> will be a war, not against particular men, but primarily against the anti-social institutions upon which their power and privilege depend.
>
> The Revolution will therefore begin by destroying, above all, all the institutions and all the organizations, churches, parliaments, tribunals, administrations, banks, universities, etc., which constitute the lifeblood of the State.[147]

And at another point he wrote that "the Social Revolution must put an end to the old system of organization based upon violence,. . . destroying once and for all the historic cause of all violences, the power and very existence of the State."[148]

These statements didn't mean that, on the other hand, Bakunin assumed that there would be no destruction of physical property whatsoever in a social revolution. He recognized that much as would be the case with personal violence, the working classes could be expected initially to visit their anger upon the physical manifestations of their oppression as well. Thus buildings which housed landlords, state administration, and the church might well be sacked in a revolution's first days. Indeed, Bakunin commented that the working classes would willingly destroy their own "villages and towns" if "the exigencies of defense or victory" required it.[149] One should note, however, that both types of physical destruction were understood by Bakunin to be direct consequences of a revolution's first phase—one of spontaneous anger, the other of military necessity—and that both would be, at best, only incidental to the attainment of a revolution's real goal.

The systematic and complete destruction that Bakunin demanded was of the abstract instrumentalities of the state and state power, as well as of all institutions that sanctioned or protected social domination. This was to include the "confiscation" of all property and wealth held by the privileged classes, as well as the burning of "all deeds and property" that had legitimated such holdings.[150] As a concrete example of these intentions, Venturi cited Bakunin's response to one revolt in Italy: "The Italian peasants have now begun a genuine revolution. When they succeed in seizing a town, they burn all the papers. Destruction of this kind must take place everywhere."[151] This type of direct action was critical, Bakunin argued, not only for the long-term success of a social revolution, but for its immediate ability to survive. Only by removing the material bases from which an armed reaction could be waged, by expropriating its wealth and dismantling its institutionalized power, could the revolution protect itself from the threat of counter-revolution: "in cutting open criminal purses, one stops reaction at its source, one destroys its means."[152] Further, Bakunin contended that material disarmament would preclude later efforts to kill off the privileged classes as individuals—efforts which would otherwise appear essential to the revolution's future security, but which would inevitably prove highly counter-productive. By stripping these classes of property and position, the revolution would remove any apparent necessity of killing them. As Bakunin succinctly put it, "We shall ruthlessly destroy positions and things so as to be able to spare human beings without endangering the revolution."[153]

Bakunin concluded that only this discriminate violence, directed against the abstract instrumentalities of class power, could resolve the self-destructive quandary of personal violence, and thereby enable a social revolution to fulfill its moral obligation to treat its opponents with compassion without undermining its own safety. There was thus no logical contradiction between his exhortations to revolutionary destruction on the one hand, and his admonition that a successful revolution must "recognize" its defeated opponents "as your brothers and invite them to live and work alongside of you upon the unshakeable foundation of social equality."[154]

Within even this sharply limited context, however, Bakunin understood revolutionary destruction to be no more than a "negative passion."[155] Its importance rested solely upon its ability to clear adequate social ground upon which to construct new socialist institutions and relationships: "there can be no revolution without a sweeping and passionate destruction, a salutary and fruitful destruction, since by means of such destruction new worlds are born and come into existence."[156] Moreover, Bakunin argued that the willingness of the working classes to undertake such negative action, as well as the long-term value of these efforts, were both predicated upon the existence of a positive, popular pre-revolutionary ideal. Those classes would never dismantle society's institutional fabric, Bakunin believed, without "at least a remote conception" of the "new order" which was to replace it.[157] Additionally, in an argument that referred back to the revolutionary association's educational responsibilities, Bakunin contended that the more faithfully this popular ideal reflected the existent level of "material and historical development, the "more salutary and effective" would be the destruction that it would inspire, "for destructive action is ever determined—not only in its essence, but the degree of its intensity, but likewise the means used by it—by the positive ideal which constitutes its initial inspiration, its soul."[158] All of these points defined the possibility, direction, and impact of negative revolutionary destruction in terms of that violence's instrumental relationship to a new, positive social structure.

In summary, Bakunin believed that revolutionary violence, as a conscious strategy, must be strictly limited to attacks against the objective institutional foundation of economic and social oppression. He additionally counseled that the form and intensity of that violence must reflect a substantial knowledge of current material development and must also embody some awareness of the new social order that would follow in its wake. Thus, in both its logic and prescribed function, Bakunin's conception of revolutionary violence was fully consistent with and supportive of his general theory of revolutionary authority.

Bakunin believed further that his desire to minimize personal violence paralleled the traditional historical behavior of the working classes. "The people are not at all cruel," he wrote, except in certain "very rare and very brief moments" of unleashed revolutionary fury, because those classes "suffer too much themselves" to exacerbate anyone else's pain.[159] Although he noted that in the past the working classes had often been manipulated by various bourgeois elements into "instruments of the systematic fury" of bourgeois interests,[160] Bakunin insisted that the motivation and instigation of such "wholesale annihilation of persons but not things"[161] had been bourgeois: "you will inevitably find that behind those masses are agitators and leaders belonging to the privileged classes."[162]

Bourgeois responsibility for such bloody attacks was historically consistent, Bakunin argued, with the bourgeoisie's frequent reliance upon personal violence in both revolutionary as well as reactionary situations. The hallmark of the bourgeois revolutionary, whether a Jacobin in 1793 or a Marxist state socialist in 1870, in Bakunin's view, was his unwillingness to alter the basic institutional structures of state domination. Consequently, Bakunin contended, even the most radical bourgeois could be concerned only with the forced replacement of the particular elite that was currently exercising state power and could do so only by physically eliminating these rivals. "It is only natural,. . . that having no intention of waging radical revolution against things they should long for bloody revolution against men."[163] In short, Bakunin concluded that in practice both revolutionary and reactionary bourgeois defined their paramount political objective to be control over the existent institutions of state power, and therefore found themselves with no structural alternative but to pursue their goal through personal attacks against those individuals and classes that obstructed their way.

Bakunin also believed that nineteenth-century bourgeois reaction to working-class insurrections had been far more "bloodthirsty" than the protection of their objective interests had warranted. He attempted to explain this savagery by suggesting that the bourgeoisie's attachment to the central symbol of bourgeois state power—private property—had transcended the realm of material necessity to that of religion. The "atrocities" committed by the bourgeois reaction of 1848 in Paris, Bakunin argued, could only be understood as an essentially religious response, in which the bourgeoisie believed itself to be "defending the sacred foundations of morality." For this class, Bakunin observed, property is their God, their only God, which long ago replaced in their hearts the heavenly God of the Christians. . . . The ruthless and desperate war which they wage for the defense of property is not only a war of interests: it is a religious war in the full meaning of the word.[164]

Thus Bakunin argued that in sharp contrast with the violence of working-class revolution, which by both objective class interest and subjective class attitude would inherently minimize human bloodshed, the violence of the bourgeoisie had been and would remain for exactly the same reasons directed against human life.

Bakunin's understanding of the proper role of violence in social revolution can be further examined through his proposals to incorporate the brigands into the Russian revolutionary movement. Again, his actual argument was at some variance from that later attributed to him by Paradox commentators like Pyziur and Avrich, and again Bakunin's true position was fully consistent with his fundamental social and revolutionary theory.

Bakunin believed that the Russian brigands, and particularly the leaders of the two most famous peasant revolts—Stenka Razin in 1670 and Pugachev in 1773—were "the first rebels, the first revolutionists in Russia."[165] In Bakunin's understanding of the term, the brigand was a political outlaw, in search of freedom as much as booty: "the brigand is always the hero, the defender, the avenger of the people, an irreconcilable enemy of the entire State regime."[166] Bakunin reinforced this political interpretation by noting that the intended goal of these two brigand-led revolts still inspired the Russian peasantry in 1869. "This ideal is the communal ownership of land with complete freedom from any sort of State control or exploitation. This was what the people strove for at the time of the False Dmitri, Stenka Razin, and Pugachev, and this is what they strive for now."[167]

In his 1869 program for a Russian social revolution, Bakunin considered the brigands to be the "third basic fact" of the pre-revolutionary environment, following only the "frequent uprisings" among the peasantry and the traditional peasant longing for a return to the "free economic commune" or the mir.[168] He proposed that the "free Cossacks" and the "enormous numbers of vagabonds, both 'holy' and otherwise" should be conscripted to serve once again as the "originator and coordinator" of a broad popular revolution.[169] In the Russian context, Bakunin argued, "popular revolution is born from the merging of the revolt of the brigand with that of the peasant."[170] However, he explicitly warned of the dangers that this course of action would present. It is "not an easy business," he wrote, to "turn the [world of brigands] into a tool for a popular revolution."[171] Their crude antagonism toward the state had to be reshaped into a consciously moral and instrumental pursuit of broad popular liberation—a transformational process the importance of which Bakunin firmly impressed upon his potential emissaries:

> Going to the brigands does not mean that one should become a brigand and nothing more than a brigand. It does not mean sharing all their. . . passions. . . which are frequently vile. No, it means instilling a new spirit and arousing a new world outlook in these wild men who are rough to the point of cruelty, but whose nature is fresh and strong,. . . and therefore open to lively propaganda.[172]

Bakunin's presentation of the Russian brigand's historical role, and of the conclusions that he extrapolated from that role and then integrated into his own revolutionary program for Russia, is fully consistent with accepted historical opinion. In fact, the account of Stenka Razin's revolt in a 1967 work by the respected French historian, Roland Mousnier, not only supports Bakunin's major contentions about the behavior and impact of the brigand in Russian history, but also provides a vantage point from which to view certain tenets of Bakunin's fundamental philosophical argument.

Stenka Razin was a Cossack, a term which originally designated any man without a permanent home or fixed occupation.[173] The Cossack movement had developed in opposition to the increasingly oppressive policies of the Moscow government in the late sixteenth and early seventeenth centuries, including measures that legally bound the peasant to his land, and which in 1652 removed the last vestige of village political autonomy by seizing the power to appoint local priests. Thousands of Russian peasants had responded to the government's efforts by fleeing to the steppelands, where they established primitive but nonetheless democratic communities "based on principles of freedom and equality," wherein "talent had free rein, where a man's worth alone won him prestige or wealth."[174]

In 1669, a band of Cossacks under Razin's leadership began raiding Russian merchant ships, and thereby placed themselves in open rebellion against the Muscovy state. Razin's revolt, however, was not directed against the tsar. It was understood at the time as an attempt to "serve the Tsar by freeing him from his criminal servants," the aristocracy and the state apparatus.[175] In all other respects, though, it became a major effort to liberate the Russian peasantry:

> Stenka Razin apparently wanted to destroy the great hereditary nobility, the governors, the bureaucracy, the essential elements of the Muscovy machinery of state throughout Russia, in order to restore freedom to the humble people, which can then only have meant freeing them from serfdom, from taxes they had not agreed to, from non-elected authorities, from obligations that did not result from freely discussed contracts.[176]

Furthermore, the Cossacks themselves were only the instigators and coordinators of what was a massive popular movement:

> The Cossacks served merely as the ferment of an immense insurrection of all the oppressed against the state and against the nobility. In a band of 15,000 rebels there were only a hundred Don Cossacks. But the Cossacks were indispensible to give courage to humble folk to revolt, and to co-ordinate the movements.[177]

As this brief sketch illustrates, Bakunin's interpretation of the brigand's role in Russian revolutionary history, as well as his own desire to once again incorporate the brigand into a popular insurrection, were both historically legitimate arguments. Bakunin's attribution of a democratic and egalitarian potential to the Russian brigands, and his perception of them as necessary instigators and coordinators among a willing but otherwise unprepared peasantry, were well-founded in previously recorded events. Moreover, as noted earlier, one can discern within Stenka Razin's revolt several themes which, filtered through a nineteenth-century lens, permeated the core of Bakunin's revolutionary theory. Bakunin's proposals to free popular life from the oppressive institutions of a centralized state and to create in its place a system based on localized collective responsibility, his critique of the symbiotic relation between church and state, and his delineation of the requirements for pre-revolutionary education and organization all reflected in some degree issues and conditions central to the development of this peasant revolt.

Bakunin's historically appropriate conception of the Russian brigand was apparently confused by several Paradox commentators with the Romantic image of brigandage common to late eighteenth- and early nineteenth-century bourgeois culture, to which Bakunin's notion bore scant resemblance. Among the more disenchanted bourgeois intellectuals of that period, the folklore of outlaw bands had apparently become hopelessly entwined with their own intense longing for an unspecified but nonetheless complete individual freedom which they feared they had somehow lost. Schiller's *The Robbers* (1782), for example, presented what Lichtheim described as "an enthusiastic glorification of brigandage."[178] Even Alexander Herzen, in an early fascination with Schiller and the Romantics, believed that "the artist and the brigand" were the "supreme exemplars of human dignity and freedom because they recognized no law but their own unfettered genius."[179] This fundamentally escapist notion of the brigand, with its strong overtones of individualistic self-pity, was quite different from Bakunin's political interest in a potential agent of collective popular liberation.

The distinction was missed entirely, however, by most Paradox commentators. Preferring to tar Bakunin as a proponent of mindless violence, Pyziur described Bakunin as having "elevated destruction itself into the rank of a program," and wrote of Bakunin's interest in brigands: "Bakunin's decision to use criminals in the revolutionary cause was prompted . . . by his desire to see, at any price, the all-destructive revolution and the catastrophe of the existing civilized world."[180] Paul Avrich made reference to Bakunin's "demonic visions of fire and brimstone,"[181] and elsewhere described him as being animated by a "dream of immediate and universal destruction, the leveling of all existing values and institutions," which Avrich then argued Bakunin intended to attain through a "peasant jacquerie. . . a revolt of the uncivilized masses driven by. . . an unquenchable thirst for revenge."[182] And Max Nomad titled his chapter on Bakunin "The Apostle of Pan-Destruction," which Pyziur then adopted as an "epithet" which he argued Bakunin "richly deserved."[183]

The most charitable interpretation of these statements would be to attribute them to their authors' apparent inability to differentiate Bakunin's conception of revolutionary violence against "positions and things" from the Romantic distortions of bourgeois culture, or perhaps from the worst fears of the propertied classes. Bakunin's own explanation would center upon the unwillingness of such commentators to equate civilization with anything other than the institutions of the bourgeois state.

It remains for this discussion of Bakunin's notion of revolutionary violence only to contrast his position with those of Sorel and Fanon, two other theorists with whose work Bakunin's arguments are sometimes confused. Sorel believed that revolutionary violence must have precisely the opposite characteristics from those that Bakunin proposed. Sorel construed violence to be the necessary mechanism through which the working classes could restore history to Marx's inevitable march toward irreconcilable class contradictions. Violence was essential to force the "cowardly" middle classes to stiffen their resolve, deny the working classes' demands, heighten the contradictions between the two classes and thus prepare the social revolution. It was conceptualized to resemble "acts of war," in that it was to be "carried on without hatred and without the spirit of revenge."[184]

For Sorel, therefore, revolutionary violence was first and foremost an instrumental strategy: its function was theoretical, to force the material processes of history to reach their preordained Marxist conclusion. Consistent with this abstract orientation, violence for Sorel was to be thoroughly dispassionate, merely another useful tool—passion and revenge would clutter the strategy with human rather than revolutionary concerns. Third, Sorel would employ violence specifically to outrage and horrify the middle classes, inevitably requiring that violence to assume a personal, more or less terrorist cast. Finally, and implicit within all three prior points, Sorel conceptualized violence as a technique with which to provoke a revolution, and consequently understood it to be an operating tactic of an elite cadre in the pre-revolutionary period. On every point, Sorel's position was the antithesis of that of Bakunin.

Bakunin's conception of revolutionary violence must also be clearly distinguished from that of Franz Fanon. Bakunin believed that personal violence would necessarily have a negative impact—morally upon those who engaged in it, and politically upon the ultimate success of the entire revolution. Fanon, on the contrary, argued that, within a specifically colonial context, personal violence was a positive "cleansing force" —psychologically in that it freed the native from his "inferiority complex" and "despair," and politically in that this new psychological freedom would increase the participatory and egalitarian aspects of post-revolutionary society.[185] Clearly, even allowing for the difference of situation, Fanon's argument was quite the reverse from that of Bakunin. Bakunin called for destruction of institutions to clear *social* ground; Fanon demanded the destruction of human beings in order to overcome individual *psychological* barriers.

With Bakunin's theory of revolutionary authority, and the role of revolutionary violence within it, now fully fleshed, it is now possible to examine Bakunin's relationship to Nechaev and to the 1869 *Catechism* in particular. The fundamental charge, leveled by liberal bourgeois and Marxist commentators alike, has been that by this association and in this document Bakunin demonstrated conclusively his belief in the revolutionary efficacy of personal violence, of a nihilistic "pan-destruction," and thereby confirmed the ultimate practical consequences of his political doctrine. A thorough knowledge of Bakunin's thought as against that of Nechaev, however, coupled with an understanding of the historical context within which they both operated, leads one to conclude that this accusation cannot be sustained.

Prior to his flight to Geneva in early March, 1869, and his first encounter with Bakunin, Nechaev had formulated a revolutionary plan for Russia and had taken the initial steps to carry it through. In conjunction with another young Russian radical, Tkachev, he had begun to organize students in a movement which Venturi described as a "return" to the "Machiavellism of Ishutan."[186] Their joint manifesto, *A Program of Revolutionary Action*, written before Nechaev's departure, paralleled in its bitter tone and nihilist content many of the more fanatic sections of the 1869 *Catechism*. Venturi offered from it the following citation concerning the revolutionary's single-minded dedication to the cause: "Those who join the organization must give up every possession, occupation, or family tie, because families and occupations might distract members from their activities."[187] Further, their *Program* outlined a revolutionary timetable, calling for the establishment of a hard-core of students by May 1, 1869, efforts that summer to organize artisans in the smaller provincial towns, followed that autumn and winter by an organization of the popular mass. During this developmental period, according to Venturi, their *Program* called for the revolutionaries to "establish their regulations and 'catechism'."[188]

Thus Nechaev's *Program* both closely paralleled the content of the later

Catechism, and actually predicted when that second document would be written. This circumstantial evidence is strengthened by the direction Nechaev's written work took after Bakunin broke with him in June, 1870. Citing Venturi,

> [Nechaev] described his ideal of a Communist and regulated life down to the smallest detail. Bakunin's anarchism was left on one side to reveal the Communist and egalitarian kernal that Tkachev was later to theorize and that Nechaev had perhaps taken from the Babeufism of some of his Russian companions and from "Russian Jacobinism."[189]

The theoretical consistency that can be observed between the 1869 *Catechism* and Nechaev's positions both prior to and after the writing of that document must be contrasted with the flagrant contradiction between the *Catechism*'s negativist violence and any other manuscript, speech, or action attributed to Bakunin. This tension is most evident in precisely the most fanatical passages cited to demonstrate the *Catechism*'s viciousness. One might compare, for example, Section 13 of that document with the structure and direction of Bakunin's entire system of social thought:

> He is not a revolutionist if he is attached to anything in this world, if he can stop before the annihilation of any situation, relation, or person belonging to this world—everybody and everything must be equally hateful to him.[190]

Venturi himself, although professing to be satisfied with the evidence attributing the *Catechism* to Bakunin, noted that the central theme of a second, allegedly "jointly authored pamphlet" was "terrorism, which until then hadn't formed part of Bakunin's program," and further noted that after he had terminated his association with Nechaev "Bakunin returned to the ideas which he had already expounded."[191]

Beyond these strictly circumstantial factors, one must also weigh Bakunin's own statements of theoretical disagreement with Nechaev. In a letter to all his revolutionary contacts after his break with Nechaev, in which Bakunin renounced Nechaev and warned his associates to do the same, Bakunin argued that Nechaev had attempted to build a revolutionary organization upon "Machiavelli's policies" and the "Jesuit system":

> For the body—only violence; for the soul—lies. Truth, mutual trust, real solidarity, exist only among a dozen people who make up the sancta sanctorum of the society. All the rest serve as a blind soulless weapon. . . . It is allowed, indeed it is even a duty, to cheat them, to compromise them, and in cases of necessity to have them killed.[192]

In this passage Bakunin summarized and excoriated the primary nihilist concept put forth within the disputed *Catechism*: the absolute obligation of the true revolutionary to renounce all human emotion and morality for the advancement of the cause. To argue that Bakunin wrote that *Catechism* would thus require one to insist that in these lines just cited Bakunin was indignantly denouncing concepts that he himself had both believed and expounded only six months prior.

In another letter, this to Talandier on July 24, 1870—several weeks after the letter cited above—Bakunin wrote that not only had Nechaev employed despicable methods in his own previous Russian organization, but that when this information belatedly became known to Bakunin (principally Nechaev's murder of Ivanov in Moscow), "this poor Nechaev is still so naive, so childish, in spite of his systematic perversity, that he believed it possible to convert me—he even went so far as to beg me to agree to develop his theory in a Russian paper which he had proposed to me to establish."[193] Here Bakunin not only castigated Nechaev's theoretical argument as perverse, but he explicitly indicated that the "theory" of justifiable revolutionary murder which Nechaev propounded was held solely by Nechaev, and that he had no desire to "convert."

Additionally, in Bakunin's earlier letter of June 2, 1870, to Nechaev himself, written just prior to their rupture, Bakunin described in detail the fundamental theoretical as well as methodological points that divided his position from that of Nechaev. Bakunin directly criticized Nechaev's understanding of both the external behavior and the internal structure of a revolutionary association, arguing that its members must be

> *filled with moral purpose.* Your system will only corrupt them, and make them traitors to you and exploiters of the people. . . . you follow the Jesuitical teaching and systematically kill all individual, human feelings in them and all their personal sense of justice—as if feeling and justice could be impersonal.[194]

Bakunin also admonished Nechaev to remember that the Russian peasantry "are not a blank sheet of paper on which any sort of secret society, even for instance your communists, can write whatever program they like," and he challenged Nechaev to realize that "any effort to impose our ideas on the people which might be opposed to their instincts signifies a desire to enslave them to a new sovereignty."[195] Bakunin concluded this attack upon Nechaev's theoretical argument by leveling a veiled threat against what Bakunin believed would be the authoritarian political consequences of Nechaev's conception of a post-revolutionary state: "It will be necessary to make sure," Bakunin warned, "the day after the people's victory, that there is no establishment of any sort of State control over the people, even one that appears to be revolutionary itself, even yours."[196]

It is important to a fair evaluation of the dispute over the authorship of the 1869 *Catechism* to recognize the depth of theoretical disagreement demonstrated in this letter. Bakunin castigated Nechaev for advocating ideas and methods that rather transparently reflected the same smug authoritarian and putschist assumptions about popular revolutions that Bakunin's collectivist anarchism had always rejected. He faulted Nechaev for destroying the individual revolutionary's moral ties to both his fellow revolutionaries and to the working classes, for presuming that a revolutionary association could arbitrarily impose its own intellectually determined program upon a supine and incompetent population, and for intending to establish a centralized, authoritarian, and rigidly egalitarian form of Babeufian state after a successful revolution. Moreover, all of these putschist notions, which in these letters Bakunin flatly disowned as having no relationship at all to his own work, were at the very theoretical core of both the 1869 *Catechism* itself, and of Nechaev's written work both prior to and after his short association with Bakunin. One must consider the additional fact that Bakunin's call for revolutionary violence against bourgeois positions and things only, and his insistence that violence against human beings be held to an absolute minimum, simply bears no resemblance to the vicious terrorist methods proudly advocated in both Nechaev's 1869 *Program* and the 1869 *Catechism.*

It is impossible to discern at this late date what impact the Paradox school's distorted and distortionary interpretation of Bakunin's political argument might have played in developing the notion that Bakunin somehow wrote the 1869 *Catechism.* It is of course true that the misinformed accusations these commentators made about Bakunin's allegedly terrorist approach to revolution reflect the same assumptions about Bakunin's intentions that could lead one logically to view the *Catechism* as also being his handiwork.

In the final analysis, however, there would appear to be little need for intensive speculation about the historical source of the accusation that Bakunin wrote the *Catechism.* Such information is only of secondary importance when ranged against the broad theoretical abyss that separates Bakunin's collectivist-anarchist argument from the putschist notions proffered in that document—an abyss which can be corroborated both in Bakunin's letters on the subject and Nechaev's other written work. Consequently, if one approaches this question with an informed understanding of Bakunin's overall philosophical and political argument, one can quite fairly conclude that the 1869 *Catechism* was written by Nechaev alone.

Having dismissed the authorship issue, one should consider Bakunin's reasons for choosing to ally himself with Nechaev for that eighteen-month period. Once one sets aside the assumption that this alliance was based on a common theoretical approach to revolution, it becomes easier to see a different kind of logic in Bakunin's willingness to link up with an individual like Nechaev. In his writings about Russia, Bakunin had regularly noted that structural conditions peculiar to that country would require revolutionary leaders of extraordinary personal energy and ability. This necessity had been a primary motivation behind Bakunin's desire to integrate the Cossack brigands into a new revolutionary movement. Bakunin's letters, as well as the observations of others who knew Bakunin, indicate that it had been the apparent presence of such character traits in Nechaev that had attracted Bakunin to him.

In a letter to Herzen, written almost three years before Bakunin first met Nechaev, he analyzed the then-current unrest in Russia in terms which anticipated both the political emergence of individuals like Nechaev and the efforts that would be required to guide those individuals into productive revolutionary activity. Reacting to Karakozov's recent attempt to assassinate the tsar, Bakunin wrote that although he too, like Herzen, was opposed to regicide, "I am not at all surprised that. . . in the stress of the present situation. . . a man has come forward who is less philosophically sophisticated and therefore has more energy than we have, and who imagines that the Gordian Knot can be cut at one stroke." Bakunin then argued that Herzen must redirect the editorial content of his newspaper, the *Bell*, toward precisely these types of individuals, so as to harness their immense energy into a more morally responsible and politically effective revolutionary movement:

> Seek a new public among the young people, among the half-educated pupils of Chernyshevsky and Dobrolyubov, among the Bazarovs and the Nihilists, for they have life and energy and strong, straightforward determination. . . . This is the public that needs a blaze of light, and you cannot frighten it by telling the truth. Preach practical discretion and caution to it, but give it the whole truth.[197]

In effect, in both its analysis of the problem and in its proposed solution, this letter directly anticipated the major issues that the appearance of a Nechaev would create, and it demonstrated the logical basis upon which three years hence Bakunin would become interested in working with such an individual.

More specifically, in much of his correspondence either to or about Nechaev, Bakunin defended his attraction to Nechaev in terms of Nechaev's tremendous personal energy, of his (Bakunin's) own inability to muster an equivalent level of strength, and of the centrality of such men of action to the success of the revolutionary movement in Russia. In his long letter to Nechaev of June 2, 1870, in which he detailed their fundamental theoretical incompatability, Bakunin still obliquely praised Nechaev's strength and determination. Referring to the need to incorporate Cossack brigands into the movement, Bakunin wrote:

> I admit that I am completely unfit for such a task. In order to take it on and bring it to a successful conclusion, one must have the nervous strength of a

legendary hero, passionate conviction and iron will. Maybe there are such people among your ranks. But people of our generation and our background are of no use.[198]

In the letter to Talandier renouncing Nechaev, Bakunin again had positive words for Nechaev's energy and directly identified that characteristic as the primary source of the bond between himself and Nechaev:

It is still true that Nechaev is one of the most active and energetic men that I have ever encountered. When it comes to serving that which he calls the cause, he hesitates nor stops before nothing and shows himself as pitiless toward himself as toward all others. This was the principal quality which attracted me and which made me pursue this alliance for so long a time.[199]

Lastly, in a letter to Ogarev in November, 1872, written after Nechaev's arrest and deportation back to Russia, Bakunin argued that despite his other personal failings Nechaev's stamina would prevent him from becoming a traitor to the revolutionary movement. "An inner voice tells me that Nechaev, who is lost beyond salvation and who, no doubt, knows it, will this time muster up all his original energy and steadfastness out of the depths of his nature, which is confused, depraved but not base. He will not betray anything or anybody, but will die a hero."[200]

Bakunin's perception of Nechaev's personal qualities was shared by others in his circle in Switzerland. Michael Sazhin, in his *Reminiscences*, wrote of Nechaev's "collosal energy, his fanatical devotion to the revolutionary cause, his character of steel, his indefatigable ability to work."[201] And James Guillaume, Bakunin's editor, wrote that Bakunin had become involved with Nechaev out of his "admiration for Nechaev's savage energy."[202] Their observations provide outside confirmation for Bakunin's own analysis. It would consequently seem proper for one to conclude that Bakunin's reasons for allying himself with Nechaev were in fact quite independent of any shared set of revolutionary principles, as has been considered the case by most Paradox commentators (see the discussion of Nechaev in chapter 1). Instead, their relationship had grown out of Bakunin's belief in the importance of men of strong temperament to the Russian revolutionary movement, in the inability of individuals from educated backgrounds like himself to fulfill that role, and in his perception of Nechaev as having the requisite temperament and background. Moreover, it was only within this context that Bakunin made his much-quoted comment about Nechaev, "they are magnificent, these young fanatics."[203] In sum, a close examination of the question demonstrates that the controversy over Bakunin's relationship with Nechaev, like that over the authorship of the 1869 *Catechism*, is more effective in providing information about the character of the political debate that has swirled about Bakunin's thought since his death than it is in pointing up some fatal flaw within the structure of his political argument.

A Revolutionary Program for Europe

Having examined both Bakunin's general theory of social revolution and the basic process by which he believed such a revolution could be achieved, the practical value of this theory can be assessed by explaining its application to the particular condition of the working classes in Europe in 1870.

Bakunin argued that a specific revolutionary program could be successful only if it could satisfactorily address all of the theoretical criteria established by his basic theories of social revolution and of revolutionary authority. More precisely, a revolutionary program must adequately resolve the two fundamental problems of the contemporary working class: their ignorance as to the real causes of their situation, and their inability to organize themselves into an instrumental revolutionary force. And the program must accomplish this task within the same set of historically generated constraints that had left the working classes with insufficient educational and organizational skills to begin with.

Bakunin divided these historical limitations upon a revolutionary program into two basic categories: constraints upon the substance of the program's goals, and constraints upon the approach which that program could employ if it was to attain those goals. The first limitation, on the program's content, reflected the restrictions Bakunin had placed on all forms of educational "propaganda": its conceptual framework must faithfully mirror the historically defined instincts of the class being addressed. A program could remain "revolutionary, alive, active, and true" only insofar as it "expresses" and "formulates popular instincts that have been worked out by history."[204] In pragmatic terms, this criterion strictly limited a program's scope and orientation. "You cannot convert anyone," Bakunin cautioned, "who does not feel the need for conversion, whose position does not inevitably force him in that direction."[205]

Bakunin's second limitation on a revolutionary program, on its approach, similarly reflected the impact of the working classes' past and present material history on their readiness for social revolution. He argued that a program must acknowledge the working classes' current social existence, its "actual daily life," and accept for its own point of departure the limited historical knowledge and perspective of those classes.[206] A program must incorporate within its substantive structure "a living and tangible comprehension" of the "daily, completely isolated and individual" manner in which both peasants and urban workers experienced economic hardship.[207] Moreover, a properly constructed program must accommodate itself to two particular consequences of these classes' atomized and exploited situation. First, most members of the working classes were somewhat uncomfortable in dealing with general or abstract theories about society. On the contrary, their attitudes and behaviors were usually "carried away only by the power and logic of facts, apprehending and envisioning most of the time only their immediate interests or moved only by their monetary, more or less blind passions."[208] And second, the few theoretical assumptions which these classes did accept had been taught to them by institutions of the bourgeois state. Under the "influence of religious, political, and social ideas which governments and priests had tried to inculcate into them," many segments of the working classes would immediately "repel with defiance and anger" any attempt to convert them to an overtly different theory of society.[209] Bakunin concluded therefore that while the working classes' fundamental beliefs were based on their historically engendered socialist instinct, these classes' conscious theoretical perspective had been reduced by the same historical forces to little more than "religious and political prejudices" that were bourgeois inspired and thus "militated against their own interests."[210]

Bakunin believed that a revolutionary program could only overcome this apparent contradiction if it addressed itself exclusively to the concrete conditions of the working classes' immediate existence. By completely avoiding all questions of broad social and revolutionary theory, a program could cultivate these classes' historical instinct toward socialism while adroitly evading their socially induced prejudices. It should concentrate on practical economic and social issues, reaching each worker at the level of "his own job and working conditions within it in his own locality," so as to enlist his "natural common sense and daily experience" in the program's own educational effort.[211] In sum, Bakunin argued that a properly constructed revolutionary program must reflect the working classes' past and present material conditions not only in its selection of revolutionary ideals but also in the particular focus it gave those goals when it transformed them into revolutionary propaganda.

Since a revolutionary program had to have a practical focus if it was to successfully "educate and organize" the working classes, and since there was a substantial disparity of condition and attitude between the urban and the rural sectors of the working classes, Bakunin felt obliged to devise two separate programs so as to be able to appeal to both components equally.

Bakunin's program for the urban working classes was constructed upon two prior assumptions. The first was that there were two separate factions within those classes, differentiated by wages and position: the well-to-do workers with "better paying occupations" and concomitantly "semi-bourgeois" affectations of "ambition and vanity,"[212] as against what Bakunin termed the "flower of the proletariat,"[213] the miserable illiterate "rabble" which "sustains the whole world by its labor" yet hardly received bare sustenance in return.[214] Bakunin's program was consciously oriented toward this poorer, far more numerous faction, which he believed was more structurally revolutionary both by its lack of cultural contamination from the bourgeois world and its more directly antagonistic material position vis-à-vis the privileged classes.[215]

The second assumption Bakunin built into his program for the urban working classes concerned these classes' proposed primary role in sparking off the entire process of social revolution. Bakunin argued that in 1870 Europe only the urban workers "today unite in themselves the instinct, the clear consciousness, the idea, and the conscious will of the Social Revolution," and that consequently these workers must be brought to seize the "initiative in this revolutionary movement."[216] A proper program for the urban classes must therefore generate a broadly based revolutionary structure capable of appealing to the rural peasantry as well as the urban worker.

With these two basic presumptions in mind, Bakunin chose the International Workingmen's Association (IWA) as the most appropriate vehicle to implement this urban program. Only the International, he argued, could effectively channel the expressive chaos of an urban rebellion into a disciplined social force capable of challenging the bourgeois state. Only a broad, internationally based organization could ensure that the working classes would be ready with a collectively organized structure of social authority prepared, as a parallel power, to supplant the bourgeois state:

> so that when the Revolution, brought about by the natural force of circumstances, breaks out, there will be a real force at hand which knows what to do and by virtue thereof is capable of taking the Revolution into its own hands and imparting to it a direction salutary for the people: a serious, international organization of worker's organizations of all countries, capable of replacing the departing political world of the States and the bourgeoisie.[217]

Bakunin felt further that the kind of strong, materially based, and revolutionary International that was required had to be composed of local, autonomous trade union sections. In an argument in direct contradistinction to both Marx's insistence upon a strong executive council and Lenin's subsequent admonitions about the limitations of trade union consciousness, Bakunin contended that only the local section could successfully absorb existent worker dissatisfaction and transform it into an effective revolutionary force. Moreover, only the local section could organize a social revolution that would be decentralized and non-authoritarian, and that consequently could incorporate the long-term moral and practical advantages of local political authority. In short, Bakunin believed that only a fully decentralized International could be hospitable to the forms of mutual interaction and collective self-discipline that were for him the essential prerequisite of a liberatory social revolution.

One immediate organizational advantage of concentrating upon local sections, Bakunin argued, was that the outline of such sections could already be seen in many factories and shops, expressed in the "solidarity of economic demands for redress" which had developed from "the daily experience of the worker's world."[218] The founding of a local IWA section would simply represent the formal consolidation of an existent spontaneous process, and therefore "the worker is already a member before he is even aware of it, completely naturally."[219] By organizing itself in this fashion, the International was relying upon a "framework" generated "not by a theory" but rather by the "actual development of economic facts,"[220] and could consequently claim to be "the purest expression of the collective interest" of the urban working classes.[221]

This emphasis upon the local section would have the additional benefit of strengthening the urban working classes' existent sense of economic solidarity. Such solidarity, Bakunin believed, was the touchstone of a revolutionary movement because it could focus the working classes' heretofore disparate social force into a directed political power. "Once this solidarity is seriously accepted and established," Bakunin wrote, "it produces everything else."[222] Economic solidarity could so clarify the political situation that "the least educated, least prepared, most submissive worker" would find himself "pulled constantly forward" until he became "revolutionary, anarchist, and atheist, often without knowing himself how it happened."[223] In short, Bakunin argued that economic solidarity could best transform the urban working classes' "socialist instinct" into the necessary "revolutionary consciousness." And economic solidarity could be produced most effectively within the autonomous local section: "only the trade union sections can give their members this practical education and consequently only they can draw into the organization of the International the masses of the proletariat."[224]

Beyond these short-term tactical advantages, an organizational emphasis upon the autonomous local section also had several philosophical and moral benefits. Through their decentralized structure, these local sections could in effect fuse Bakunin's concept of mutual interaction into the very core of the urban working classes' revolutionary movement. Thus the benefits of this organizational approach would be apparent, Bakunin argued, in both the more appropriate substance as well as in the more participatory process of decision making that would take place.

In terms of the substance of policy decisions, Bakunin contended that a structure of autonomous local sections would ensure that the revolutionary organization's policies matched the needs of local workers. A local factory unit would tend to make its decisions inductively, "following a natural course of development" by which it "begins with the fact in order to arrive at idea," and would thereby arrive at decisions that would most accurately reflect its workers' current situation.[225] In contrast, Bakunin argued that a pre-eminent Central Council, of the variety advocated by Marx, would inevitably make its decisions deductively, "following, on the contrary, the course of ideal or abstract development" by which it would "begin with the idea in order to arrive at the fact," and by so doing arrive at theoretically elegant but completely impractical solutions that ignored the workers' actual situation.[226]

In terms of the political process involved in reaching these decisions, Bakunin believed that a federation of autonomous local sections would encourage precisely the liberatory values of collective self-discipline that lay at the very center of the working classes' socialist instinct. If the International were organized in this decentralized fashion, each worker would have an essentially equal amount of authority over its policy decisions and equal access to the information required to make those decisions. "All questions touching the International," Bakunin insisted, including those bearing on "its institutions and the real state of its organizations," would be "discussed boldly" in "frank and public discussion."[227] Policy decisions would be the product of the "identity and natural equilibrium of interests" that would be realized through "the salutary effect of the free circulation and advocacy of ideas."[228] In effect, such an organizational structure would satisfy Bakunin's prior theoretical insistence that a truly liberatory post-revolutionary society could only be achieved by a fully participatory pre-revolutionary movement. As Bakunin bluntly summarized his logic, "the International can become an instrument of the emancipation of humanity only when it has emancipated itself first."[229]

Bakunin argued that the only organizational alternative to his decentralized approach—Marx's notion of a strong General Council—would inevitably duplicate within the International the worst class characteristics of the bourgeois state. If decision-making authority were so centralized, the International would shortly be "split into two camps," one comprising a "few score leaders" who were well-informed, and the other consisting of the "vast majority" of members "whose only science reduces itself to a blind faith in the theoretical and practical wisdom of its leaders."[230] In effect, Bakunin concluded, Marx's unfettered General Council would inevitably transform the International into "a sort of oligarchic State,"[231] which left Bakunin's own proposals to structure the International as a federation of autonomous local sections as the sole acceptable solution.

Bakunin believed that the local section's various organizational needs could be best met through a single operational tactic: the general strike. Workers' strikes, he argued, could concurrently (1) arouse, instruct, and subsequently organize workers within the section's trade area; (2) tighten up the section's internal structure, and thus prepare it to oppose and eventually replace the state; and (3) attain immediate economic relief—higher wages and shorter hours—for its membership. Like numerous other socialist theoreticians, then, Bakunin conceptualized the mass strike as the key catalyst in bringing about a social revolution. However, unlike most others, Bakunin put this traditional socialist weapon in the service of his specifically collectivist-anarchist principles and goals.

Strikes, Bakunin believed, inevitably clarified the objective class character of capitalist society, and of the economic and social situation of the urban working classes within it. A strike always "broadens and deepens" the economic and political "gulf" between worker and capitalist, demonstrating to the workers "in the most perceptible manner that their interests are absolutely incompatible with the interests of the capitalists and property-owners."[232] In turn, such recognition stimulates the worker's more or less dormant "socialist instinct," for "strikes awaken in the masses all the social-revolutionary instincts which reside deeply in the heart of every worker," and they thereby quicken the worker's interest in the local section's ongoing educational activities.[233] A general strike was thus able to accelerate the process through which the urban worker's "socialist instinct" could be transformed into "reflected socialist thought," and to help these classes come to recognize the necessity of a social revolution. "Strikes are necessary," Bakunin concluded, "to such an extent that without them it would be impossible to arouse the masses for a social struggle, nor would it be possible to have them organized."[234]

Secondarily, strikes could serve to strengthen the internal cohesion of the participating local sections. By raising their members' consciousnesses, a general strike would heighten the members' awareness of the indispensability of the International for their struggle and reinforce their commitment to their section. Additionally, by highlighting the difficulties of a protracted social struggle, a strike would emphasize to each section its need for an effective internal structure. "Strikes spell war," Bakunin argued, and by their seriousness convince "all workers in the most graphic and perceptible manner of the necessity of a strict organization to attain victory."[235]

It should be noted that, unlike Marx, Bakunin believed that a general strike must retain an "exclusively economic character."[236] This orientation mirrored the limited theoretical focus of the trade union section itself, and Bakunin believed that it would have at least three specific benefits. First, the local section's economic emphasis directed working-class activity away from what Bakunin considered the debilitating influences of "bourgeois politics." By concentrating solely upon building economic solidarity by making strictly economic demands, the section restricted working-class contact with bourgeois elements to isolated and easily exposed attempts by bourgeois radicals to deter specific economic actions. Second, Bakunin's revolutionary organization was constructed entirely of decision-making units located within the material production process itself. This system of social authority avoided the formation of exclusively political units which, split off from the physical process of production, then required an administrative apparatus with which to implement decisions and monitor their effect. Bakunin apparently hoped that by working exclusively at the economic level he could eliminate the structural pre-conditions for a post-revolutionary state bureaucracy. And third, an economic strike also held out the possibility of some small improvement in the urban working classes' immediate material situation. Strikes were important, Bakunin wrote, "in order to render existence somewhat more tolerable."[237] All of these advantages, Bakunin believed, could be derived from a strategy of exclusively economic general strikes organized at the local section level.

This, then, was Bakunin's revolutionary program with which to "educate and organize" the urban working classes in 1870 Europe. It called for the existent International Workingmen's Association to be reorganized into autonomous local sections, which were to concentrate on nurturing their members' immediate economic concerns into a general strike. And while Bakunin was adamantly insisting that the focus of these autonomous local sections must be exclusively economic, his proposals for both the International's overall structure as well as for the operational procedures within it clearly emphasized the highly political principles of mutual interaction and collective self-discipline upon which Bakunin had rested his entire social philosophy.

Despite his emphasis upon the primacy of the urban working classes' revolutionary role, Bakunin didn't believe that these classes could carry out a successful social revolution by themselves. He argued that although these classes had to be the conscious cutting edge of the movement, they had to secure the wholehearted support and active participation of the peasantry if they were to succeed either morally or practically. "As long as the workers of the land, the peasants, will not give their hand to the workers of the city for a common revolutionary action, all the revolutionary efforts of the cities shall be condemned to inevitable fiascos."[238] Bakunin therefore believed that a revolutionary program for the urban working classes was incomplete unless it included an equally well designed program with which to educate and organize the peasantry.

As Bakunin presented it, a revolutionary peasantry was an essential component of both the moral integrity and the practical political strategy of a social revolution. The moral argument was derived from Bakunin's contention that, objectively speaking, the peasantry within any European capitalist country were only "rural proletarians."[239] As he had indicated in his critique of capitalism, Bakunin believed that commercially generated exchange value as well as the Marxist category of industrially created surplus value was based in the objective exploitation of human labor. Therefore, hired farm laborers and even small freeholders who live by their own labor were systematically defrauded of their labor's true value, and were equally as economically "enslaved" as their urban counterparts.[240] Bakunin concluded that, in view of their joint status as exploited manual labor, there could be "no real conflict of interests" between worker and peasant: "in the presence of the bourgeois exploiter, the worker must feel himself the brother of the peasant."[241] A social revolution consequently had as great a moral obligation to obtain economic justice for the peasantry as for the urban working classes.

The peasantry were a necessary component of a social revolution, however, for more than moral concerns. Bakunin argued strongly that within the 1870 European capitalist state, the political allegiance of the peasantry was the single critical determinant of that state's stability. Most particularly in France and Germany, "the peasants constitute the principal, almost sole, foundation upon which the safety and power of the State now rest."[242] Thus the peasantry must be incorporated into the revolutionary movement for the most pragmatic of strategic reasons: in order to defeat the bourgeois state, the state had to be deprived of its peasant "army."

Bakunin realized that such a separation would be difficult to engineer. A peasant program would have to transform what had heretofore been the stoutly reactionary peasant classes into a more or less conscious group of revolutionary socialists. Moreover, it would have to do so in the face of the bourgeois state's assiduous long-term efforts to cultivate the peasantry's affection. Such a peasant program was possible, Bakunin concluded, but only if it adhered strictly to his basic criteria for all revolutionary programs: it must speak clearly and directly to the immediate economic concerns of the peasantry at the local village level, avoiding all abstract or theoretical arguments. And it must be fully cognizant of the peasantry's past and present material situation, and of the attitudes and beliefs which they have as a result acquired.

A properly constructed peasant program, Bakunin believed, must respond to two fundamental aspects of the peasantry's attitudes and beliefs—of its psychological make-up—which appear at first glance to be mutually contradictory. On the one hand, the peasantry carried two deep-set and historically generated "instincts" which represented the rural variant of all working classes' "socialist instinct." Forced to "survive by the labor of their arms," they had developed intense attitudes which had over the years taken on the trappings of biological instinct: a "hatred" for all the "privileged fainéants" who were protected by the bourgeois state, and a strong longing for a just peasant society based on the "sacred rights of labor."[243] These two instincts, Bakunin believed, embodied the requisite qualities of personal self-respect and political self-determination such that, when confronted by the "intolerable realities" of bourgeois exploitation, they created a firm psychological foundation for a socialist peasantry. "These instincts are profoundly socialist," he wrote, "because they express the irrepressible conflict between the workers and the exploiters of labor, and the very essence of socialism, the real, natural inner core of all socialism, lies there."[244] This analysis provided the historical and psychological context to Bakunin's otherwise rather curious statements that the poorer of the European peasantries were "revolutionary and socialist without knowing it themselves."[245]

However, on the other hand, the peasantry's socialist instinct had been severely attenuated within the bourgeois state. The combined impact of what had been required for their economic survival and the sustained ideological propaganda of bourgeois institutions had, Bakunin argued, diverted the peasantry into an ill-fitting but nonetheless reactionary posture. In effect, although the peasantry's current reactionary stance was only superficial, it was quite logically comprehensible in terms of their past and present economic situation.

Bakunin explained the peasant's basic dilemma with the observation that each peasant had to fend for himself economically, despite the varying degree of social cooperation that might be present within his village. If he was to survive in the long run, each peasant was forced to defend his own individual economic interest even if that interest wasn't a small plot of land but only the vainglorious dream of some day acquiring one. Bakunin described the atomistic consequences of the capitalist marketplace for the peasantry in particularly trenchant terms:

> Who in present-day society is not grasping, in this sense that he passionately clings to what little of value he has been able to amass, and which guarantees to him, in the prevailing economic chaos and in this society which is without pity for those who die of starvation, his existence and that of his family?[246]

Bakunin concluded, therefore, that in terms of their material position, the peasantry's current economic "individualism" was "just as natural" a historically induced attitude as was the "communism" of the completely dispossessed urban worker.[247]

In turn, this socially created economic individualism placed the peasant in immediate economic opposition to any socialist program that would deprive him of his land, while making him immediately receptive to all kinds of bourgeois propaganda about the sanctity of individual economic rights. When confronted with a socialist theory that (a) demanded the immediate and complete collectivization of all property, (b) was to be administered by a centralized urban-worker-controlled state, and (c) was presented as an alien and abstract theory, the peasant wasn't interested. On the contrary, such an approach logically enough led the peasant to identify all the more strongly with the bourgeois position. Most importantly, the peasant's increased allegiance to the bourgeoisie would occur despite the fundamental economic fact that he was combining forces with his true exploiter in order to defeat his true liberator, and despite his own deeply held hatred for the bourgeoisie and his desire for a socialist peasant society.

Bakunin cited the French peasantry's overwhelming support of Louis Bonaparte as a perfect case in point. That affection, he argued, was no more than a "negative expression of their hatred against the landed gentry and the city bourgeoisie."[248] For the peasantry to change from this overtly reactionary to a revolutionary position, therefore, required only a properly constructed program that could reclaim and restore the peasantry's most fundamental attitudes and beliefs. These "Bonapartist sympathies," Bakunin concluded, "are merely the surface symptoms of the socialist instinct led astray by ignorance and exploited by malice, a skin disease which will yield to the heroic treatment of revolutionary socialism."[249]

The central issue for a well-designed peasant program, then, was exactly the same question Bakunin had posited as the challenge for any revolutionary program: to evade the peasantry's present, superficial, but nevertheless historically appropriate individualist ideology by addressing itself, through their immediate economic concerns, to their more deeply held desires for a just socialist society. Moreover, an effective program would have to undertake this effort without imposing any external authority or controls upon the peasantry from outside their own villages. In terms of its procedural approach, a peasant program like an urban program had to adhere to Bakunin's fundamental principles of mutual interaction and collective self-discipline.

This non-authoritarian approach to the transformation of the peasantry from reactionary bulwark to revolutionary socialist broke decisively, in Bakunin's opinion, with both the Marxist desire to simply impose a social revolution on the peasantry, and the sense of social superiority with which the urban working classes traditionally regarded their rural counterparts. Against the state socialist concept of "imposing Communism" upon the peasantry through an urban-based state apparatus, Bakunin raised all his criticisms of arbitrary political authority. Morally, such an approach would reduce the peasantry to the status of slaves, even if this program's goal was the true end of the peasantry's own historical development. And strategically, this statist program would create a dangerously powerful class of military leaders within the revolution itself while simultaneously forfeiting the entire peasantry to the bourgeoisie:

> They would arouse and arm against themselves the whole mass of peasants, and in order to put down the peasant revolt, they would find themselves compelled to have recourse to a vast armed force, well organized and well disciplined. As a result they would give an army to the reaction, and would beget, would form a

caste of reactionary militarists, of ambitious generals, in their own midst. The State machine thus reinforced, they would soon have a leader to drive that machine—a dictator, an Emperor.[250]

Similarly, Bakunin argued that the urban worker's conviction of his own "superior intelligence and education" was no more than a "doctrinaire bourgeois prejudice," which would have an equally inimical effect on the peasantry's politics.[251] In fact, this urban disdain and the resultant hatred of the worker that it bred in the peasant had long since produced negative consequences: Bakunin suggested that this "fatal antagonism" had already "paralyzed" the European socialist movement for a century.[252] Both of these urban-oriented, authoritarian approaches would have to be avoided, Bakunin believed, for a peasant program to achieve its revolutionary purpose.

The solution Bakunin presented followed his central admonition that a revolutionary program must not attack the bourgeois state with abstract arguments but rather should "undermine in fact the power of the State."[253] His strategy, simply put, was to harness the peasantry's bourgeois-cultivated "cupidity."[254] Believing that the peasant's perceived self-interest concealed a more fundamental socialist instinct, Bakunin argued that a revolutionary program would "push them in the direction of their own instincts" if it moved to satisfy the peasantry's short-term material demands.[255] More interestingly, the immediate self-interest of the peasantry would directly conflict with the essential economic interests of the bourgeoisie. By encouraging the peasantry to seize what they required, a revolutionary program could help transform their reactionary economic individualism into a major force for social revolution. "The solution," Bakunin proposed, "lies in establishing a line of revolutionary conduct which reverses the situation, which would not only prevent the peasants' individualism from pushing them into reaction, but which, on the contrary, would make it instrumental in the triumph of the revolution."[256]

The centerpiece of Bakunin's program was a peasant seizure of the land. "They love the land," he argued, "so let them take all of it."[257] Through this single act, the peasantry would find themselves directly confronting the immediate economic interests of all three rural elements of the bourgeoisie: the large landowners, the church, and the state itself. A land seizure would serve to alienate the peasantry from both the local state institutions and those who administered them, as well as to drive a material wedge between the peasantry and the local priesthood. In short order, Bakunin argued, a land seizure would transform the peasantry into agents of socialist revolution by provoking a broad-scale class conflict in the countryside.

Additionally, the peasant program Bakunin constructed around this action reflected the principal theoretical tenets of his general theory of social revolution. First, a land seizure would replace the institutional framework of the bourgeois state with *de facto* political arrangements based on the informal hierarchies of personal influence found in most villages: it would encourage the development of collective self-discipline among the peasantry. Second, the central notion of a land seizure highlighted the program's emphasis upon violence against "positions and things" rather than human beings. Third, within this program the external role of Bakunin's revolutionary association—and, by extension, of the urban working classes in general—would be minimal and informal, limited primarily to the role of educational propagandists. And most important, the very action proposed by the program would have a major educational as well as organizational spin-off: much like the function of the general strike for the urban worker, a land seizure would simply set the process of social revolution in motion so that the peasantry could then seize hold of their own future.

Bakunin's revolutionary theory is more practically focussed than that of Marx, and Bakunin's insistence upon self-activity and self-administration throughout the revolutionary process clearly belies Engels' taunt in "On Authority" about a revolution's inherently "authoritarian" nature. This is not to argue that Bakunin's application of the principles of mutual authority and collective self-discipline is completely unproblematic. Both the ability of Bakunin's revolutionary association to remain only a Cincinnatus-style political militia and the likelihood of the peasantry's rapid establishment of a system of rural cooperatives would appear to be predicated upon specific social assumptions which may not be as assured as Bakunin thought them to be. It is nonetheless fair to conclude that Bakunin had a rich and complex revolutionary theory, that was both consistent in its theoretical structure and evocative in its character and emphasis of later twentieth-century revolutionary arguments.

5 *Bakunin and Marx*

Bakunin's relationship to Marx was substantially more complex than has been commonly supposed. Beyond the specifically political challenge that Bakunin raised within the First International, which has been the subject of numerous commentaries, there lies his broadly based attack upon Marx's political and social thought, which remains scarcely acknowledged much less evaluated. One can attribute some portion of this disparity, of course, to the sheer fascination of a pitched political battle between two founders of European socialism. And one might also be tempted to cite many commentators' apparent lack of knowledge about the actual content and character of Bakunin's thought. Regardless of its source, however, this exclusive concentration upon their actual political struggle within the First International has obscured Bakunin's most telling blows. For although he always described himself as a disciple of Marx, in the sense that Marx had been the first to put forward a socialist economic determinism, Bakunin was at the same time a most severe and penetrating critic of Marx and Marxist political doctrine. Further, and quite contrary to the suggestions of various psycho-historians like Joll and Nomad, Bakunin's theoretical criticism of Marx was not an unimportant by-product of their political dispute, but was rather its cause. Lastly, and most importantly for present-day political thought, it is much more within Bakunin's theoretical, not his political, critique of Marx that one can discover the broad outline of an attack upon Marx's Hegelian notion of the state. Consequently, this chapter will focus primarily upon the character and implications of Bakunin's theoretical divergence from Marx.

What divided Bakunin's central political argument from Marx's was, simply put, the question of social authority. This issue was the substantive core of nearly every disagreement between them, from practical questions concerning the establishment of workers' parties or the abolition of inheritance, to broader differences over the character of historical development or the correct relationship of mankind to the natural world. One should note, however, that this theoretical disagreement about the proper character of social authority bore little resemblance to the mythologized version that has been promoted by many commentators. Such accounts inevitably pitted Marx, the rational party disciplinarian against Bakunin, the absolutist despot, who was simultaneously the sworn Stirnerian enemy of all social structure. Quite the contrary, the real disagreement revolved around questions about the sources of social authority, their consequent relative legitimacy, and the implications they carried for a whole range of social and political problems.

Bakunin's basic approach to all questions of social authority grew out of his fusion of Lamarckian evolutionary theory with Feuerbach's anthropological naturalism. By injecting a strictly materialist but progressive conception of historical change into Feuerbach's sentient, conscious image of mankind, Bakunin was able to develop a notion of a fixed and immutable natural authority that totally determined all aspects of human existence, and yet still carve out within those naturally manifested limits a volitional zone within which mankind could consciously order the structure of human society. It was upon this theoretical substructure that Bakunin grounded his arguments about mutual interaction, animal and rational will, and collective self-discipline. The central intention of his position was to enable each individual to exert a maximal authority over the conditions that defined his own life, by acting within and through the dominant natural authority of his social group and of the physical world as a whole. For Bakunin, therefore, the question of social authority was not one of the existence of that authority per se, but rather of disaggregating that authority by source, structure, and amenability to human intervention.

Bakunin's conception of individual freedom, and of the consequent distribution of social authority required to attain that freedom, became the philosophical base from which he attacked Marx. Bakunin argued quite explicitly that Marx never transcended his Hegelian foundations, and was thus never able to overcome the abstracted and authoritarian bias of Hegelian metaphysics. Despite his professed and serious economic materialism, which Bakunin shared and lauded, Marx remained, in Bakunin's eyes, a "metaphysician" who retained the "idealist" belief that "thought is prior to life, and abstract theory is prior to social practice."[1] More specifically, Bakunin argued that Marx had distorted his study of economics by his insistence upon injecting the Hegelian dialectic into it:

But to all this M. Marx added two new elements: the most abstracted and subtle dialectic—which he borrowed from the Hegelian school and frequently pushed to the point of roguishness and perversion—and the communist point of departure.[2]

Bakunin argued further that Marx's appropriation of the dialectic had saddled Marx with an incorrect model of historical change. Marx was so steeped in the notion of a dialectical transformation of the state that he believed the European working class could make a successful revolution only by themselves seizing the modern bourgeois national state. Consequently, Bakunin wrote, Marx interpreted every movement toward state centralization of social authority to be a "great revolutionary advance,"[3] regardless of the human cost both in consolidating that new nation-state, and in subsequently attacking and destroying it. For Marx, the "bloody defeats of peasant rebellions in Germany and the rise of despotic states in the Sixteenth Century,"[4] as well as "the triumph of Catholicism in France in the Sixteenth and Seventeenth Centuries,"[5] were important events in the historical movement toward their opposite, a proletarian revolution. Bakunin also pointed to Marx's argument that, in their own period, Bismarck's centralization of Germany into the central bulwark of European reaction had nonetheless served the revolutionary cause.[6] Bakunin concluded that for Marx, "the State, of little matter which, even Bismarck's, is the Revolution."[7]

From Bakunin's own theoretical point of view, Marx was totally incorrect in this reliance upon the state as such as an agent of working-class revolution. Working not from a dialectical but rather an evolutionary perspective on the process of historical change, Bakunin perceived the rise of the state as a major imposition upon the free mutual interaction of those subjected to it, and he contemptuously dismissed the dialectical view that "considered the triumphs of the State as those of social democracy" as a "Marxist sophism" and a "disgusting and revolting absurdity."[8] Additionally, Bakunin chided Marx for his cold-blooded willingness to accept the horrors of history "indifferently" since, from a dialectical perspective, such outrages would necessarily speed the coming of the revolution. Bakunin believed that, quite the contrary, "we must carefully refrain from praising and admiring" those events that by historical or economic circumstance were "inevitable" but were nonetheless in "flagrant opposition to the supreme goal of history. . . the triumph of man's humanity."[9]

Marx's conception of historical development, Bakunin believed, was simply one applied instance of Marx's fundamentally authoritarian approach to all questions of social authority. Firmly fixed in the idealist and abstracted notions of Hegelian metaphysics—as represented by his appropriation of Hegel's central methodological device, the dialectic—Marx conceptualized all issues of social authority in terms of the purpose for which that authority was utilized. Rather than perceiving it as a force that could be derived from various sources and have varying impacts, Marx's notion of social authority confronted popular life as a seamless, unitary whole, which, as Engels argued explicitly in his 1873 polemic "On Authority" (and as Marx confirmed in numerous correspondence during the same period), presented mankind with only the option of total acceptance or total rejection. Here, Bakunin's argument against Marx clearly paralleled Feuerbach's attack on Hegel's dialectic as equally incapable of tolerating the diversity of "co-ordination and co-existence" in space, but instead opting for the much more restrictive principle of "succession and sub-ordination" implicit within "exclusive time."[10]

The theoretical divergence between Bakunin and Marx was very evident in their respective notions of the national state. Bakunin's central philosophical conception of mutual interaction led him to consider the state as such to represent only an unnecessary and arbitrary interference with the ongoing process of daily life. Regardless of specific institutional structure or social orientation, Bakunin argued,

> if there is a State, there must necessarily be domination, and therefore slavery; a State without slavery, overt or concealed, is unthinkable—and that is why we are enemies of the State.[11]

For Marx, though, the question of the state wasn't a question of the state as such, except in some far-distant and extremely ill-defined sense of its "withering away." Moreover, Marx never considered the national state, even when he referred to its final transcendence from a true Socialist State to pure communism and its requisite "administration of things," as having been an oppressive or distastefully bloody entity. On the contrary, consistent with his dialectical presumption, Marx seemed to view the state with the dispassionate eye of the objective clinician, concerned only to anticipate properly its inevitable passing into a more historically advanced and complete phase of human development. In effect, the same institution which for Bakunin epitomized the negative consequences of all authoritarian impositions upon "real life," had for Marx a simple objective status as a series of necessary steps through which the dialectic must by its nature pass. It was therefore quite appropriate for the question of the state to serve as the concrete vehicle upon which to focus and order their broader, philosophical disagreement over the character of social authority in general.

Bakunin's central attack upon what he understood to be Marx's Hegelian-induced authoritarianism was concentrated upon Marx's notion of a revolutionary state. Marx, he argued, was a proponent not of a liberation of the popular classes from all externally imposed economic exploitation and political oppression, but rather of a distinctly more limited arrangement of "prescriptive, authoritarian socialism"[12] which Bakunin labeled "State Communism."[13] Marx's doctrine presumed that the "supreme objective of all his efforts" would be the establishment of a "Great People's State,"[14] which would fulfill the direct charge of the 1848 Manifesto by basing its economic structure upon "the organization of labor by the State."[15] This economic first principle would, Bakunin argued, carry several clear consequences for the overall structure of economic relations within Marx's proposed state:

> *Labor financed by the State*—such is a fundamental principle of *authoritarian communism,* of State Socialism. The State, *having become the sole proprietor,*. . . will have become the sole capitalist, banker, money-lender, organizer, director of all national work, and distributor of its profits.[16]

Bakunin contended that, if such a highly centralized economic structure was to operate productively, state communism would require "an extremely complicated government" with which to "administer" the popular classes "economically."[17] Both in its need to regulate all economic activity, therefore, as well as in its fundamental character as a political state, Marx's revolutionary regime would find itself "governing and administering the masses politically,"[18] with all the concomitant exploitation and oppression, just like those bourgeois regimes that preceded it.

This analysis of Marx's position was directly rooted in the dichotomy between Marx's unitary notion of social authority and Bakunin's own more segmented approach. For Marx, a new revolutionary state would be liberatory not as a result of any substantial modifications the new state would make upon the actual exercise of coercive force—it would have at its disposal equally as much force as the bourgeois state which it replaced—but it would be liberatory due to the changed purpose for which that coercive state power would now be employed. The new state power, instead of serving the particular interests of one economic class among several, as Marx (and Bakunin) believed the case had been within all prior states, would benefit the sole class which could transcend its particular or partial interests to become what Marx termed a "universal class." By utilizing state power to secure its universalized interests, the proleteriat would necessarily transcend all particularist or class-based arrangements, and its "dictatorship" would consequently represent the first stage in a new "social" era of human history.

Bakunin believed, however, that Marx's approach had ignored certain central structural characteristics of all political states, regardless of their specific social intentions. Marx's designation of his new state as "revolutionary" would in no way alter the necessary set of relationships that governed the behavior of all states both internally, with regard to their own populations, and externally, with other states. Indeed Bakunin argued that, as in the case of science, a Marxist state would in at least some respects be an even more oppressive political institution than the bourgeois regimes it intended to depose.

In terms of its relations with its own internal population, Bakunin contended, a Marxist state would, like all other states, necessarily develop a "small privileged minority" in whose particular interest the state would be principally maintained.[19] Like all other ruling elites in all other states, the first obligation of the new elite would be to institutionalize its own position of economic privilege and political power. This self-concern would be evident both in its daily disposition of resources as well as in its fierce resistance to any challenge to its continuation: "no dictatorship can have any other aim except to perpetuate itself."[20]

Bakunin argued further that a Marxist state, like all others, represented an arbitrary man-made force that had been abstracted from everyday popular life and set above it. Regardless of its genesis, this new elite could only function as a "machine" that was artificially imposed upon daily life, "governing the masses from above."[21] It would in fact be, Bakunin believed, a massive machine: "In order to be able to carry out its great economic and social mission, this State will have to be very far-reaching, very powerful and highly centralized."[22] This new state's centralized and mechanical character would have at least two specific negative consequences for its relationship to the popular classes within it. First, since all effective decision making would be located within an inaccessible state machine, any and all popular freedoms would exist only at the suffrance of that state. Within such a political structure, Bakunin argued, human freedom would be "purely formal, doled out, measured, and regulated by the State."[23]

And secondly, Bakunin contended that a Marxist state would view science not as a vehicle for popular freedom but rather as an important tool through which the state could impose and maintain its own intellectual domination. For Marx, Bakunin argued, scientific knowledge would be the property of the state, and that state would "impose science on the people"[24] in the form of externally framed, uncomprehended, yet fixed directives required for the maintenance of a centralized, state-run economy. This hierarchical and explicitly unitary perspective concerning science grew "quite logically" from Marx's fundamentally idealist presumption that thought preceded life, for "since thought, theory and science are, for the present at least, the property of only a very few people, those few should rule social life."[25] However, Bakunin continued, far from in any respect liberating the working classes, this political appropriation of scientific knowledge would only compound the inability of those classes to control the conditions of their lives. The new revolutionary state would in effect become the "reign of the scientific mind,"[26] which, for its own greater productive efficiency, would divide the mass of people into two armies—industrial and agricultural armies under the direct command of the State engineers who will constitute a new privileged scientific-political class.[27]

Moreover, in such an unrestrained political environment, science's inherently abstracted and insensitive—indeed oblivious—character would have free rein, at tremendous human cost. Thus a Marxist state, Bakunin argued, although it would remove the despotism of bourgeois capitalist institutions, would erect in its place a "despotism savant" that, in "penetrating into the very spirit of men and corrupting their thought at the source,"[28] would create "the most aristocratic, despotic, arrogant, and contemptuous of all regimes."[29] This state appropriation of science would consequently leave the individual worker or peasant even more removed from economic decision making, more alienated from the products of his labor, and substantially more oppressed than he had previously been under even a capitalist state. It would be, Bakunin concluded, "A barracks regime for the proletariat, in which a standardized mass of men and women workers would wake, sleep, work and live by rote."[30]

Bakunin also argued that Marx's revolutionary state, precisely because it was a state, would find itself constantly entangled in military adventures with and against its neighboring states. "Whoever says State," Bakunin wrote, "necessarily implies a particular limited State," since only a Napoleon might dream of governing a "universal State."[31] Bakunin then followed out what he believed was the inevitable consequence of the intrinsic nature of any state: "State means *a* State, and *a* State confirms the existence of *several* States, and *several* States means rivalry, jealousy, and incessant, endless war. The simplest logic bears this out, and so does the whole of human history."[32] Furthermore, exactly as was the case with every other state, the material requirements necessary to such external endeavors would in turn force a Marxist state to place various internal controls upon its own population.

Having argued that Marx's new revolutionary state would resemble all other states in both internal structure and external behavior, Bakunin readily took issue with Marx's disclaimer that his new state would be different in that it would be a popular or "People's State." This distinction, Bakunin argued, was predicated on nothing more than the liberal/bourgeois idea of universal suffrage, by which the working classes would "elect its so-called representatives and rulers."[33] Such an argument could be sustained only if one ignored the past experience of all bourgeois parliamentary systems, in which once they were elected, workers "cease to be workers and begin to look down upon the toiling people."[34] Bakunin insisted instead that this institutionalization of political power could only create a new group of governors, who would develop the same anti-popular concerns, and the same concomitant devices through which to evade popular accountability, common to every other governing elite. Within Marx's new state, he argued, the working classes would exercise their power only by

> proxy, which means entrusting it to a group of men elected to represent and govern them, which in turn will unfailingly return them to all the deceit and subservience of representative or bourgeois rule. After a brief flash of liberty or orgiastic revolution, the citizens of the new State will wake up slaves, puppets and victims of a new group of ambitious men.[35]

This could occur because Marx's so-called People's State, just like the regimes it replaced, understood the question of democratic control to be no more than the selection of a "small handful of privileged individuals" by "throngs herded together on election day and ever ignorant of why and whom they elect."[36] The only substantive distinction between Marx's state and its predecessors, in Bakunin's eyes, was that in the new revolutionary state the same oligarchic political consequences could more easily masquerade themselves as "the ostensible expression of a people's will,"[37] a distinction that imbued the new state with an even more unfortunate character. In view of its fundamentally despotic character, Bakunin argued, there was no legitimacy whatsoever in Marx's claim to have structured a liberatory or "popular" state. On the contrary, Bakunin insisted that by the intrinsic nature of the state as such, it could never be harnessed for the true interests of the popular classes: the notion of a "People's State," he concluded, was "a ridiculous contradiction, a fiction, a lie."[38]

This fundamental disagreement between Bakunin and Marx over the proper structure for social authority was not confined to issues concerning Marx's support for a revolutionary state. The same theoretical dichotomy also underlay, for instance, their dispute over the correct short-term path to a socialist revolution. Marx's concentration on a seizure of the existent state by the working classes, as against Bakunin's focus on the necessity of dismantling that state, were simply logical concomitants of their central positions. This theoretical disagreement also informed their dispute as to whether the working classes ought to organize parliamentary political parties, so that they might then attempt to seize the bourgeois state by partially or perhaps in some countries entirely peaceful political means. Further, one can clearly see these theoretical contours in each of the various arguments about the proper internal structure of the International itself—for example, the degree to which the General Council should issue policy directives. One can even perceive the outlines of this basic disagreement over social authority in Marx's personal disdain for non-Germanic populations, and in the increasingly anti-German tone that Bakunin adopted in his own writings.

In effect, all these disputes over specific policies and programs were essentially case studies of a more fundamental conceptual disagreement over the proper structure of revolutionary social authority. They were simply reflections of what Bakunin himself had recognized, and very directly described to Herzen in 1869—fully a year before Marx's "Confidential Circular" signaled the formal opening of hostilities within the International—as "a question of principle, the question of State Communism."[39]

The divergent assumptions of Bakunin's and Marx's respective conceptions of a liberatory social authority were not in any way coincidental, either in source or content. On the contrary, these distinctions were clearly and firmly grounded in the separate solutions through which each man resolved the philosophic problem posed by the limited contemplative character of Feuerbach's anthropological naturalism. As discussed in the theoretical section in chapter 2, while Marx turned to the dialectic for what he termed an "energizing principle," Bakunin chose to incorporate a Lamarckian notion of evolutionary change so as to acquire what he called a "spontaneous living fact." Moreover, Bakunin then utilized the theoretical principles derived from conjoining Lamarck and Feuerbach to lambast Marx for the same sins for which Feuerbach himself had attacked Hegel. Consequently, the central question that Bakunin's critique of Marx raises for contemporary political theory concerns Marx's appropriation of Hegel's central methodological principle: had Marx also, along with the dialectic, implicitly adopted the absolute and unitary notion of social authority found in Hegel's universal state? In effect, had Marx not only appropriated Hegel's dialectic, but with it the notion of an absolute universal state toward which Hegel believed the dialectic was ceaselessly moving?

One possible answer to this question lies in Marx's *Critique of Hegel's Philosophy of Right*, in which he subjected Hegel's political philosophy to post-Feuerbachian scrutiny. Marx's purpose in undertaking this work seemed to be to demonstrate that Hegel's final acceptance of the Prussian bureaucratic state could not be justified in terms of Hegel's own philosophical postulates. However, Marx's method of argument—that Hegel's specific, concretized political conclusions contradicted the philosophical system upon which it was predicated—clearly indicated that Marx's quarrel was with Hegel's political application of his system, not with the system itself. Avineri, in *The Social and Political Thought of Karl Marx*, argued just this point: "The object of Marx's criticism is therefore the same as the one implied in his letter to Ruge: Hegel's idea of the state merely reflected modern constitutional monarchy; as such, it failed to live up to its own theoretical standards."[40] Indeed, Marx disagreed not with Hegel's notion of a universal state, nor with Hegel's notion that such a state would be led by a universal class, but rather only with Hegel's particular choice of a universal class. Marx argued, qua Avineri, that "only the universal can be rational, and the monarch's will, by definition, negates universality."[41] Consequently, where Hegel had considered that the bureaucratic class which administered the Prussian state represented the general interests of civil society as a whole, and had therefore transcended its particular class interests to speak for the universal concerns of the state itself as its "universal class," Marx insisted that the bureaucratic class represented only the monarch's will, and thus remained a particular rather than a universal class. According to Avineri,

> Hegel had thought that the bureaucracy, as a universal class, would [liberate men from class]; Marx rightly pointed out that universality can be meaningful only if it applies to all, and not to a particular class. To Marx, a class cannot be truly universal unless it is everybody's class.[42]

Marx further pursued this critique by arguing that the existence of a bureaucratic class per se, far from indicating that the state had attained its universal potential, only confirmed its alienated and particularist structure. In this attack he again demonstrated that he accepted Hegel's notion that a state could in fact be properly universal, and that such a universal state was in fact the appropriate ultimate goal of human history as embodied within the dialectic. "According to Marx," Avineri wrote, "bureaucracy can be abolished only when the state becomes the real, and not the apparent, general interest. . . . The state is thus degraded to a private interest with others of the same sort, its claim to universality deprived of justification."[43] Beyond the problem of how a universal state could survive without a bureaucracy, the important issue here for Bakunin's critique of Marx is that, once again, Marx had predicated his criticism of Hegel upon an argument that called not for the *dissolution* of Hegel's system, but rather for its fulfillment. As Avineri observed,

> But if Marx does not accept the Hegelian identification of bureaucracy with universality, he still retains the dialectical concept of a "universal class," i.e., a partial social stratum which is, however, an ideal subject of the universal concept of the Gemeinwesen.[44]

Indeed, Avineri argued that Marx's entire approach to Hegel's political conclusions was to demonstrate that Hegel's philosophical system necessarily required the transcendence of Hegel's particularized "modern" state. In essence, Marx's argument was that to maintain the integrity of Hegel's philosophy, it was essential to jettison his particular version of the universal state.

Marx's full acceptance of Hegel's fundamental philosophical structure, and specifically Hegel's notion of a universal state, is readily apparent in the solution Marx proposed to Hegel's political dilemma. There was indeed a universal class, but it was the proletariat and not the bureaucratic class, and there was indeed a dialectical means by which that universal class could establish its universal state, but it was universal suffrage rather than bureaucratic edict. Both of these proposals were predicated upon a strict adherence to a dialectical perception of history, and were in fact of value to Marx solely for their capacity to satisfy it: just as Bakunin had argued, Marx's interest in sentient individuals within the real physical world was for their ability to fulfill the prior ordinations of abstract philosophy.

The proletariat's central attraction for Marx was precisely its capacity to satisfy the philosophical requirements of the dialectic. Its role in Marx's early thought was as a vehicle which could bring about the necessary *aufgehoben* from Hegel's falsely labeled bureaucratic state to a truly universal state within the criteria of Hegel's own definition. "For Marx," Avineri argued, "the proletariat was never a particular class, but the repository of the Hegelian 'universal class'," and in consequence it wasn't surprising that Marx "does not reveal much empathy" for their sentient human plight.[45] Further, since Marx believed he had properly identified the proletariat as the "final realization of universality,"[46] Marx's concept of the "dictatorship of the proletariat" could be fully justified as the completion of the dialectic's journey through history: it was the universal state. Thus this dictatorship's policies, as spelled out in the 1848 Manifesto some five years after Marx wrote the *Critique*, represented not the invalid attempts of a particular class to impose exploitation and domination—as Marx would describe prior bourgeois states—but rather man's liberation into his true nature as what Marx later described as a "universally developed individual."[47] The dictatorship of this new universal class, Avineri wrote, would involve only

> the wielding of state power for the attainment of universal goals. By applying this policy the proletarian state will be the first state in history to use political power for universal and not partial ends. This program thus realizes the Hegelian postulate about the universality of the state.[48]

In short, the proletariat is of importance not in its immediate, sentient existence as suffering human beings but, on the contrary, because it "carries out the universal postulates of philosophy."[49] Feuerbach could not have found a more clear-cut example of the sacrifice of living beings to a dominant idealist abstraction.

Beyond this notion of the proletariat as the true universal class, Marx also retained the presumptions of Hegel's universal state in his depiction of the path by which this class was to attain state power. And although one could argue that Marx's devotion to universal suffrage was not as complete as Bakunin and, here, Avineri wish to make it appear—that is, that Marx still retained the notion of violent revolution in at least some circumstances—both Bakunin and Avineri base their arguments as much on Marx's firm support for Lassalle's Social Democratic Workers Party in Germany and on Marx's tendentious struggle to maintain the principle of parliamentary political organization within the charter of the First International as on his strictly theoretical writings.

Avineri observed that, for Marx, universal suffrage was a "dialectical weapon"[50] by which the proletariat could force the bourgeois (read "Hegelian") state to transcend itself into a properly universal state. He cited a quotation from the *Critique* in which Marx argued that universal suffrage would destroy the distinction between civil society and the state upon which the Hegelian (read "bourgeois") state was predicated: "Within the abstract political state the reform of the suffrage is hence a claim for the dissolution of the political state, as well as for the dissolution of civil society."[51] The act of the bourgeois state in granting universal suffrage, for Marx, would thus be its last act as a partial bourgeois state. This would take place, Avineri argued, because the fact of universal suffrage would destroy the existence of differentially allocated private property, and thus the basis of class:

> Since class is based on property, and property is by nature differential, the disappearance of class differences depends upon the disappearance of property as the determinant of status. That is why Marx postulated universal suffrage. He argued that property is meaningless and ceases to exist once it ceases to determine status.[52]

Avineri concluded this exposition by making explicit the relationship that he believes Marx saw between universal suffrage and, through the consequent transcendence of the partial to the universal state, Marx's conception of that universal state. In Marx's evaluation of 1848 France, Avineri wrote,

> [Universal suffrage] was promulgated out of what Marx calls the radical illusions which thought that universal suffrage could co-exist with a bourgeois society. For Marx, these two are incompatible. . . . By itself, universal suffrage would ultimately lead to communism.[53]

Here again, from the perspective of a Bakuninist critique, Marx had opted for a position that satisfies the philosophical requirements of the dialectic but does not address the concrete conditions of the real world. While universal suffrage would overturn the specifically *formal* nature of the particularist Hegelian or bourgeois state, in that the separation of civil society from state power would indeed be rectified, Marx ignored all the real-world informal structures and techniques whereby both elected and unelected minority elites maintain political control. Bakunin would argue that Marx ignored every real question about the true character of state power: the capacity of a fixed elite to manipulate information (scientific or otherwise), the oligarchic tendency toward institutional self-perpetuation, and many other consequences of bourgeois political systems.

Far more important than the degree to which Marx's dedication to the dialectic pointed up his inadequate understanding of bourgeois politics, however, was the loophole which the dialectic had opened concerning the issue of property. Clearly, once differential private property had been eliminated (suspending for the moment all questions about the capacity of universal suffrage to achieve such a result), there were two distinctly opposite techniques by which the new revolutionary society could handle the reallocation of that property—of the means of production. For Marx, working from the notion of a universal state, ruled by a universal class as in Hegel, the logical disposition of this property was to assign it to the state: since the state now represented the general or universal interest of the entire society, it could best administer the economic infrastructure of the society in accordance with that general interest. Bakunin, of course, perceived the issue differently. Lacking the justificatory notion of an absolute universal state, indeed working from the contrary notion that all states, of whatever social or class composition, will necessarily induce economic exploitation and political domination, Bakunin argued that this new revolutionary state would indeed "universalize" the situation of the proletariat, but only in the sense of leaving not just the proletariat but everyone in the state (save its new elite) both economically alienated and politically disenfranchised. To be sure, this new state would have resolved the dichotomy between civil society and the universal state that had plagued bourgeois/Hegelian society, but only by fusing every class into a massive, all-encompassing state. Thus Marx might have found the solution to the problem posed by the Hegelian dialectic, but he hadn't dealt with the real issues of human liberation: the transcendence of private property doesn't in any sense necessarily lead to direct individual and collective control over the conditions of social or economic existence. The dialectic had been fulfilled, but man remained enslaved. As Bakunin succinctly summarized the entire question, the "social revolution" which the working classes longed for was "infinitely broader than that which is promised by the German or Marxist programme."[54]

Similarly, it was Marx's commitment to the dialectic and an absolute universal state that informed his perversely constructed notion of "social labor." In the last section of the *Eighteenth Brumaire*, Marx defied nearly every description of urban life by arguing that only within the confines of the industrial factory could man engage in socially controlled labor:

the farmer was an economically isolated and inferentially anti-social creature mired in the "idiocy of rural life." That the most economically as well as socially alienating of all possible environments, in which the individual worker couldn't control any aspect of his life or labor, should become "social," while the traditional locus of all notions of both unalienated human labor and fulfilling social ties—the rural community—should become an abomination suited only for dismemberment, reflected more than Marx's own *burgerlichte* disdain for the peasantry. Rather, it is a further example of Marx's unwavering commitment to the dialectic, and to a Hegelian conception of reality above and beyond all other practical or political considerations. Factory labor was "social" because it satisfied the specific economic conditions required by the dialectic, because it created a deprived social class that could universalize its deprived condition by depriving all classes within a universal state and would necessarily be, by Hegelian definition, man's highest social accomplishment. Because the reification of private capital would be replaced by a newly reified state capital, the worker's labor, qua Marx, would no longer be alienated, since it would accrue to the new universal state of which the worker would be, again by Hegelian definition, the putative director. Whether agricultural labor might or might not have been stupefying wasn't at issue: for Marx, the central concern was that the perhaps even more stultifying conditions within the urban factory were more conducive to the realization of the dialectic's philosophical hegemony. In effect, it was only from the prison of the dialectic that Marx could laud as "social" the prison of the factory.

There would seem, in sum, to be two major points which one could draw from this discussion of Bakunin and Marx. First, there would appear to be a strong correspondence between those characteristics of Marx's social and political thought that Bakunin excoriated as authoritarian, and those elements that Marx had appropriated from Hegelian philosophy. And second, it would seem probable that Bakunin was able to point to this connection, if only implicitly, as a result of his own distance from Hegel's system.

6 *Bakunin's Theory of Collectivist Anarchism: A Preliminary Assessment*

On its most fundamental level, Bakunin's political philosophy was an argument against the institutionalization of social authority. He attacked every form of official authority on the grounds that it was neither politically legitimate nor socially efficacious. A fixed formal structure of authority could never be politically legitimate because it was always the instrument of a self-interested ruling class: formal authority, by definition, was inextricably linked to domination and exploitation. And a formal structure of authority could never be socially efficacious because it was inherently incapable of capturing the overwhelming complexity and diversity of human life within its narrowly prescribed framework.

The only form of social authority which could be both legitimate and efficacious was a process of natural or mutual authority—what Bakunin's Lamarckian frame of reference led him to describe as mutual interaction. Rooted in the fundamental motive force of the entire physical world, a system of mutual authority governed through a permanent process of reciprocal persuasion among political, economic, and social (although not intellectual) equals. Mankind could achieve its full human and social potential only by replacing artificial institutional forms of social authority, based upon class coercion, with a strictly non-institutional system of mutual interchange among equals patterned after the structure of the natural world. This, then, was the central argument of Bakunin's collectivist anarchism: that a truly participatory system of social organization must be constructed upon the permanent opposition of mutual to official forms of authority.

As the dominant concept within Bakunin's political philosophy, this argument against the institutionalization of social authority bound the different components of his thought together into a cohesive whole. Whether one looks at his theory of human freedom, his analysis of bourgeois society, his critiques of state and of science, or his theory of social revolution, Bakunin's position was always underscored by his conceptualization of natural authority. A close and careful analysis of Bakunin's political writings, therefore, reveals something quite different from the fragmented, internally contradictory theory attributed to him by Paradox commentators. Rather, Bakunin's work presents a fully fleshed theory of man's political universe, and provides a soundly constructed collectivist-anarchist response to both authoritarian Marxism and libertarian-individualist anarchism.

Bakunin's theoretical legacy is a rich one. Not only did he develop a unique and important conceptual framework, but he employed that structure to break new analytic ground in several key aspects of socialist theory. Bakunin's understanding of the state, of bureaucracy, of science, of a revolutionary vanguard, and of a revolutionary peasantry all represented major contributions to critical thought.

Bakunin's theory of the state, as noted in chapter 2, is grounded on the notion that the state as such is an artificial construct. Indeed, the thrust of Bakunin's argument goes beyond the assertion that the state is not socially necessary, to argue that the state is in fact an *anti-social* construct. Bakunin focussed his attention on the mailed understructure of the state: its reliance upon political repression and economic exploitation, its dependence upon a permanent bureaucracy, its evolution toward military dictatorship. The argument is not that other, moderating behavior doesn't exist, but rather that such behavior represents only a superficial veneer. When a state comes under severe pressure—as it inevitably must, in Bakunin's view—the conditions for its survival require that it strip away this benign surface to reveal its irreducibly violent core.

Bakunin's argument allows for no exemptions, no "special cases" based upon a state's legitimating ideology. Whether a state is socialist or capitalist, democratic or authoritarian, even large or small, the sole issue is the degree to which that state has advanced toward this ultimate, final stage of development. Clearly some will develop along this continuum less rapidly than others, restrained by demographic, cultural, or political factors of various types. The central point of Bakunin's analysis, however, is that all states carry within them this violent understructure, and that they all tend toward a final military stage in which this understructure overwhelms all other less malevolent state functions.

There are several interesting theoretical concomitants of this argument. First, there can be, from this perspective, no such entity as a "good" state: *all* states are in the process of evolving toward absolutism. There are only states which are at present less evil than others. In turn, the notion of a renegade or outlaw state ceases to be meaningful. The task of international diplomacy, from this perspective, becomes not one of enticing dangerous states back into the peace-loving international fold, but rather one of preventing less bellicose states from following their basic instinct to act violently. According to Bakunin's analysis of state morality, the most hideous forms of state action against its own citizens— Stalin's slaughter of the Kulaks, Hitler's incineration of the Jews, Pol Pot's decimation of Cambodia—simply symbolize the state fulfilling its potential, reaching its final form. Ultimately, Bakunin's theory of the state suggests that the phrase "democratic government" may be a contradiction in terms. Since states by definition are concerned primarily with questions of self-perpetuation, self-expansion, and self-aggrandizement, in direct contradiction to the fundamental interests of most of its citizens, it makes little sense to speak of such an institutionalized entity as one that can be democratically controlled by its citizenry.

These arguments may seem rather extreme, yet there is a kernel of truth within them that is difficult to deny. Numerous events in the twentieth century tend to confirm Bakunin's view of the state—not the least of which has been the evolution of the totalitarian and centrally planned socialist state. Moreover, as Bakunin himself contends, the alacrity with which all states go to war suggests that there is indeed a pathological element within the state's institutional psyche. Far from becoming less relevant, this argument has become considerably more important with the advent of nuclear weapons and with the consequent capacity of states to trigger not just regional wars but also the vaporization of the entire planet.

Less difficult to accept—but no less provocative an argument at its time—was Bakunin's insistence that the modern state was inherently bureaucratic. His analysis of the state led him to conclude that its inertial tendencies toward both self-interest and self-perpetuation would force Marxist and bourgeois states alike to assume a "machinelike" bureaucratic form. Further, his own system of mutual and unstructured social authority allowed him to propose an alternative organizational framework which, he argued, could not develop into a bureaucratic administrative apparatus. Thus in 1870, some forty years before Weber concluded that bureaucratic rationalization was the inevitable consequence of the industrial division of labor, or Michels concluded that the emergence of a new elite was the inevitable consequence of technical expertise within mass organizations, Bakunin's argument about mutual authority led him to attempt a non-bureaucratic and a non-oligarchic theory of post-industrial social authority. Weber, to be sure, accounted for the possibility of such an approach with his admission that the progressive rationalization of society could be halted by a "reversion. . . to small-scale organization" in all areas of human activity.[1] However, Weber's subsequent theoretical observation does not detract from either the originality or the importance of Bakunin's argument and Bakunin's contention that "there is no middle path between rigorously consistent federalism and bureaucratic government"[2] remains an effective summary of the anti-authoritarian argument against the modern centralized state.

Equally as important for the development of a modern anti-authoritarian argument was Bakunin's critique of science. For Bakunin, science, like the state, was an inherently abstract enterprise. However, unlike the state, science was a legitimate indeed essential human undertaking, which had a critical role to play in mankind's development. For science to fulfill its mandate, however, it had to be kept at arms length from politics in two important respects. First, scientific activity had to be freed of its ruling-class fetters, which, Bakunin argued, had distorted it into a tool of the state's privileged classes. Second, and more broadly, Bakunin's Feuerbachian concern with the fate of the sentient individual led him to insist that science be permanently precluded from determining political policy. Thus, in Bakunin's view, the task of re-directing science toward its proper social role was twofold: science had to be freed of its false ruling-class bias, and it had to be employed appropriately as only "the compass of life," not its arbiter. If society could thus assert political control over the content and function of science, Bakunin believed, science would strengthen the principle of mutual authority rather than destroy it.

Bakunin's insistence upon the importance of restraining scientific hegemony, like his arguments about the nature of the state and of state bureaucracy, has become increasingly relevant as the twentieth century has unfolded. A number of similar arguments against the political character of scientific activity have been made since Bakunin wrote, and they have been put forward from a number of different perspectives. Bookchin, for instance, has called for the miniaturization of modern technology, so that science might be placed in the service of decentralized democratic interests.[3] Similarly, a constellation of public interest groups has attacked the so-called Green Revolution in Third World agriculture, demanding that agricultural science be directed instead toward the development and distribution of appropriate technology for nutritional self-sufficiency. Moreover, the anti-nuclear movement within Western capitalist countries has at its foundation a critique of science that is fundamentally Bakuninist in its insistence upon public control over nuclear decision-making processes. The increasing relevance of Bakunin's approach again suggests the prescient character of his theoretical work.

While Bakunin's critique of the state, of bureaucracy, and of science are more universally applicable, there are several aspects of his specifically revolutionary theory that also represent an important contribution to critical thought. Two of the more salient are Bakunin's notion of a revolutionary vanguard and his conception of the peasantry's revolutionary role.

The sole function of a vanguard, in Bakunin's theory, was to serve as a "midwife" to the working classes' socialist instinct. Consistent with his underlying theory of natural authority, this revolutionary association was to act upon the working classes "informally," relying exclusively upon the natural influence of its members' social and strategic knowledge. For Bakunin, the vanguard was simply a facilitator of the working classes' own revolutionary activity.

Bakunin's argument was premised upon his more general belief that abuses of social authority stemmed not from human personalities, but rather from improperly constructed social institutions. Through the specific character of the revolutionary association's relationship to the working classes, Bakunin believed, precisely those structural prerequisites necessary to the exercise of arbitrary authority had been eliminated. The influence of the revolutionary association was, by definition, premised on developing those attitudes and beliefs that were already accepted by those who were to be influenced. Bakunin's major point about revolutionary education was that it could succeed only if it incorporated and reinforced the fundamental, historically created desires of the working classes. Consequently, members of the association would find it futile to attempt to lead the working classes in directions for which they had not been historically prepared.

Additionally, Bakunin emphasized the educational rather than the coercive aspects of the association's role in the training of its members. He stressed that the members' selfless and invisible role, in conformance with the historical desires of the working classes, would result in the achievement of "true power" rather than only its shallow authoritarian "trappings." Bakunin thus concluded that the proper relationship between the association and the working classes was assured by the intrinsic character of the system of mutual influence which created and sustained that relationship.

Bakunin's vanguard theory is clearly different from that found within previous coup-d'état-oriented theories of revolution, such as those of Babeuf, Buonarroti, and Blanqui. More importantly, Bakunin diverged substantially from the basic Marxist notion of the proletariat as vanguard and dramatically from the Leninist notion that came to dominate many twentieth-century socialist movements. Precisely because Bakunin did not construct his revolutionary association as a separate political entity outside the revolutionary classes, he did not have to concoct a theoretical excuse for its revolutionary activities, nor fabricate a device by which to re-integrate this external force into the body of a liberated populace. Thus, through his initial conceptualization of the issue, Bakunin eliminated the possibility that his revolutionary theory could have the anti-democratic consequences that we now associate with the vanguard approach adopted by Lenin.

Bakunin also added a new dimension to the theory of social revolution with his discussion of the role of the peasantry. There had, of course, been various pre-industrial or utopian socialist theories of revolution that had sought to incorporate the peasantry. Bakunin's work was, however, the first effort within the post-industrial socialist camp to view the peasantry as something more than a bulwark of reaction. Contrary to Marx, Lassalle, and others within the First International, Bakunin argued that the peasantry must first be weaned from the bourgeoise before an urban working-class revolution could succeed. Moreover, Bakunin's outline of a land seizure provided a strategy for this process which could have an effectiveness equivalent to that of the urban workers' general strike.

In his attention to the revolutionary importance of the peasantry, Bakunin foreshadowed the subsequent development of revolutionary theory. The Land and Freedom movement in Russia during the 1880's, and even Lenin's party slogan in the early twentieth century, reflected Bakunin's earlier emphasis upon the importance of the peasantry. Furthermore, as the possibility of social revolution spread beyond Russia to less industrialized countries that did not have a sizable urban proletariat, such as China, the emphasis on the role of the peasantry grew still greater. Thus Bakunin's vision of a revolutionary role for the peasantry within more advanced Western European countries had, in a sense, paved the theoretical ground for the development of an exclusively peasant-based form of revolutionary socialism.

It is important to emphasize that Bakunin's understanding of social revolution was not a particularly sanguinary one. Quite contrary to the Babeuvian notion with which Paradox commentators saddled him, Bakunin's revolutionary theory was designed to minimize bloodshed. This was especially true of his charge to the revolutionary association to limit outbreaks of violence against individuals on the part of the peasantry. While still maintaining the primacy of a spontaneous social revolution based on the full participation of the working classes, Bakunin had insisted on both moral and practical grounds that only institutions, not individuals, should be the target.

Bakunin's approach to the issue of revolutionary violence was the antithesis of that taken by later theorists like Sorel and Fanon. Moreover, Bakunin's explicit arguments against gratuitous violence separate him quite definitively from the cold-blooded efforts of most terrorist organizations. From those who practiced "propaganda by the deed" in the late nineteenth century, to the more recent Baader-Meinhof and Brigadi Rossi movements in Western Europe, the many terrorist groups that have sought to spark revolution through personal attacks on individuals have little theoretical kinship with Bakunin's view of political violence. In fact, one of the most striking aspects of Bakunin's argument is its consistently humanist bias. Thus it makes little sense to tar Bakunin's political thought with the pan-destructionist brush favored by most Paradox commentators.

Bakunin's overall contribution to critical theory, however, transcends the value of these separate critiques or arguments. The central importance of his work lies in his success in welding each of these different conceptual elements together into a coherent political position which he then deployed both negatively, to attack the underlying authoritarianism of Marxian socialism, and positively, to propose a more participatory framework for a popular revolutionary movement.

Turning first to the negative, Bakunin's fundamental disagreement with Marx and Marxist theory revolved around the proper character of social authority. Working from his notions of mutual authority and human self-consciousness, Bakunin criticized Marx's understanding of the transition to socialism as inadequate and incomplete. Marx's revolutionary theory, Bakunin argued, called for the elimination of only one particular economic component of the several institutional barriers to human self-fulfillment, and would leave intact other equally oppressive structures of social control. Bakunin's critique further suggested the likelihood that Marx had incorporated Hegel's notion of the absolute state, as well as Hegel's dialectical method, into his revolutionary theory.

By focussing his general critique of the state—and of its scientific and bureaucratic extensions—on Marx's theory of social authority, Bakunin could conclude that Marx's approach would produce not a socialist society but rather an extremely oppressive system of "state communism." Bakunin's fundamental argument against formal political institutions led him to argue that a Marxist state would inevitably become an intellectual and bureaucratic class dictatorship, which would adopt equally if not more immoral policies than those of its bourgeois predecessors.

Far from being a frivolous *ad hoc* attack on Marx, as some commentators have suggested, Bakunin's argument penetrated to the wellsprings of Marxist theory. Writing in the early 1870's, well before the advent of Bolshevism, Bakunin insisted that the conceptual core of Marxian socialism was an anti-democratic centralism that would lead not to socialist liberation but to a heavy-handed state capitalism. Bakunin's critique of Marxism thus strongly suggests that the critical anti-democratic flaw in the structure of twentieth-century communist states does not reflect some Leninist or Stalinist (or specifically Russian) breach of faith with Marxian principle. Rather, from the perspective of Bakunin's analysis, this oppressive and bureaucratic dimension can be observed directly within Marx's own political argument—within the most central formulation of the Marxian socialist enterprise. In this view, the failure of socialism within the Eastern European bloc speaks to the inadequacies not of its implementors, but of the fundamental political theory itself.

Bakunin's critique of the centralist bias within Marx's thought also has important implications for the tenor of late twentieth-century political discourse. If Bakunin's argument is correct, it will no longer suffice for Marxists like George Lichtheim to obfuscate the character of numerous popular and present-day organizing efforts by claiming that they are "semi-Marxist." On the contrary, as Murray Bookchin has argued quite persuasively, it will be necessary to both acknowledge and accept the inappropriateness of attempting to tack decentralized participatory modes of political behavior onto what is a fundamentally authoritarian Marxian substructure.[4] Bakunin's basic argument can thus have a substantial impact upon how present-day political thinkers evaluate the structure and purpose of numerous twentieth-century revolutionary movements.

In sum, the broad conceptual basis of Bakunin's political thought contradicts the intellectual commonplace that anarchism is not so much a political theory as an emotional reaction to industrialization. On the contrary, Bakunin has provided a theoretical grounding that places collectivist anarchism well within the mainstream of useful political analysis. If there is an argument against the validity of the collectivist-anarchist vision of the world, it must now be made on the basis of disagreement with the specific premises of a consistent theoretical argument. With Bakunin's work, then, the anarchist perception of reality gained the stature of a full-fledged political philosophy, worthy of equal consideration among the various political perspectives on the modern world. It is this contribution that makes Bakunin the true father of modern anarchism.

Notes

Chapter 1

1. Bakunin, "Protestation of the Alliance," in *The Political Philosophy of Bakunin: Scientific Anarchism*, ed. G. P. Maximoff (New York: Free Press, 1964), p. 314.
2. Ibid., p. 313.
3. Bakunin, "Politics of the International," in Maximoff, *Political Philosophy*, p. 312.
4. Ibid., p. 313.
5. Bakunin, "Federalism, Socialism, and Anti-Theologism," in *Bakunin on Anarchy*, trans. and ed. Sam Dolgoff (New York: Vintage, 1971), p. 139.
6. E. H. Carr, *Michael Bakunin* (New York: Vintage, 1961), p. 451.
7. Ibid., p. 112.
8. Ibid.
9. Max Nomad, *Apostles of Revolution* (New York: Collier Books, 1961), p. 190.
10. Ibid.
11. Ibid., p. 198.
12. Ibid., p. 151.
13. James Joll, *The Anarchists* (New York, Grosset and Dunlap, 1966), p. 26.
14. Ibid., p. 49.
15. Ibid., pp. 84, 85.
16. Ibid., pp. 84-85.
17. George Woodcock, *Anarchism* (Cleveland: World Publishing, 1962), p. 171.
18. Joll, *The Anarchists*, p. 87.
19. Edmund Wilson, *To the Finland Station* (Garden City: Doubleday Anchor, 1953), p. 279.

20. Ibid.
21. Paul Avrich, *The Russian Anarchists* (Princeton: Princeton University Press, 1971), p. 27.
22. Joll, *The Anarchists*, p. 84.
23. Woodcock, *Anarchism*, p. 174.
24. Bakunin, "Reaction in Germany," in *Michael Bakunin: Selected Writings*, trans. Steven Cox and Olive Stevens, and ed. Arthur Lehning (New York: Grove Press, 1973), p. 58.
25. Woodcock, *Anarchism*, p. 150.
26. Albert Camus, *The Rebel* (New York: Vintage, 1956), p. 158.
27. Bakunin, "Appeal to the Slavs," in Woodcock, *Anarchism*, p. 155.
28. Robert G. Wesson, *Soviet Communes* (New Brunswick: Rutgers University Press, 1963), p. 59.
29. Camus,*The Rebel*, p. 160.
30. Woodcock, *Anarchism*, p. 174.
31. Eugene Pyziur, *The Doctrine of Anarchism of Michael A. Bakunin* (Chicago: Henry Regnery Co., 1968), p. 3.
32. Martin Malia, *Alexander Herzen and the Birth of Russian Socialism* (New York: Grosset and Dunlap, 1971), pp. 417-18.
33. Carr, *Bakunin*, p. 452.
34. Pyziur, *Doctrine of Anarchism*, p. 146.
35. Carr, *Bakunin*, p. 193.
36. Paul Avrich, "Preface," in Dolgoff, *Bakunin on Anarchy*, p. xxiii.
37. Nomad, *Apostles*, p. 213.
38. Pyziur, *Doctrine of Anarchism*, p. 147.
39. Camus, *The Rebel*, p. 159.
40. Ibid.
41. George Lichtheim, *A Short History of Socialism* (New York: Praeger, 1971), p. 214.
42. Ibid., pp. 124, 208.
43. Ibid., pp. 203, 129.
44. Franz Mehring, *Karl Marx* (Ann Arbor: University of Michigan Press, 1973), p. 453.
45. Bakunin, "Federalism, Socialism, and Anti-Theologism," in Maximoff, *Political Philosophy*, p. 86.

Chapter 2

1. Bakunin, *Archives Bakounine*, vol. 3: *Etatisme et Anarchie*, trans. Marcel Brody and ed. Arthur Lehning (Leiden: E. J. Brill, 1967), p. 317.
2. *Bakunin, God and the State*, trans. Benjamin Tucker (New York: Dover Press, 1970), p. 72.
3. Certainly, Bakunin had read Feuerbach's *The Essence of Christianity* as avidly as any other young Hegelian, and while he may have read Lamarck's *Philosophie Zoologique* as a youth he may also have encountered Lamarck's concept of evolution in his extensive readings in the area of French socialism.
4. Ludwig Feuerbach, *Preliminary Theses on the Reform of Philosophy*, in Zawar Hanfi, "Introduction," *The Fiery Brook: Selected Writings of Ludwig Feuerbach*, trans. and ed. Zawar Hanfi (Garden City: Doubleday Anchor, 1972), pp. 31-32.

5. Feuerbach, *Preliminary Theses*, in Hanfi, *The Fiery Brook*, p. 157.

6. Ibid., p. 159.

7. Feuerbach, *The Essence of Christianity*, in Hanfi, "Introduction," *The Fiery Brook*, p. 32.

8. Feuerbach, *Towards a Critique of Hegel's Philosophy*, in Hanfi, "Introduction," *The Fiery Brook*, pp. 13-14.

9. Hanfi, "Introduction," *The Fiery Brook*, p. 35.

10. Feuerbach, *Preliminary Theses*, in Hanfi, "Introduction," *The Fiery Brook*, p. 37.

11. Hanfi, "Introduction," *The Fiery Brook*, p. 21.

12. Bakunin, "Philosophical Considerations," in Maximoff, *Political Philosophy*, p. 100.

13. Jean Baptiste Lamarck, in Richard Burkhardt, *The Spirit of System* (Cambridge: Harvard University Press, 1977), p. 157.

14. Bakunin, *God and the State*, p. 74.

15. Lamarck, *Philosophie Zoologique*, in Burkhardt, *The Spirit of System*, p. 157.

16. Bakunin, *God and the State*, p. 14.

17. Lamarck, *Philosophie Zoologique*, in Burkhardt, *The Spirit of System*, p. 152.

18. Ibid., p. 147.

19. Bakunin, "Philosophical Considerations," in Maximoff, *Political Philosophy*, p. 98.

20. Ibid.

21. Ibid.

22. Ibid.

23. Lamarck, in Burkhardt, *The Spirit of System*, p. 131.

24. Bakunin, "The Paris Commune and the Idea of the State," in Lehning, *Selected Writings*, p. 207.

25. Ibid.

26. Bakunin, "Philosophical Considerations," in Maximoff, *Political Philosophy*, p. 99.

27. Lamarck, in Burkhardt, *The Spirit of System*, p. 169.

28. Bakunin, "The Paris Commune and the Idea of the State," in Lehning, *Selected Writings*, p. 208.

29. Bakunin, "Philosophical Considerations," in Maximoff, *Political Philosophy*, p. 100.

30. Bakunin, "Knouto-Germanic Empire," in Maximoff, *Political Philosophy*, p. 333.

31. Bakunin, *God and the State*, pp. 9-10.

32. Ibid., p. 21.

33. Bakunin, "Philosophical Considerations," in Maximoff, *Political Philosophy*, pp. 100-101 (Bakunin's italics).

34. Bakunin, "The Paris Commune and the Idea of the State," in Lehning, *Selected Writings*, p. 196.

35. Bakunin, "Knouto-Germanic Empire," in Lehning, *Selected Writings*, p. 149.

36. Ibid.

37. Bakunin, "Federalism, Socialism, and Anti-Theologism," in Dolgoff, *Bakunin on Anarchy*, p. 106.

38. Bakunin, *God and the State*, p. 28.

39. Ibid.

40. Bakunin, "The Politics of the International," in K. J. Kenafick, *Michael Bakunin and Karl Marx* (Melbourne, 1948), p. 100.

41. Bakunin, "Progress of the Alliance," in Maximoff, *Political Philosophy*, p. 340.

42. Bakunin, "Knouto-Germanic Empire," in Dolgoff, *Bakunin on Anarchy*, p. 238.

43. Bakunin, "Knouto-Germanic Empire," in Maximoff, *Political Philosophy*, p. 241.

44. Ibid.

45. Bakunin, "Federalism, Socialism, and Anti-Theologism," in Maximoff, *Political Philosophy* p. 101 (Bakunin's italics).

46. Bakunin, "Integral Education," in Maximoff, *Political Philosophy*, p. 102.

47. Ibid., p. 101.

48. Bakunin, "Program of the Alliance," in Maximoff, *Political Philosophy*, p. 339.

49. Bakunin, "Philosophical Considerations," in Maximoff, *Political Philosophy*, p. 53.

50. Ibid.

51. Bakunin, "Federalism, Socialism, and Anti-Theologism," in Maximoff, *Political Philosophy*, p. 95.

52. Bakunin, *God and the State*, p. 28.

53. Bakunin, "Knouto-Germanic Empire," in Maximoff, *Political Philosophy*, p. 166.

54. Ibid., p. 158.

55. Bakunin, "Knouto-Germanic Empire," in Lehning, *Selected Writings*, p. 151.

56. Bakunin, "Knouto-Germanic Empire," in Maximoff, *Political Philosophy*, p. 166.

57. Bakunin, "Knouto-Germanic Empire," in Lehning, *Selected Writings*, p. 151.

58. Bakunin, "Federalism, Socialism, and Anti-Theologism," in Maximoff, *Political Philosophy*, p. 155.

59. Bakunin, "Knouto-Germanic Empire," in Lehning, *Selected Writings*, p. 154.

60. Bakunin, "Philosophical Considerations," in Lehning, *Selected Writings*, pp. 95-96.

61. Ibid.

62. Ibid., p. 91.

63. Ibid.

64. Bakunin, "The Political Theology of Mazzini," in Kenafick, *Bakunin and Marx*, p. 224.

65. Bakunin, "Knouto-Germanic Empire," in Maximoff, *Political Philosophy*, p. 165.

66. Bakunin, "The Intrigues of Mr. Utin," in Maximoff, *Political Philosophy*, p. 158.

67. Ibid., p. 159.

68. Bakunin, "Progress of the Alliance," in Maximoff, *Political Philosophy*, p. 339.

69. Bakunin, "Knouto-Germanic Empire," in Lehning, *Selected Writings*, p. 151.

70. Bakunin, *God and the State*, pp. 28-29 (Bakunin's italics).

71. Bakunin, "Philosophical Considerations," in Maximoff, *Political Philosophy*, p. 91.

72. Bakunin, "The Paris Commune and the Idea of the State," in Lehning, *Selected Writings*, p. 196.

73. Bakunin, "Federalism, Socialism, and Anti-Theologism," in Maximoff, *Political Philosophy*, p. 148.

74. Bakunin, "Protestation of the Alliance," in *Oeuvres*, ed. James Guillaume, 6 vols. (Paris: P. V. Stock, 1895-1913), 6:38.

75. Bakunin, "Politics of the International," in Kenafick, *Bakunin and Marx*, p. 101.

76. Bakunin, "Protestation of the Alliance," in Maximoff, *Political Philosophy*, p. 264.

77. Bakunin, "Protestation of the Alliance," in Guillaume, *Oeuvres*, 6:87.

78. Bakunin, "Politics of the International," in Kenafick, *Bakunin and Marx*, p. 101.

79. Bakunin, "Integral Education," in Maximoff, *Political Philosophy*, p. 330.

80. Bakunin, "Program of the Alliance," in Maximoff, *Political Philosophy*, p. 341.

81. Bakunin, "Knouto-Germanic Empire," in Dolgoff, *Bakunin on Anarchy*, p. 237.

82. Bakunin, "Knouto-Germanic Empire, in Maximoff," *Political Philosophy*, p. 165.

83. Bakunin, "Knouto-Germanic Empire," in Lehning, *Selected Writings*, p. 147.

84. Bakunin, "The Political Theology of Mazzini," in Kenafick, *Bakunin and Marx*, p. 227.

85. Bakunin, "The Paris Commune and the Idea of the State," in Lehning, *Selected Writings*, p. 197.

86. Bakunin, "Knouto-Germanic Empire," in Maximoff, *Political Philosophy*, pp. 339-40.

87. Bakunin, "Federalism, Socialism, and Anti-Theologism," in Maximoff, *Political Philosophy*, p. 94 (Bakunin's italics).

88. Bakunin, "Knouto-Germanic Empire," in Maximoff, *Political Philosophy*, p. 165.

89. Bakunin, "Program of the Alliance," in Maximoff, *Political Philosophy*, pp. 156-57.

90. Bakunin, in Pyziur, *Doctrine of Anarchism*, p. 121.

91. Ibid., p. 119.

92. Bakunin, "Federalism, Socialism, and Anti-Theologism," in Lehning, *Selected Writings*, p. 109.

93. Bakunin, in Pyziur, *Doctrine of Anarchism*, p. 120.

94. Bakunin, "Principles and Organization of the International Brotherhood," in Lehning, *Selected Writings*, p. 76.

95. Bakunin, "Philosophical Considerations," in Maximoff, *Political Philosophy*, p. 92.

96. Ibid., p. 104.

97. Bakunin, "Knouto-Germanic Empire," in Guillaume, *Oeuvres*, 1:294-95.

98. Bakunin, "Philosophical Considerations," in Maximoff, *Political Philosophy*, p. 104.

99. Bakunin, "Knouto-Germanic Empire," in Guillaume, *Oeuvres*, 1:294.

100. Bakunin, "Philosophical Considerations," in Maximoff, *Political Philosophy*, p. 104.

101. Ibid.

102. Bakunin, "Federalism, Socialism, and Anti-Theologism," in Maximoff, *Political Philosophy*, p. 95.

103. Ibid., p. 94.

104. Ibid.

105. Bakunin,, "Philosophical Considerations," in Maximoff, *Political Philosophy*, p. 97.

106. Ibid., p. 98.

107. Bakunin, "Federalism, Socialism, and Anti-Theologism," in Maximoff, *Political Philosophy*, p. 95.

108. Ibid (Bakunin's italics).

109. Bakunin, "Knouto-Germanic Empire," in Lehning, *Selected Writings*, p. 147.

110. Bakunin, "Intrigues of Mr. Utin," in Maximoff, *Political Philosophy*, p. 334.

111. Bakunin, *God and the State*, p. 41.

112. Bakunin, "Federalism, Socialism, and Anti-Theologism," in Maximoff, *Political Philosophy*, p. 93.

113. Ibid., pp. 93-94.

114. Bakunin, "Program of the Alliance," in Maximoff, *Political Philosophy*, p. 339.

115. Bakunin, in Kenafick, *Bakunin and Marx*, p. 104.

116. Bakunin, "Knouto-Germanic Empire," in Lehning, *Selected Writings*, p. 149.

117. Bakunin, "The Paris Commune and the Idea of the State," in Lehning, *Selected Writings*, p. 196.

118. Bakunin, "Knouto-Germanic Empire," in Lehning, *Selected Writings*, p. 149.

119. Ibid.

120. Bakunin, "Politics of the International," in Kenafick, *Bakunin and Marx*, p. 100.

121. Bakunin, "Program of the Alliance," in Maximoff, *Political Philosophy*, p. 340.

122. Ibid.

123. Bakunin, "Politics of the International," in Kenafick, *Bakunin and Marx*, p. 100.

124. Bakunin, "Knouto-Germanic Empire," in Lehning, *Selected Writings*, p. 152.

125. Bakunin, "Federalism, Socialism, and Anti-Theologism," in Guillaume, *Oeuvres*, 1:204.

126. Bakunin, "Principles and Organization of the International Brotherhood," in Lehning, *Selected Writings*, p. 67.

127. Bakunin, "Politics of the International," in Kenafick, *Bakunin and Marx*, pp. 194-95.

128. Bakunin, "Program of the Alliance," in Maximoff, *Political Philosophy*, p. 338.

129. Bakunin, "Knouto-Germanic Empire," in Maximoff, *Political Philosophy*, p. 253.

130. Ibid.

131. Ibid., p. 255.

132. Ibid., p. 254.

133. Ibid., p. 78.

134. Ibid., p. 259.

135. Ibid.

136. Ibid.

137. Ibid., pp. 259-60.

138. Ibid., p. 259.

139. Ibid., p. 260.

140. Ibid., pp. 253-54.

141. Ibid., p. 259.

142. Bakunin, "Principles and Organization of the International Brotherhood," in Lehning, *Selected Writings*, p. 65.

143. Bakunin, "1866 Revolutionary Catechism," in Dolgoff, *Bakunin on Anarchy*, p. 76.

144. Bakunin, "Knouto-Germanic Empire," in Lehning, *Selected Writings*, pp. 152-53.

145. Bakunin, "Knouto-Germanic Empire," in Maximoff, *Political Philosophy*, p. 260.

146. Ibid.

147. Ibid.

148. Ibid.

149. Bakunin, "Knouto-Germanic Empire," in Lehning, *Selected Writings*, p. 148.

150. Bakunin, "Philosophical Considerations," in Maximoff, *Political Philosophy*, p. 104.

151. Ibid., p. 96.

Chapter 3

1. Bakunin, "God and the State," in *Oeuvres* 1:288.

2. Bakunin, "Federalism, Socialism, and Anti-Theologism," in *Oeuvres* 1:171 (Bakunin's italics).

3. Bakunin, "Knouto-Germanic Empire," in Maximoff, *Political Philosophy*, p. 160.

4. Bakunin, "Federalism, Socialism, and Anti-Theologism," in Dolgoff, *Bakunin on Anarchy*, p. 144.

5. Bakunin, *Etatisme et Anarchie*, p. 222.

6. Bakunin, *Statism and Anarchism*, in Maximoff, *Political Philosophy*, p. 210.

7. Bakunin, "Knouto-Germanic Empire," in Kenafick, *Bakunin and Marx*, p. 45.

8. Bakunin, "Letter to the Internationalists of the Jura-Switzerland," in *Oeuvres* 1:226-27.

9. Ibid.

10. Bakunin, "Science and the Urgent Revolutionary Task," in Maximoff, *Political Philosophy*, p. 365.

11. Bakunin, "God and the State," in *Oeuvres* 1:324.

12. Bakunin, "Knouto-Germanic Empire," in Maximoff, *Political Philosophy*, p. 144.

13. Bakunin, "Federalism, Socialism, and Anti-Theologism," in Maximoff, *Political Philosophy*, p. 208.

14. Bakunin, "Knouto-Germanic Empire," in Lehning, *Selected Writings*, p. 151.

15. Bakunin, "Federalism, Socialism, and Anti-Theologism," in Lehning, *Selected Writings*, p. 95.

16. Bakunin, *Statism and Anarchism*, in Maximoff, *Political Philosophy*, p. 210.

17. Bakunin, "Federalism, Socialism, and Anti-Theologism," in Dolgoff, *Bakunin on Anarchy*, p. 137.

18. Bakunin, "The Bear of Berne and the Bear of St. Petersburg," in Maximoff, *Political Philosophy*, p. 141.

19. Bakunin, "Federalism, Socialism, and Anti-Theologism," in Lehning, *Selected Writings*, p. 103.

20. Bakunin, "Argument Against Marx," in Lehning, *Selected Writings*, p. 265 (Bakunin's italics).

21. Bakunin, "Federalism, Socialism, and Anti-Theologism," in Lehning, *Selected Writings*, p. 103.

22. Bakunin, *Statism and Anarchism*, in Maximoff, *Political Philosophy*, p. 212.

23. Bakunin, "Federalism, Socialism, and Anti-Theologism," in Lehning, *Selected Writings*, pp. 102-3.

24. Ibid., p. 103 (Bakunin's italics).

25. Bakunin, "Knouto-Germanic Empire," in *Oeuvres* 4:450.

26. Bakunin, "Letters to a Frenchman," in *Oeuvres* 2: 250.

27. Bakunin, *Statism and Anarchism*, in Maximoff, *Political Philosophy*, p. 211.

28. Bakunin, *Statism and Anarchism*, in Dolgoff, *Bakunin on Anarchy*, p. 337.

29. Bakunin, "Knouto-Germanic Empire," in *Oeuvres* 4: 493.

30. Bakunin, "Protestation of the Alliance," in Maximoff, *Political Philosophy*, p. 212.

31. Ibid., p. 213.

32. Ibid., p. 212.

33. Bakunin, "Knouto-Germanic Empire," in *Oeuvres* 4:493.

34. Bakunin, "The Bear of Berne and the Bear of St. Petersburg," in Maximoff, *Political Philosophy*, p. 256.

35. Bakunin, *Etatisme et Anarchie*, p. 244.

36. Ibid., pp. 242-43.

37. Bakunin, "Federalism, Socialism, and Anti-Theologism," in Maximoff, *Political Philosophy*, p. 224.

38. Bakunin, "Writing Against Marx," in Lehning, *Selected Writings*, p. 265 (Bakunin's italics).

39. Bakunin, "The Paris Commune and the Idea of the State," in Lehning, *Selected Writings*, p. 205.
40. Ibid.
41. Bakunin, *God and the State*, p. 84.
42. Ibid.
43. Bakunin, "Letters on Patriotism," in Maximoff, *Political Philosophy*, p. 227.
44. Ibid., p. 232.
45. Ibid.
46. Bakunin, "Letters to a Frenchman," in Maximoff, *Political Philosophy*, p. 233.
47. Bakunin, "Federalism, Socialism, and Anti-Theologism," in Lehning, *Selected Writings*, p. 136.
48. Ibid.
49. Ibid., pp. 136-37.
50. Ibid., p. 137.
51. Bakunin, "Federalism, Socialism, and Anti-Theologism," in *Oeuvres* 1:146.
52. Ibid., p. 159 (Bakunin's italics).
53. Bakunin, "Federalism, Socialism, and Anti-Theologism," in Lehning, *Selected Writings*, p. 138.
54. Ibid., p. 137.
55. Ibid., p. 138.
56. Bakunin, "The Paris Commune and the Idea of the State," in Lehning, *Selected Writings*, p. 207.
57. Bakunin, "Federalism, Socialism, and Anti-Theologism," in *Oeuvres* 1:159-60 (Bakunin's italics).
58. Ibid., p. 160.
59. Bakunin, "The Paris Commune and the Idea of the State," in Lehning, *Selected Writings*, p. 206.
60. Bakunin, "Knouto-Germanic Empire," in Lehning, *Selected Writings*, p. 140.
61. Bakunin, "Federalism, Socialism, and Anti-Theologism," in *Oeuvres* 1:149.
62. Ibid., p. 150.
63. Bakunin, "The Bear of Berne and the Bear of St. Petersburg," in Maximoff, *Political Philosophy*, p. 139.
64. Bakunin, "Federalism, Socialism, and Anti-Theologism," in *Oeuvres* 1:177 (Bakunin's italics).
65. Ibid., p. 148 (Bakunin's italics).
66. Bakunin, "The Bear of Berne and the Bear of St. Petersburg," in Maximoff, *Political Philosophy*, p. 139.
67. Bakunin, "Federalism, Socialism, and Anti-Theologism," in Maximoff, *Political Philosophy*, p. 75 (Bakunin's italics).
68. Bakunin, "Protestation of the Alliance," in Dolgoff, *Bakunin on Anarchy*, p. 152.
69. Bakunin, "Federalism, Socialism, and Anti-Theologism," in *Oeuvres* 1:155-56.
70. Bakunin, "Federalism, Socialism, and Anti-Theologism," in Maximoff, *Political Philosophy*, p. 75.

71. Bakunin, "Protestation of the Alliance," in Maximoff, *Political Philosophy*, p. 307.

72. Bakunin, "Knouto-Germanic Empire," in Lehning, *Selected Writings*, p. 158.

73. Ibid., p. 155.

74. Ibid., p. 158.

75. Ibid (Bakunin's italics).

76. Bakunin, "Knouto-Germanic Empire," in Maximoff, *Political Philosophy*, p. 70.

77. Ibid., p. 80.

78. Ibid., p. 70.

79. Bakunin, "Federalism, Socialism, and Anti-Theologism," in Maximoff, *Political Philosophy*, p. 59.

80. Bakunin, *God and the State*, p. 55.

81. Ibid., p. 62.

82. Bakunin, *Etatisme et Anarchie*, p. 383.

83. Bakunin, *God and the State*, pp. 60-61.

84. Bakunin, *Etatisme et Anarchie*, p. 311.

85. Bakunin, *God and the State*, p. 30.

86. Ibid., p. 59.

87. Ibid., pp. 31-32.

88. Bakunin, *Etatisme et Anarchie*, p. 311.

89. Bakunin, "Integral Education," in Maximoff, *Political Philosophy*, p. 196.

90. Bakunin, "The Lullers," in *Oeuvres* 5:117.

91. Bakunin, "The Lullers," in Maximoff, *Political Philosophy*, p. 82.

92. Bakunin, *God and the State*, p. 55 (Bakunin's italics).

93. Bakunin, "Knouto-Germanic Empire," in Maximoff, *Political Philosophy*, p. 70.

94. Bakunin, *God and the State*, p. 59 (Bakunin's italics).

95. Ibid., p. 62.

96. Ibid.

97. Bakunin, *Statism and Anarchism*, in *The Essential Works of Anarchism*, ed. Marshall Schatz (New York: Bantam Books, 1971), p. 157.

98. Bakunin, "Knouto-Germanic Empire," in Lehning, *Selected Writings*, p. 157.

99. Bakunin, *God and the State*, p. 63.

100. Ibid., p. 63.

101. Bakunin, *Etatisme et Anarchie*, p. 317.

102. Bakunin, "Letters to a Frenchman," in Lehning, *Selected Writings*, p. 233.

103. Ibid.

104. Bakunin, "Principles and Organization of the International," in Lehning, *Selected Writings*, p. 78.

105. Ibid.

106. Bakunin, "Federalism, Socialism, and Anti-Theologism," in Maximoff, *Political Philosophy*, p. 119.

107. Bakunin, "Report to the Commission on the Question of Inheritance Right," in Maximoff, *Political Philosophy*, p. 244.

108. Bakunin, "Philosophical Considerations," in Maximoff, *Political Philosophy*, pp. 183, 185.

109. Bakunin, "Protestation of the Alliance," in Maximoff, *Political Philosophy*, p. 306.

110. Bakunin, "Knouto-Germanic Empire," in Kenafick, *Bakunin and Marx*, p. 189.

111. Marx, *Grundrisse*, ed. and trans. David McLellan (New York: Harper & Row, 1971), p. 142.

112. Bakunin, *Etatisme et Anarchie*, p. 211.

113. Bakunin, *Statism and Anarchism*, in Maximoff, *Political Philosophy*, p. 184.

114. Ibid (Bakunin's italics).

115. Bakunin, "Protestation of the Alliance," in *Oeuvres* 6:60.

116. Bakunin, "Letters to a Frenchman," in Maximoff, *Political Philosophy*, p. 293.

117. Bakunin, "World Revolutionary Alliance of Social Democracy," in Maximoff, *Political Philosophy*, p. 385.

118. Marx, *Grundrisse*, p. 79.

119. Ibid., p. 115.

120. Bakunin, "Knouto-Germanic Empire," in Maximoff, *Political Philosophy*, p. 180.

121. Ibid.

122. Bakunin, "Federalism, Socialism and Anti-Theologism," in Maximoff, *Political Philosophy*, p. 191.

123. Bakunin, *Statism and Anarchism*, in Maximoff, *Political Philosophy*, p. 189.

124. Bakunin, "Science and the Urgent Revolutionary Task," in Maximoff, *Political Philosophy*, p. 355.

125. Ibid., p. 353.

126. Marx, *Grundrisse*, p. 131.

127. Ibid., pp. 131, 120-21, 18.

128. Bakunin, "Philosophical Considerations," in Maximoff, *Political Philosophy*, p. 187.

129. Bakunin, "Knouto-Germanic Empire," in Kenafick, *Bakunin and Marx*, p. 193.

130. Ibid.

131. Bakunin, "Program of the Alliance," in Maximoff, *Political Philosophy*, p. 342.

132. Ibid.

133. Bakunin, "Science and the Urgent Revolutionary Task," in Maximoff, *Political Philosophy*, p. 355.

134. Bakunin, "Knouto-Germanic Empire," in Maximoff, *Political Philosophy*, p. 343.

135. Bakunin, "Protestation of the Alliance," in Maximoff, *Political Philosophy*, p. 310.

136. Bakunin, "Federalism, Socialism, and Anti-Theologism," in Maximoff, *Political Philosophy*, p. 113.

137. Bakunin, "Protestation of the Alliance," in Maximoff, *Political Philosophy*, p. 310.

138. Bakunin, "Science and the Urgent Revolutionary Task," in Maximoff, *Political Philosophy*, p. 355.

139. Bakunin, "Report to the Commission on the Question of Inheritance Right," in Maximoff, *Political Philosophy*, p. 244.

140. Bakunin, "Principles and Organization of the International Brotherhood," in Lehning, *Selected Writings*, p. 80.

141. Bakunin, "Federalism, Socialism, and Anti-Theologism," in Maximoff, *Political Philosophy*, p. 192.

142. Bakunin, "Knouto-Germanic Empire," in Maximoff, *Political Philosophy*, p. 342.

143. Bakunin, "Principles and Organization of the International Brotherhood," in Lehning, *Selected Writings*, p. 82.

144. Bakunin, *Etatisme et Anarchie*, p. 221.

145. Bakunin, "The Lullers," in Maximoff, *Political Philosophy*, p. 197.

146. Bakunin, "The Bear of Berne and the Bear of St. Petersburg," in *Oeuvres* 2:39.

147. Bakunin, "Protestation of the Alliance," in Maximoff, *Political Philosophy*, p. 212.

148. Bakunin, "Knouto-Germanic Empire," in Lehning, *Selected Writings*, p. 153.

149. Bakunin, *Etatisme et Anarchie*, p. 347.

150. Bakunin, "The Bear of Berne and the Bear of St. Petersburg," in Maximoff, *Political Philosophy*, p. 218.

151. Bakunin, "Politics of the International," in Maximoff, *Political Philosophy*, p. 214.

152. Bakunin, "Knouto-Germanic Empire," in Maximoff, *Political Philosophy*, p. 215.

153. Bakunin, "The Bear of Berne and the Bear of St. Petersburg," in Maximoff, *Political Philosophy*, p. 220.

154. Ibid.

155. Bakunin, "Knouto-Germanic Empire," in Maximoff, *Political Philosophy*, p. 217.

156. Bakunin, "Germany and State Communism," in *Archives Bakounine*, Vol. II: *Michel Bakounine et les Conflits dans L'Internationale 1872*, ed. Arthur Lehning (Leiden: E. J. Brill, 1965), p. 109.

157. Bakunin, "The Bear of Berne and the Bear of St. Petersburg," in Maximoff, *Political Philosophy*, p. 219.

158. Ibid., p. 220.

159. Bakunin, "Protestation of the Alliance," in *Oeuvres* 6:33.

160. Bakunin, "Letter Composed at Marseilles," in Kenafick, *Bakunin and Marx*, p. 160.

161. Bakunin, "Protestation of the Alliance," in *Oeuvres* 6:34.

162. Bakunin, "Policy of the International," in *Oeuvres* 5:190 (Bakunin's italics).

163. Bakunin, "Knouto-Germanic Empire," in *Oeuvres* 4:439.

164. Bakunin, "Integral Education," in Maximoff, *Political Philosophy*, p. 336.

165. Bakunin, "Knouto-Germanic Empire," in Maximoff, *Political Philosophy*, p. 216.

166. Bakunin, "Letter to La Liberte," in Lehning, *Selected Writings*, p. 260.

167. Bakunin, "Integral Education," in Maximoff, *Political Philosophy*, p. 337.

168. Bakunin, "Protestation of the Alliance," in *Oeuvres* 6:35.

169. Bakunin, *Statism and Anarchism*, in Lehning, *Selected Writings*, p. 267.

170. Bakunin, "Knouto-Germanic Empire," in *Oeuvres* 4:445.

171. Bakunin, "Letters to a Frenchman," in Maximoff, *Political Philosophy*, p. 291.

172. Bakunin, "Letters to La Liberte," in Lehning, *Selected Writings*, p. 260.

Chapter 4

1. Bakunin, "Federalism, Socialism, and Anti-Theologism," in *Oeuvres* 1:59.

2. Bakunin, "Knouto-Germanic Empire," in Dolgoff, *Bakunin on Anarchy*, p. 301.

3. Bakunin, "Organization of the International," in Maximoff, *Political Philosophy*, p. 374.

4. Bakunin, "Knouto-Germanic Empire," in *Oeuvres* 4:415.

5. Bakunin, "Protestation of the Alliance," in Maximoff, *Political Philosophy*, p. 302.

6. Ibid., p. 311.

7. Bakunin, "A Circular Letter to My Friends in Italy," in Maximoff, *Political Philosophy*, p. 377.

8. Bakunin, "Knouto-Germanic Empire," in Maximoff, *Political Philosophy*, p. 217.

9. Bakunin, "Politics of the International," in *Oeuvers* 5:179.

10. Bakunin, *Statism and Anarchism*, in Maximoff, *Political Philosophy*, p. 376.

11. Bakunin, "Politics of the International," in Maximoff, *Political Philosophy*, p. 315.

12. Bakunin, "Science and the Urgent Revolutionary Task," in Maximoff, *Political Philosophy*, p. 361.

13. Bakunin, "Politics of the International," in Maximoff, *Political Philosophy*, p. 315.

14. Bakunin, "Knouto-Germanic Empire," in *Political Philosophy*, p. 369.

15. Bakunin, "Knouto-Germanic Empire," in *Oeuvres* 4: 451.

16. Bakunin, *Etatisme et Anarchie*, p. 369.

17. Bakunin, "Knouto-Germanic Empire," in *Oeuvres* 4:451.

18. Bakunin, *Statism and Anarchy*, in Schatz, *Essential Works*, p. 167.

19. Bakunin, "Intrigues of Mr. Utin," in Maximoff, *Political Philosophy*, p. 335.

20. Bakunin, "Letters to a Frenchman," in Dolgoff, *Bakunin on Anarchy*, p. 194.

21. Bakunin, "Knouto-Germanic Empire," in *Oeuvres* 4:453-54.

22. Ibid., p. 454.

23. Ibid., p. 453.

24. Ibid., p. 463.

25. Pyziur, *Doctrine of Anarchism*, p. 65.

26. Bakunin, "Science and the Urgent Revolutionary Task," in Maximoff, *Political Philosophy*, p. 360.

27. Ibid.

28. Ibid.

29. Bakunin, "Letters of a Frenchman," in *Oeuvres* 4:29.

30. Bakunin, "Knouto-Germanic Empire," in Maximoff, *Political Philosophy*, p. 215.

31. Bakunin, "The Political Theology of Mazzini," in Kenafick, *Bakunin and Marx*, p. 220.

32. Bakunin, "Knouto-Germanic Empire," in Maximoff, *Political Philosophy*, p. 215.

33. Bakunin, "Federalism, Socialism, and Anti-Theologism," in Lehning, *Selected Writings*, p. 104.

34. Bakunin, "Letters to a Frenchman," in Maximoff, *Political Philosophy*, p. 371.

35. Bakunin, *Statism and Anarchism*, in Maximoff, *Political Philosophy*,, p. 370.

36. Bakunin, "Science and the Urgent Revolutionary Task," in Maximoff, *Political Philosophy*, p. 357.

37. Bakunin, "Politics of the International," in Maximoff, *Political Philosophy*, p. 315.

38. Bakunin, "Science and the Urgent Revolutionary Task," in Maximoff, *Political Philosophy*, p. 351.

39. Ibid.

40. Ibid.

41. Ibid., p. 352.

42. Bakunin, "Letters to a Frenchman," in Maximoff, *Political Philosophy*, p. 378.

43. Bakunin, *God and the State*, p. 64.

44. Bakunin, "Science and the Urgent Revolutionary Task," in Maximoff, *Political Philosophy*, p. 355.

45. Bakunin, "Politics of the International, in Maximoff, in *Political Philosophy*, p. 315.

46. Bakunin, "Letters to a Frenchman," in *Oeuvres* 4:19-20.

47. Bakunin, "Protestation of the Alliance," in Maximoff, *Political Philosophy*, p. 308.

48. Ibid.

49. Bakunin, "Knouto-Germanic Empire," in *Oeuvres* 4:452.

50. Bakunin, "Letters to a Frenchman," in Maximoff, *Political Philosophy*, p. 397.

51. Bakunin, *Etatisme et Anarchie*, p. 309.

52. Bakunin, *Statism and Anarchism*, in Dolgoff, *Bakunin on Anarchy*, p. 327.

53. Bakunin, "Programme and Purpose of the Revolutionary Organization of International Brothers," in Lehning, *Selected Writings*, p. 172.

54. Bakunin, *Les Conflits dans L'Internationale*, pp. 75-76.

55. Bakunin, "Politics of the International," in *Oeuvres* 5:197.

56. Bakunin, "Programme and Purpose of the Revolutionary Organization of International Brothers," in Lehning, *Selected Writings*, p. 172.

57. Bakunin, "Protestation of the Alliance," in Maximoff, *Political Philosophy*, p. 302.

58. Bakunin, letter to Nechaev of June 2, 1870, in Lehning, *Selected Writings*, p. 183.

59. Bakunin, "Principles and Organization of the International Brotherhood," in Lehning, *Selected Writings*, p. 92.

60. Bakunin, "A Circular Letter to My Friends in Italy," in Maximoff, *Political Philosophy*, p. 377.

61. Bakunin, *Statism and Anarchism*, in Maximoff, *Political Philosophy*, p. 202.

62. Ibid., pp. 202-3.

63. Bakunin, "Programme and Purpose of the Revolutionary Organization of International Brothers," in Lehning, *Selected Writings*, p. 170.

64. Murray Bookchin, *Post-Scarcity Anarchism* (Berkeley: Ramparts Press, 1971), p. 14.

65. Bakunin, "Letters to a Frenchman," in *Oeuvres* 2:227-28.

66. Ibid., pp. 234-35.

67. Bakunin, "Letters to a Frenchman," in Maximoff, *Political Philosophy*, p. 395.

68. Bakunin, "Letters to a Frenchman," in *Oeuvres* 2:228.

69. Bakunin, "Letters to a Frenchman," in Maximoff, *Political Philosophy*, p. 401.

70. Bakunin, letter to Nechaev of June 2, 1870, in Lehning, *Selected Writings*, p. 191 (Bakunin's italics).

71. Bakunin, in Pyziur, *Doctrine of Anarchism*, p. 129.

72. Bakunin, in Nomad, *Apostles of Revolution*, p. 228.

73. Bakunin, letter to Nechaev of June 2, 1870, in Lehning, *Selected Writings*, p. 188.

74. Bakunin, "Programme and Purpose of the Revolutionary Organization of International Brothers," in Lehning, *Selected Writings*, p. 172.

75. Bakunin, "Protestation of the Alliance," in *Oeuvres* 6:86.

76. Ibid.

77. Ibid., pp. 85-86.

78. Bakunin, letter to Nechaev of June 2, 1870, in Lehning, *Selected Writings*, p. 193.

79. Bakunin, "Protestation of the Alliance," in Maximoff, *Political Philosophy*, p. 317.

80. Ibid.

81. Bakunin, *God and the State*, p. 33.

82. Bakunin, letter to Nechaev of June 2, 1870, in Lehning, *Selected Writings*, p. 191.

83. Bakunin, "Principles and Organization of the International Brotherhood," in Lehning, *Selected Writings*, p. 72.

84. Bakunin, "Letters to a Frenchman," in Maximoff, *Political Philosophy*, p. 398.

85. Bakunin, "Report on the Alliance," in Maximoff, *Political Philosophy*, p. 317.

86. Bakunin, letter to Albert Richard of April 1, 1870, in Maximoff, *Political Philosophy*, pp. 379-80.

87. Ibid., p. 379.

88. Bakunin, "A Circular Letter to My Friends in Italy," in Maximoff, *Political Philosophy*, p. 380.

89. Bakunin, "Principles and Organization of the International Brotherhood," in Lehning, *Selected Writings*, p. 93.

90. Bakunin, in Pyziur, *Doctrine of Anarchism*, p. 89.

91. Bakunin, *Statism and Anarchy*, in Schatz, *Essential Works*, pp. 182-83.

92. Bakunin, "Principles and Organization of the International Brotherhood," in Lehning, *Selected Writings*, p. 93.

93. Ibid.

94. Ibid., p. 87.

95. Bakunin, "Programme and Purpose of the Revolutionary Organization of International Brothers," in Lehning, *Selected Writings*, p. 172.

96. Bakunin, "Principles and Organization of the International Brotherhood," in Lehning, *Selected Writings*, p. 93.

97. Bakunin, letter to Nechaev of June 2, 1870, in Lehning, *Selected Writings*, p. 189.

98. Ibid., p. 194.

99. Bakunin, letter to Albert Richard of April 1, 1870, in Lehning, *Selected Writings*, p. 180.

100. Bakunin, letter to Nechaev of June 2, 1870, in Lehning, *Selected Writings*, p. 194.

101. Bakunin, "A Circular Letter to My Friends in Italy," in Kenafick, *Bakunin and Marx*, pp. 244-45.

102. Bakunin, letter to Albert Richard of April 1, 1870, in Lehning, *Selected Writings*, p. 181.

103. Ibid., pp. 181-82.

104. Ibid., p. 181.

105. Bakunin, "A Circular Letter to My Friends in Italy," in Maximoff, *Political Philosophy*, p. 374.

106. Bakunin, "A Circular Letter to My Friends in Italy," in Kenafick, *Bakunin and Marx*, pp. 244-45.

107. Bakunin, "To All These Gentlemen," in Nomad, *Apostles of Revolution*, pp. 193-94.

108. Bakunin, letter to Albert Richard of April 1, 1870, in Lehning, *Selected Writings*, p. 181.

109. Bakunin, letter to Nechaev of June 2, 1870, in Lehning, *Selected Writings*, p. 192.

110. Ibid., pp. 192-93 (Bakunin's italics).

111. Cincinnatus was a Roman farmer and general who lived about 450 B.C. Twice called from his farm to lead the army into battle, he twice voluntarily surrendered his military command and returned to his farm.

112. Bakunin, "Programme and Purpose of the Revolutionary Organization of International Brothers," in Lehning, *Selected Writings*, p. 172.

113. Bakunin, "A Circular Letter to My Friends in Italy," in Maximoff, *Political Philosophy*, p. 380.

114. Bakunin, letter to Nechaev of June 2, 1870, in Lehning, *Selected Writings*, p. 189.

115. Ibid., p. 190.

116. Ibid.

117. Bakunin, "Letters to a Frenchman," in *Oeuvres* 4:19.

118. Alan B. Spitzer, *Old Hatreds and Young Hopes: The French Carbonari against the Bourbon Restoration* (Cambridge: Harvard University Press, 1971), p. 230.

119. Ibid., pp. 232-33.

120. George Lichtheim, *The Origins of Socialism* (New York: Praeger, 1969), p. 167.

121. Frederick Engels, in his introduction to the 1888 edition of the *Communist Manifesto.*

122. Pope Leo XIII, in Julius Braunthal, *History of the International*, vol. 1: 1864-1914 (New York: Praeger, 1961), p. 162.

123. Bakunin, "Paris Commune and the Idea of the State," in Lehning, *Selected Writings*, p. 200.

124. Bakunin, letter to Nechaev of June 2, 1870, in Lehning, *Selected Writings*, p. 188.

125. James Guillaume, in Carr, *Bakunin*, p. 371.

126. Bakunin, letter to Nechaev of June 2, 1870, in Lehning, *Selected Writings*, p. 182.

127. Bakunin, "Philosophical Considerations," in Maximoff, *Political Philosophy*, p. 413.

128. Bakunin, "1866 National Catechism," in Dolgoff, *Bakunin on Anarchy*, p. 100.

129. Bakunin, "The Bear of Berne and the Bear of St. Petersburg," in Maximoff, *Political Philosophy*, p. 372.

130. Bakunin, "A Circular Letter to My Friends in Italy," in Maximoff, *Political Philosophy*, p. 413.

131. Bakunin, "Programme and Purpose of the Revolutionary Organization of International Brothers," in Lehning, *Selected Writings*, p. 168.

132. Bakunin, "Letter Composed at Marseilles," in Kenafick, *Bakunin and Marx*, p. 125.

133. Bakunin, "A Circular Letter to My Friends in Italy," in Maximoff, *Political Philosophy*, p. 413.

134. Bakunin, "Programme and Purpose of the Revolutionary Organization of International Brothers," in Lehning, *Selected Writings*, p. 167.

135. Bakunin, "Philosophical Considerations," in Maximoff, *Political Philosophy*, p. 414.

136. Bakunin, "Programme and Purpose of the Revolutionary Organization of International Brothers," in Lehning, *Selected Writings*, p. 168.

137. Bakunin, "Letter Composed at Marseilles," in Kenafick, *Bakunin and Marx*, p. 125.

138. Bakunin, "Letters to a Frenchman," in Maximoff, *Political Philosophy*, p. 399.

139. Bakunin, "Philosophical Considerations," in Maximoff, *Political Philosophy*, p. 414.

140. Bakunin, "Programme and Purpose of the Revolutionary Organization of International Brothers," in Lehning, *Selected Writings*, p. 168.

141. Bakunin, "Philosophical Considerations," in Maximoff, *Political Philosophy*, p. 413.

142. Bakunin, letter to Nechaev of June 2, 1870, in Lehning, *Selected Writings*, p. 183.

143. Bakunin, "Protestation of the Alliance," in *Oeuvres* 6:79.

144. Bakunin, "The Lullers," in Maximoff, *Political Philosophy*, p. 270.

145. Bakunin, "A Circular Letter to My Friends in Italy," in Maximoff, *Political Philosophy*, p. 413.

146. Bakunin, "Programme and Purpose of the Revolutionary Organization of International Brothers," in Lehning, *Selected Writings*, p. 169.

147. Bakunin, "1866 National Catechism," in Dolgoff, *Bakunin on Anarchy*, p. 100.

148. Bakunin, "The Paris Commune and the Idea of the State," in Maximoff, *Political Philosophy*, p. 373.

149. Bakunin, *Statism and Anarchism*, in Maximoff, *Political Philosophy*, p. 381.

150. Bakunin, "1866 National Catechism," in Dolgoff, *Bakunin on Anarchy*, p. 100.

151. Bakunin, in Franco Venturi, *Roots of Revolution* (New York: Grosset and Dunlap, 1966), p. 369.

152. Bakunin, "Letter Composed at Marseilles," in Kenafick, *Bakunin and Marx*, p. 125.

153. Bakunin, "Programme and Purpose of the Revolutionary Organization of International Brothers," in Lehning, *Selected Writings*, p. 167.

154. Bakunin, "A Circular Letter to My Friends in Italy," in Maximoff, *Political Philosophy*, p. 377.

155. Bakunin, *Statism and Anarchism*, Maximoff, *Political Philosophy*, p. 381.

156. Ibid.

157. Bakunin, "Protestation of the Alliance," in Maximoff, *Political Philosophy*, p. 381.

158. Ibid.

159. Bakunin, "Philosophical Considerations," in Maximoff, *Political Philosophy*, p. 413.

160. Ibid.

161. Bakunin, "World Revolutionary Alliance of Social Democracy," in Maximoff, *Political Philosophy*, p. 283.

162. Bakunin, "Philosophical Considerations," in Maximoff, *Political Philosophy*, pp. 413-14.

163. Bakunin, "Programme and Purpose of the Revolutionary Organization of International Brothers," in Lehning, *Selected Writings*, p. 169.

164. Bakunin, "Knouto-Germanic Empire," in Maximoff, *Political Philosophy*, p. 134.

165. Bakunin, *Statism and Anarchism*, in Dolgoff, *Bakunin on Anarchy*, p. 347.

166. Bakunin, in Venturi, *Roots of Revolution*, p. 369.

167. Bakunin, letter to Nechaev of June 2, 1870, in Lehning, *Selected Writings*, p. 184.

168. Ibid., p. 185.

169. Ibid.

170. Bakunin, cited in Venturi, *Roots of Revolution*, p. 369.

171. Bakunin, letter to Nechaev of June 2, 1870, in Lehning, *Selected Writings*, p. 187.

172. Ibid.

173. Roland Mousnier, *Peasant Uprisings in Seventeenth-Century France, Russia, and China*, trans. Brian Pearce (New York: Harper and Row, 1970), pp. 159ff.

174. Ibid., p. 160.

175. Ibid., p. 223.

176. Ibid.

177. Ibid., p. 227.
178. George Lichtheim, *The Origins of Socialism* (New York: Praeger, 1969), p. 169.
179. Malia, *Birth of Russian Socialism*, p. 59.
180. Pyziur, *Doctrine of Anarchism*, pp. 3, 84.
181. Paul Avrich, *The Russian Anarchists* (Princeton: Princeton University Press, 1971), p. 27.
182. Avrich, in his preface to Dolgoff, *Bakunin on Anarchy*, p. xvi.
183. Pyziur, *Doctrine of Anarchism*, p. 3.
184. Georges Sorel, *Reflections on Violence*, trans. T. E. Hulme and J. Roth (New York: Collier, 1970), p. 115.
185. Tony Smith, "Idealism and People's War," *Political Theory* 1(November 1973): 442.
186. Venturi, *Roots of Revolution*, p. 362.
187. Nechaev, "1868 Catechism," in Venturi, *Roots of Revolution*, p. 363.
188. Venturi, *Roots of Revolution*, p. 363.
189. Ibid., p. 383.
190. Nechaev, "1869 Catechism," in Nomad, *Apostles of Revolution*, p. 232.
191. Venturi, *Roots of Revolution*, pp. 370, 434.
192. Bakunin, in Venturi, *Roots of Revolution*, p. 386.
193. Bakunin, letter to Talandier of July 24, 1870, in Kenafick, *Bakunin and Marx*, p. 128.
194. Bakunin, letter to Nechaev of June 2, 1870, in Lehning, *Selected Writings*, pp. 189-90 (Bakunin's italics).
195. Ibid., pp. 184, 190.
196. Ibid., p. 191.
197. Bakunin, letter to Herzen and Ogarev of July 19, 1866, in Lehning, *Selected Writings*, pp. 61-62.
198. Bakunin, letter to Nechaev of June 2, 1870, in Lehning, *Selected Writings*, p. 187.
199. Bakunin, letter to Talandier of July 24, 1870, in *Les Conflicts dans L'Internationale*, p. xlix.
200. Bakunin, letter to Ogarev of November, 1872, in Nomad, *Apostles of Revolution*, p. 251.
201. Michael Sazhin, *Reminiscences*, in Nomad, *Apostles of Revolution*, p. 247.
202. James Guillaume, "Michael Bakunin: A Biographical Sketch," in Dolgoff, *Bakunin on Anarchy*, p. 40.
203. Bakunin, letter to Guillaume of April 13, 1869, in Venturi, *Roots of Revolution*, p. 364.
204. Bakunin, letter to Nechaev of June 2, 1870, in Lehning, *Selected Writings*, p. 190.
205. Bakunin, "Policy of the International," in Kenafick, *Bakunin and Marx*, p. 91.
206. Bakunin, "Protestation of the Alliance," in *Oeuvres* 6:84.
207. Ibid., p. 71.
208. Bakunin, "Protestation of the Alliance," in Maximoff, *Political Philosophy*, p. 303.
209. Bakunin, "Protestation of the Alliance," in *Oeuvres* 6:72.

210. Bakunin, "Politics of the International," in Dolgoff, *Bakunin on Anarchy*, p. 165.

211. Bakunin, "Protestation of the Alliance," in *Oeuvres* 6:71.

212. Bakunin, "Letters to a Frenchman," in *Oeuvres* 2:168.

213. Bakunin, "Knouto-Germanic Empire," in *Oeuvres* 4:414.

214. Bakunin, "Politics of the International," in Maximoff, *Political Philosophy*, p. 312.

215. Bakunin, "Knouto-Germanic Empire," in *Oeuvres* 4:414.

216. Bakunin, "Letters to a Frenchman," in Maximoff, *Political Philosophy*, p. 204.

217. Bakunin, "Politics of the International," in Maximoff, *Political Philosophy*, p. 323.

218. Bakunin, "Knouto-Germanic Empire," in *Oeuvres* 4:421.

219. Bakunin, "Protestation of the Alliance," in *Oeuvres* 6:56.

220. Bakunin, "Protestation of the Alliance," in Maximoff, *Political Philosophy*, p. 307.

221. Bakunin, "Politics of the International," in Maximoff, *Political Philosophy*, p. 323.

222. Bakunin, "Protestation of the Alliance," in *Oeuvres* 6:75.

223. Ibid.

224. Ibid., pp. 75-76.

225. Bakunin, "Protestation of the Alliance," in Maximoff, *Political Philosophy*, p. 303.

226. Ibid.

227. Bakunin, "Report on the Alliance," in Maximoff, *Political Philosophy*, p. 321.

228. Bakunin, "A Circular Letter to My Friends in Italy," in Maximoff, *Political Philosophy*, p. 321.

229. Bakunin, "Protestation of the Alliance," in Maximoff, *Political Philosophy*, p. 320.

230. Ibid.

231. Ibid.

232. Bakunin, "World Revolutionary Alliance of Social Democracy," in Maximoff, *Political Philosophy*, p. 384.

233. Ibid.

234. Ibid.

235. Ibid.

236. Bakunin, "Politics of the International," in Maximoff, *Political Philosophy*, p. 321.

237. Bakunin, "The Double Strike in Geneva," in Maximoff, *Political Philosophy*, p. 322.

238. Bakunin, "Germany and State Communism," in *Les Conflicts dans L'Internationale*, p. 119.

239. Bakunin, "Letters to a Frenchman," in *Oeuvres* 2:246.

240. Ibid.

241. Ibid., p. 236.

242. Bakunin, "Letters to a Frenchman," in Maximoff, *Political Philosophy*, p. 203.

243. Bakunin, "Letters to a Frenchman," in *Oeuvres* 4:17-18.
244. Bakunin, "Letters to a Frenchman," in *Oeuvres* 2:221.
245. Bakunin, "Letters to a Frenchman," in *Oeuvres* 4:16.
246. Bakunin, "Letters to a Frenchman," in *Oeuvres* 2:229.
247. Ibid., pp. 229-30.
248. Ibid., p. 229.
249. Ibid., p. 219.
250. Bakunin, "Letters to a Frenchman," in Maximoff, *Political Philosophy*, p. 399.
251. Bakunin, "Letters to a Frenchman," in *Oeuvres* 2:240.
252. Ibid., p. 222.
253. Ibid., p. 217.
254. Ibid., p. 229.
255. Ibid., p. 242.
256. Ibid., p. 230.
257. Ibid., p. 242.

Chapter 5

1. Bakunin, *Statism and Anarchism*, in Maximoff, *Political Philosophy*, pp. 283-84.
2. Bakunin, *Etatisme et Anarchie*, p. 317.
3. Bakunin, "Letter to La Liberté," in Lehning, *Selected Writings*, p. 254.
4. Ibid.
5. Bakunin, "Knouto-Germanic Empire," in *Oeuvres* 4:462.
6. Bakunin, "Writing against Marx," in Lehning, *Selected Writings*, pp. 263-64.
7. Bakunin, *Etatisme et Anarchie*, p. 321.
8. Bakunin, "Knouto-Germanic Empire," in *Oeuvres* 4:461.
9. Ibid., pp. 456-57.
10. Feuerbach, *Towards a Critique of Hegel's Philosophy*, in Hanfi, "Introduction," *The Fiery Brook*, pp. 13-14.
11. Bakunin, *Statism and Anarchism*, in Maximoff, *Political Philosophy*, p. 237.
12. Bakunin, "Federalism, Socialism, and Anti-Theologism," in Lehning, *Selected Writings*, p. 103.
13. Bakunin, letter to Herzen of October, 1869, in James Joll, *The Anarchists* (New York: Grosset and Dunlap, 1966), p. 105.
14. Bakunin, "Writing Against Marx," in Lehning, *Selected Writings*, p. 264.
15. Bakunin, "Letter to La Liberté," in Lehning, *Selected Writings*, p. 253.
16. Bakunin, "Letters to a Frenchman," in *Oeuvres* 4:61-62 (Bakunin's italics).
17. Bakunin, "Writing Against Marx," in Lehning, *Selected Writings*, p. 266.
18. Ibid.
19. Bakunin, *Statism and Anarchism*, in Maximoff, *Political Philosophy*, p. 287.
20. Bakunin, *Statism and Anarchy*, in Lehning, *Selected Writings*, p. 270.
21. Bakunin, *Statism and Anarchism*, in Maximoff, *Political Philosophy*, p. 211.
22. Bakunin, "Letter to La Liberté," in Lehning, *Selected Writings*, p. 258.
23. Bakunin, "Paris Commune and the State," in Lehning, *Selected Writings*, p. 196.
24. Bakunin, "Paris Commune and the State," in Maximoff, *Political Philosophy*, p. 300.
25. Bakunin, *Statism and Anarchism*, in Maximoff, *Political Philosophy*, p. 284.

26. Bakunin, "Writing against Marx," in Lehning, *Selected Writings*, p. 266.
27. Bakunin, *Statism and Anarchism*, in Maximoff, *Political Philosophy*, p. 289.
28. Bakunin, "Letter to the Comrades of the Jura Federation," in *Les Conflits dans L'Internationale*, p. 28.
29. Bakunin, "Writing against Marx," in Lehning, *Selected Writings*, p. 266.
30. Bakunin, "Letter to La Liberté," in Lehning, *Selected Writings* p. 259.
31. Bakunin, "Writing against Marx," in Lehning, *Selected Writings*, p. 264.
32. Ibid (Bakunin's italics).
33. Bakunin, *Statism and Anarchism*, in Maximoff, *Political Philosophy*, p. 287.
34. Ibid.
35. Bakunin, "Letter to La Liberté," in Lehning, *Selected Writings*, p. 255.
36. Bakunin, *Statism and Anarchism*, in Maximoff, *Political Philosophy*, p. 284.
37. Ibid., p. 287.
38. Bakunin, "Protestation of the Alliance," in Maximoff, *Political Philosophy*, p. 286.
39. Bakunin, letter to Herzen of October, 1869, in Joll, *The Anarchists*, p. 105.
40. Shlomo Avineri, *The Social and Political Thought of Karl Marx* (New York: Cambridge University Press, 1968), p. 16.
41. Ibid., p. 15.
42. Ibid., p. 37.
43. Ibid., p. 24.
44. Ibid., p. 57.
45. Ibid., pp. 62, 63.
46. Ibid., p. 59.
47. Marx, *Grundrisse*, p. 70.
48. Avineri, *Social and Political Thought*, pp. 206-7.
49. Ibid., p. 61.
50. Ibid., p. 37.
51. Marx, *Critique of Hegel's Philosophy of Right*, in Avineri, *Social and Political Thought*, pp. 36-7.
52. Avineri, *Social and Political Thought*, p. 38.
53. Ibid., p. 213.
54. Bakunin, "Letter to La Liberté," in Lehning, *Selected Writings*, p. 259.

Chapter 6

1. Max Weber, *The Theory of Social and Economic Organization*, edited with an Introduction by Talcott Parsons (New York: Free Press, 1947), p. 339.
2. Bakunin, "Federalism, Socialism, and Anti-Theologism," in Lehning, *Selected Writings*, p. 95.
3. Murray Bookchin, *Post-Scarcity Anarchism* (Berkeley: Ramparts Press, 1971).
4. Murray Bookchin, "Beyond Neo-Marxism," *Telos* No. 36 (Summer 1978): 5-28.

Bibliography

Source Materials

Bakunin, Michael, *Archives Bakounine*. Arranged and edited by Arthur Lehning. 3 volumes. Volume 1: *Michel Bakounine et Italie, 1871-72*. Volume 2: *Michel Bakounine et les Conflits dans L'Internationale, 1872*. Volume 3: *Etatisme et Anarchie*, translated by Marcel Brody. Leiden: E. J. Brill, 1961-1967.

Bakunin, Michael, *God and the State*. Translated by Benjamin Tucker, with a new Introduction and Index of Persons by Paul Avrich. New York: Dover Press, 1970.

Bakunin, Michael. *Oeuvres*. Edited by James Guillaume. 6 volumes. Paris: P. V. Stock, 1895-1913.

Dolgoff, Sam, ed. and trans. *Bakunin on Anarchy*. New York: Vintage Books, Random House, 1971.

Lehning, Arthur, ed. *Michael Bakunin: Selected Writings*. Translated by Steven Cox and Olive Stevens. New York: Grove Press, 1973.

Maximoff, G. P., comp. and ed. *The Political Philosophy of Bakunin: Scientific Anarchism*. New York: Free Press, 1964.

Schatz, Marshall, ed. and trans. *The Essential Works of Anarchism*. New York: Bantam Books, 1971.

Intellectual and Historical Sources

Avineri, Shlomo. *The Social and Political Thought of Karl Marx*. New York: Cambridge University Press, 1968.

Avrich, Paul. *Bakunin and Nechaev*. London: Freedom Press, 1974.

Avrich, Paul. *The Russian Anarchists*. Princeton: Princeton University Press, 1971.

Beecher, Jonathan, and Bienvenu, Richard, ed. and trans. *The Utopian Vision of Charles Fourier*. Boston: Beacon Press, 1972.

Berlin, Isaiah. *Karl Marx*. New York: Oxford University Press, 1963.

Berlin, Isaiah. *Russian Thinkers*. New York: Oxford University Press, 1978.

Bookchin, Murray. *Post-Scarcity Anarchism*. Berkeley: Ramparts Press, 1971.

Bookchin, Murray. "Beyond Neo-Marxism." *Telos* No. 36 (Summer 1978): 5-28.

Braunthal, Julius. *History of the International*. Volume 1: *1864-1914*. New York: Praeger, 1961.

Buber, Martin. *Paths in Utopia*. Translated by R.F.C. Hull with an Introduction by Ephraim Fischoff. Boston: Beacon Press, 1970.

Burkhardt, Richard. *The Spirit of System*. Cambridge: Harvard University Press, 1977.

Camus, Albert. *The Rebel*. Translated by Anthony Bower with a Foreword by Sir Herbert Reed. New York: Vintage Books, Random House, 1956.

Carr, Edward Hallett. *Bakunin*. New York: Vintage Books, Random House, 1961.

Cassirer, Ernst. *Rousseau, Kant, and Goethe*. Translated by James Gutmann, Paul Kristeller, and John Randall, Jr., with an Introduction by Peter Gay. New York: Harper and Row, 1963.

Edwards, Stewart, ed. *Selected Writings of P.-J. Proudhon*. Translated by Elizabeth Fraser. Garden City: Doubleday Anchor, 1969.

Fichte, Johann Gottleib. *Addresses to the German Nation*. Edited with an Introduction by George Armstrong Kelly. New York: Harper and Row, 1968.

Findlay, John Niemeyer. *The Philosophy of Hegel: An Introduction and Re-Examination*. New York: Collier Books, 1966.

Guerin, Daniel. *Anarchism*. Translated by Mary Klopper, with an Introduction by Noam Chomsky. New York: Monthly Review Press, 1970.

Habermas, Jurgen. *Toward a Rational Society*. Translated by Jeremy J. Shapiro. Boston: Beacon Press, 1971.

Hanfi, Zawar, ed. and trans. *The Fiery Brook: Selected Writings of Ludwig Feuerbach*. Garden City: Doubleday Anchor, 1972.

Himmelfarb, Gertrude. *Darwin and the Darwinian Revolution*. New York: W.W. Norton, 1968.

Jellinek, Frank. *The Paris Commune of 1871*. New York: Grosset and Dunlap, 1965.

Joll, James. *The Anarchists*. New York: Grosset and Dunlap, 1966.

Kenafick, Kenneth J. *Michael Bakunin and Karl Marx*. Melbourne, 1948.

Kohn, Hans. *Pan-Slavism: Its History and Ideology*. New York: Vintage Books, Random House, 1960.

Kramnick, Isaac. "On Anarchism and the Real World: William Godwin and Radical England." *American Political Science Review* 66 (March 1972): 114-28.

Kropotkin, Peter. *The Great French Revolution*. Translated by N. F.Dryhurst. New York: Schocken Books, 1971.

Kropotkin, Peter. *Selected Writings on Anarchism and Revolution*. Edited and Introduced by Martin A. Miller. Cambridge: M.I.T. Press, 1970.

Lichtheim, George. *Marxism*. New York: Praeger, 1965.

Lichtheim, George. *The Origins of Socialism*. New York:, Praeger, 1969.

Lichtheim, George. *A Short History of Socialism*. New York: Praeger, 1971.

Lowith, Karl. *From Hegel to Nietzsche*. Translated by David Green. Garden City: Anchor Doubleday, 1967.

Lukacs, Georg. *History and Class Consciousness.* Translated by Rodney Livingstone. Cambridge: M.I.T. Press, 1972.

Luxemburg, Rosa. *The Russian Revolution and Leninism or Marxism?* Introduced by Bertram Wolfe. Ann Arbor: Ann Arbor Paperbacks, University of Michigan Press, 1970.

McLellan, David. "Marx's View of the Unalienated Society." *Review of Politics* 31 (October 1969): 459-65.

Malia, Martin. *Alexander Herzen and the Birth of Russian Socialism.* New York: Grosset and Dunlap, 1971.

Mannheim, Karl. *Ideology and Utopia.* Translated by Louis Wirth and Edward Shils. New York: Harcourt, Brace and World, 1936.

Marcuse, Herbert. *An Essay on Liberation.* Boston: Beacon Press, 1969.

Marcuse, Herbert. *Reason and Revolution: Hegel and the Rise of Social Theory.* Boston: Beacon Press, 1968.

Marcuse, Herbert. *Soviet Marxism.* New York: Vintage Books, Random House, 1961.

Marcuse, Herbert. *Studies in Critical Philosophy.* Translated by Joris de Bres. Boston: Beacon Press, 1973.

Marx, Karl. *The Eighteenth Brumaire of Louis Bonaparte.* New York: International Publishers, 1969.

Marx, Karl. *Grundrisse.* Translated and edited by David McLellan. New York: Harper and Row, 1971.

Marx, Karl. *The Poverty of Philosophy.* New York: International Publishers, 1971.

Marx, Karl, and Engels, Frederick. *The Communist Manifesto.* 1888 Edition

Marx, Karl, and Engels, Frederick. *The German Ideology.* Edited with an Introduction by C. J. Arthur. New York: International Publishers, 1970.

Marx, Karl; Engels, Frederick; and Lenin, V.I. *Anarchism and Anarcho-Syndicalism: Selected Writings.* New York: International Publishers, 1972.

Marx, Karl, and Lenin, V.I. *Civil War in France: The Paris Commune.* New York: International Publishers, 1969.

Masters, Anthony. *Bakunin: Father of Anarchism.* New York: Saturday Review Press, 1974.

Mehring, Franz. *Karl Marx.* Ann Arbor: Ann Arbor Paperbacks, University of Michigan Press, 1973.

Mendel, Arthur, *Michael Bakunin.* New York: Praeger, 1981.

Mousnier, Roland. *Peasant Uprisings in Seventeenth-Century France, Russia, and China.* Translated by Brian Pearce. New York: Harper and Row, 1970.

Nomad, Max. *Apostles of Revolution.* New York: Collier Books, 1961.

Proudhon, Pierre-Joseph. *What Is Property?* Translated by Benjamin Tucker. New York: Dover Press, 1970.

Pyziur, Eugene. *The Doctrine of Anarchism of Michael A. Bakunin.* Chicago: Henry Regnery Company, 1968.

Resnick, Samuel. "The Political and Social Theory of Michael Bakunin." *American Political Science Review* 21 (May 1927): 270-96.

Rousseau, Jean-Jacques. *The First and Second Discourses.* Translated by Roger and Judith Masters, and edited with an Introduction by Roger Masters. New York: St. Martin's Press, 1964.

Rousseau, Jean-Jacques. *The Social Contract*. Translated, edited, and with an Introduction by Charles Frankel. New York: Hafner, 1966.

Rude, George. *The Crowd in History, 1730-1848*. New York: John Wiley and Sons, 1966.

Saint-Simon, Henri. *Social Organization: The Science of Man, and Other Writings*. Translated and edited with an Introduction by Felix Markham. New York: Harper and Row, 1964.

Scott, John Anthony, ed. and trans. *The Defense of Gracchus Babeuf*. New York: Schocken Books, 1972.

Smith, Tony. "Idealism and People's War: Sartre on Algeria." *Political Theory* 1 (November 1973): 426-49.

Sorel, Georges. *Reflections on Violence*. Translated by T. E. Hulme and J. Roth. New York: Collier Books, 1970.

Spitzer, Alan B. *Old Hatreds and Young Hopes: The French Carbonari against the Bourbon Restoration*. Cambridge: Harvard University Press, 1971.

Venturi, Franco. *Roots of Revolution*. Translated by Francis Haskell, with an Introduction by Isaiah Berlin. New York: Grosset and Dunlap, 1966.

Weber, Max. *The Theory of Social and Economic Organization*. Edited with an Introduction by Talcott Parsons. New York: Free Press, 1947.

Wesson, Robert. *Soviet Communes*. New Brunswick: Rutgers University Press, 1963.

Wilson, Edmund. *To the Finland Station*. Garden City: Doubleday Anchor, 1953.

Woodcock, George. *Anarchism*. Cleveland: Meridian Books, World Publishing, 1962.

Index

About the Author

RICHARD SALTMAN is Research Associate in Political Science in the Department of Health Policy and Management at Harvard University School of Public Health. His writing has been published in various professional journals.